BUTTERWORTHS
ANNOTATED LEGISLATION
SERVICE

STATUTES SUPPLEMENT No. 222

THE TRADE UNION AND LABOUR RELATIONS ACT 1974

By
BRYN PERRINS, M.A. (Cantab.)
Solicitor; Lecturer in Law in the University of Birmingham

LONDON
BUTTERWORTHS
1975

ENGLAND: BUTTERWORTH & CO. (PUBLISHERS) LTD.
LONDON: 88 KINGSWAY, WC2B 6AB

AUSTRALIA: BUTTERWORTHS PTY. LTD.
SYDNEY: 586 PACIFIC HIGHWAY, CHATSWOOD, NSW 2067
MELBOURNE: 343 LITTLE COLLINS STREET, 3000
BRISBANE: 240 QUEEN STREET, 4000

CANADA: BUTTERWORTH & CO. (CANADA) LTD.
TORONTO: 2265 MIDLAND AVENUE, SCARBOROUGH M1P 4S1

NEW ZEALAND: BUTTERWORTHS OF NEW ZEALAND LTD.
WELLINGTON: 26–28 WARING TAYLOR STREET, 1

SOUTH AFRICA: BUTTERWORTH & CO. (SOUTH AFRICA) (PTY.) LTD.
DURBAN: 152–154 GALE STREET

ISBN: 0 406 54735 1

PRINTED IN GREAT BRITAIN BY
BUTLER AND TANNER LTD., FROME AND LONDON

PREFACE

"The law", quoth Mr Secretary Foot, in the Commons Committee on the Trade Union and Labour Relations Bill 1974, "the law is much too serious a business to be left to the lawyers." He may be right too, but Heaven preserve us from the politicians!

The Bill had an undignified passage through Parliament: amendments lost on the casting vote of the Speaker, only to be carried after all because a Labour ghost had voted against; the Bill ignominiously fetched back from the Lords to be corrected; a Commons sitting suspended in uproar; substantial last-minute amendments by their Lordships; the final stages rushed to get the Bill on the statute book before the Summer Recess. And then, when it finally received the Royal Assent on 31 July, 1974, it could not be printed because of a strike of the Government printers. There must be a moral there somewhere?

It is now for the lawyers and others to work the Act. Most of it is clear, some of it is vague, parts of it are self-contradictory.

I have tried to write a commentary on the Act, but since it is as important for what it does not say as for what it does say, I have adopted a narrative approach, putting the Act in its context, rather than the more usual section by section account. In that way I hope I have produced something that will be of use not only to those who want an ordinary commentary, but also to those who would like a general introduction to and some account of the law of labour relations, and also, perhaps, to those who need merely a quick check on how the law has been updated. I have tried in the text to avoid any political controversy, though that can never be very far away from Labour Law.

Finally, I have tried to concentrate on the law as it is, whilst giving where appropriate some account of how it differs from what went before, and indicating the fact when some further change is likely. For, paradoxically, the Labour Government which introduced the Bill has declared itself dissatisfied with the result; and the Conservatives, who opposed it, have said that it forms a perfectly satisfactory basis of law for them and should not need amendment.

The law is much too serious a business to be left to party politicians!

There have been some important developments while the book has been in preparation. The minority Labour Government went to the country on 10 October, 1974, and was returned to power with an overall majority of three. A Consultative Document had already been issued in connection with the Employment Protection Bill (see para. [**19**]), which proposed several amendments to TULRA. It appears from the Queen's Speech that those amendments may in fact be embodied in a separate Amendment Bill, leaving the Employment Protection Bill to follow a little later. A new Companies Bill (see para. [**19**]) is still some way off.

The proposed amendments to TULRA are as follows:

Section 5 (exclusion or expulsion of member from trade union—see paras. [**159**], **181**]-[**186**]). Some amendment will be made, but the Government is still "considering with the TUC how best effective safeguards for the individual can be provided, and will be putting forward proposals as soon as possible". It is believed that the TUC would prefer that s. 5 be repealed entirely, but that the Government is anxious to retain some safeguards.

Sections 6 and 8 (6). Section 6 (rules of trade unions and employers' associations) is to be repealed on the grounds that it is unnecessary and undesirable, and that any improvements which may be necessary are best brought about by voluntary means (see paras. [**109**], [**112**]-[**117**]). It is also proposed to repeal the provision in s. 8 (6) which enables the Registrar to remove the name of an organisation from his list if its rules do not comply with TULRA (paras. [**104**]-[**107**]).

Section 13. Statutory immunity from liability in tort will be extended to inducing a breach of any contract, not just a contract of employment (paras. [**310**]-[**333**]). It is to be expected that there will be protection against liability arising from interference with contract falling short of a breach (paras. [**334**]-[**338**]) and from the corresponding threats (paras. [**345**]-[**347**]).

Section 15 (picketing—see para. [**388**]). The Government still "have this matter under review", but there is no indication of possible conclusions. It may be that there will be some right of obstruction for "official" pickets with armbands, limited to the entrances and exits of the workplace; or that may prove to be unworkable.

Section 29 (3) (overseas trade disputes). The Lords' amendment indicated in para. [**269**] will be repealed.

Section 30 (1) and Sch. 1, para. 6 (5) (unfair dismissal in a closed shop—see paras. [**485**]-[**496**]). There will be the amendments indicated in para. [**486**]: the option to join "another appropriate union" will be deleted from the definition of "union membership agreement" in s. 30 (1) (paras. [**488**] and [**489**]), and it will be fair to dismiss an employee who refuses to join a closed shop established by such an agreement, unless the employee is a conscientious objector who refuses to join any trade union on religious grounds. That will in turn modify the exceptions to Sch. 1, para. 6 (4) (dismissal for union activity—paras. [**480**]-[**484**]).

University of Birmingham BRYN PERRINS
5 November 1974

CONTENTS

TABLE OF STATUTES

References in this Table to "*Statutes*" are to Halsbury's Statutes of England (Third Edition) showing the volume and page at which the annotated text of the Act will be found. Paragraph references printed in bold type indicate where the Trade Union and Labour Relations Act 1974 is set out.

TABLE OF CASES

In the following Table references are given where applicable to the English and Empire Digest where a digest of the case will be found.

CHAPTER ONE
INTRODUCTION

[**1**] The Trade Union and Labour Relations Act 1974 (TULRA) had one main objective, succinctly stated in s. 1 (1): "The Industrial Relations Act 1971 is hereby repealed."

[**2**] There were two problems: in the first place it was desired to keep some parts of the IRA, especially the provisions for unfair dismissal, and yet, at the same time, for political reasons it was important to wipe the whole of the IRA from the statute book. Thus, TULRA repeals but immediately re-enacts some parts of the IRA. The second problem was that the IRA itself had repealed much of the earlier legislation on the subject of trade unions, and merely to repeal the IRA would have left a void. TULRA therefore fills that void.

[**3**] In outline TULRA

—repeals the IRA
—redefines trade unions and employers' associations and makes appropriate provisions for them
—restores the traditional freedom of collective bargaining
—restates the freedom to take industrial action
—revives the "right" to picket
—renews the right against unfair dismissal.

Each of these topics is discussed in more detail in the succeeding chapters, but some general points may first be made.

1. THE ROLE OF THE LAW IN LABOUR RELATIONS

[**4**] The relationship that exists between an employer and his employee is inherently one of imbalance. Economically, the employer has all the advantages, whilst the employee whose livelihood depends on his ability to sell his only asset, his labour, is at a disadvantage. The law seeks to redress the balance of power in two ways.

[**5**] First, it accords to the employee a certain status, that is to say it accords to him certain rights irrespective of anything he may have contracted for. Because of its belief in the sanctity of contract and its general policy of *laissez faire* the common law has rarely intervened in that way (the doctrine of employers' liability in tort being one notable exception), but there has been a great deal of statute law: Truck Acts, Factories Acts, the Contracts of Employment Act and the Redundancy Payments Act, for example. Rights are accorded under these Acts to the individual employee. With one important exception, individual rights are outside the scope of TULRA and hence

outside the scope of this book. The exception is the right against unfair dismissal.

[6] The other way in which the law seeks to redress the balance between employer and employed is to allow some measure of self help through the exercise of collective power. Again it is statute law, not the common law, that does it. The common law indeed is strongly opposed to the notion of collective might and holds both trade unions and employers' associations to be unlawful as being in restraint of trade, and it attacks the exercise of such collective might with the crime and the tort of conspiracy.

2. PREVIOUS LEGISLATION

[7] The common law, then, outlawed almost all trade unions and employers' associations as being in restraint of trade. Statute intervened to make them lawful. The Trade Union Act 1871, as amended in 1876, remained for a century the very basis of collective labour law. It adopted what has been called "the abstentionist theory of law", perhaps more popularly referred to as the tradition of free collective bargaining. The notion is that the law allows workers to associate in unions, and employers in employers' associations, and then leaves the two sides to sort out their own salvation without any further interference from the law. The law may be ready to assist the parties to reach an agreement with various "props" like facilities for conciliation or arbitration; or again, if either party should overstep the boundary of what is proper, the law may have to intervene to see fair play. But ideally the law would prefer not to have to intervene at all. The law, as it were, marks out the battlefield but takes no part in the fighting.

[8] That, perhaps, is how Parliament has traditionally seen the role of the law, but the common law judges have usually had other ideas. It is a fascinating exercise to see how Parliament has granted freedoms to unions and employers' associations, and how, over the years, the common lawyers manage to whittle down the freedom or even sidestep it altogether. Professor Hamson used to remark that the common law is like a crab. It may not move at all for a long time. But when you prod it, it will move. And when it moves, it can move remarkably quickly, and it usually moves sideways.

[9] That can be seen in the last century of labour relations statutes. For instance, immediately after the 1871 Act, the courts were docile for a time, but gradually they began to find ways to intervene. It seems that they decided for themselves that they must "do something about the unions". In 1901 in the two cases of *Taff Vale Rail. Co.* v. *Amalgamated Society of Railway Servants* (1900), [1901] A.C. 426 and *Quinn* v. *Leathem*, [1901] A.C. 495 the House of Lords undermined the theory of abstention. The former case, by giving a somewhat strained interpretation to the 1871 Act, jeopardised the very existence of unions by threatening their funds: free collective bargaining implies the right to take industrial action, but it is, for reasons explained in Chapter Five, almost impossible to organise industrial action without technically committing a wrong at common law. Thus union officers going about their "proper" business committed technical wrongs, and *Taff Vale* for the first time held the union as such could be liable for the wrongs of its officers. *Quinn* v. *Leathem*,

[1901] A.C. 495 added a new dimension to the danger by discovering new possibilities for the tort of conspiracy (though the common law has since resiled from that position).

[**10**] Parliament reversed *Taff Vale Rail. Co.* v. *Amalgamated Society of Railway Servants* (1900), [1901] A.C. 426 and *Quinn* v. *Leathem*, [1901] A.C. 495 in the Trades Disputes Act 1906. And it thereby provided defences against all the technical wrongs that it thought might be done in organising industrial action.

[**11**] Then the courts in *Amalgamated Society of Railway Servants* v. *Osborne*, [1910] A.C. 87, giving an even more curious interpretation to the 1871 Act, held that unions could not properly sponsor Members of Parliament. Parliament reversed that decision by the Trade Union Act 1913.

[**12**] Then in 1964 the House of Lords again shook the unions with the decision in *Rookes* v. *Barnard*, [1964] A.C. 1129; [1964] 1 All E.R. 367 by rediscovering the forgotten tort of intimidation, which apparently made any threat of industrial action potentially unlawful. And in the following year in *J. T. Stratford & Sons, Ltd.* v. *Lindley*, [1965] A.C. 307; [1964] 3 All E.R. 102 their Lordships seemed to be outflanking the 1906 Act yet again by finding other liabilities against which the Act was no sure protection.

[**13**] Parliament reversed *Rookes* v. *Barnard* by the Trade Disputes Act 1965, but the courts seemed by then to have the bit firmly between their teeth, and in several cases in the late 1960s the Court of Appeal in particular was ready to discover ever more sophisticated grounds of liability.

[**14**] Further development of the common law was overtaken by the IRA. The IRA's policy was "interventionist" and not "abstentionist", but one of the central features of that Act was to remove all industrial disputes from the jurisdiction of the common law courts because of the common law's antagonism to the exercise of collective strength. The IRA created a new specialist court instead.

3. INDUSTRIAL RELATIONS ACT 1971

[**15**] The IRA altered completely the role of the law in labour relations. It brought the law firmly down into the market place of collective bargaining. Its scheme was simple in concept:

1. Effective collective bargaining implies that we must have workers in unions and employers in employers' associations. Therefore, there must be a legal right to join a union. Further, there must be a legal right to be an active trade unionist, which will amount to a right for the unions to recruit. Hence s. 5 IRA.
2. If the unions have organised the workers, they should have a legal right to bargain for them. Hence the sole bargaining agency.
3. If the unions are bargaining for all the workers, they should be able legally to insist on the support of all the workers. Therefore there must be some form of union security agreement.
4. If the unions and employers begin to bargain, each ought to be able to rely on what the other says. Therefore collective bargains ought to be legally enforceable.

5. If the unions are going to commit themselves to a legal contract, it is only fair that they do so on the basis of accurate information about the employers' prospects. Hence the right to information.

6. If there are any disputes about these matters, it is uncivilised to resort to industrial action. Legal rights involve legal remedies, so let the National Industrial Relations Court adjudicate. It follows that industrial action must be called off until the attempt at a court settlement has been tried and failed.

[**16**] However, this apparently simple scheme was then complicated. First the insistence on the rights of the individual worker meant that s. 5 IRA had to include a legal right not to join the union, which in turn meant that there could be no legal right to a closed shop, which in turn meant that the union security agreement referred to at 3 above had to be an agency shop and not a closed shop, save in exceptional circumstances. The second complication was the insistence that the unions be formally responsible to the national interest as well as to their members: privileges in return for responsibility. That meant that the legal rights mentioned in paragraphs 1–5 above were available only to a *registered* union. Thirdly, ss. 96–98 attempted to suppress (most) unofficial wildcat strikes, sympathetic action and blacking. Suddenly to impose a system of strict legal regulation on what had previously been a rather loose informal arrangement was in any event going to be difficult, but as it happened registration was the crucial issue on which the Act foundered. The unions regarded registration as a state licence to operate, and in retrospect it can be seen that what torpedoed the IRA was the TUC's decision that TUC unions should not remain on the register. The IRA illustrates the principle that a law cannot be enforced if it is not generally accepted. Of course, when the Act was first introduced, it was then assumed that whilst the unions would not immediately like it, they would eventually lump it. That proved a miscalculation.

4. TRADE UNION AND LABOUR RELATIONS ACT 1974

[**17**] TULRA sweeps away the IRA and restores the law more or less to what it was before the IRA was passed. It therefore restores freedom of collective bargaining as traditionally understood, including freedom to take collective action. In its original version, the Bill would have extended that freedom, but Opposition amendments prevented that.

5. INTERVENTION IN THE NATIONAL INTEREST

[**18**] The law then normally refuses to interfere in collective bargaining at the behest of either side. But it may have to intervene in the national interest. One aspect is the proclamation of a state of emergency in the face of a particularly serious strike. Another aspect is price and wage restraint. Some form of statutory wage and price control is acceptable in wartime, and it has become accepted of recent years in times of economic crisis in peacetime. Such measures are, however, regarded by most as a temporary expedient and a necessary evil. A permanent "planned economy" is generally regarded as undesirable.

6. FUTURE LEGISLATION

[**19**] TULRA was envisaged as the first part of a three part package. The second part was seen as an Employment Protection Bill, codifying and improving the rights of the individual employee; and the third was a new Companies Bill to extend "industrial democracy" by which is meant some form of worker participation in management. Whether either of these measures is introduced and if so, what form they take is naturally dependent upon political fortunes.

[**20**] It is likely that some kind of worker participation will be introduced by whichever political party is in power. There are, however, deep divisions on the form it should take, and those divisions are not entirely on party political lines. The underlying issue is as ever the one of freedom and responsibility. Freedom implies responsibility and responsibility implies discipline. The political controversy therefore centres on the twin questions: to whom is responsibility owed, and, what form should discipline take? Do the unions owe a duty to their members only, or must they take reasonable account of the national interest, and indeed the employer's interests, by moderating wage demands? And who is the arbiter of reasonableness? Likewise, does a company owe a duty only to its shareholders, or must it take reasonable account of the national interest in fixing prices, and of the workers' interests in fixing wages? And again who is the arbiter of reasonableness? And if in either case there is a duty beyond pure self interest, how is that duty to be enforced? Is it to be self discipline, a moral duty; or is it to be imposed from without, a legal duty with legal sanctions?

[**21**] Those are some of the questions. Worker participation in whatever form will not of itself provide any easy answers. But it may encourage a spirit of greater co-operation.

CHAPTER TWO

REPEAL OF THE INDUSTRIAL RELATIONS ACT

[**22**] If it were not such an atrocious pun, one might say that TULRA should be subtitled "Look back *in ira*". Be that as it may, TULRA

—abolishes NIRC and its jurisdiction on 31 July, 1974 (s. 1 (3))
—repeals the remainder of the IRA on 16 September 1974 (s. 1 (1))
—immediately re-enacts parts of it (Sch. 1)
—makes transitional arrangements, especially for pending actions (Sch. 4; ss. 21–23).

[**23**] It will be remembered that the Contracts of Employment Act 1972 had already repealed and re-enacted the IRA, ss. 17–19 and Sch. 2. (Some Northern Ireland provisions had gone too.) Further, ss. 56 and 57 (disclosure of information) and s. 113 (tribunals to have jurisdiction over contracts of employment), and in each case certain related provisions, were never operative. TULRA deals with the rest.

[**24**] Institutions, like industrial tribunals and the Industrial Arbitration Board, which existed before the IRA, are retained, but the Commission on Industrial Relations is abolished. Likewise, Acts of Parliament other than the IRA itself are not affected in substance, though there are consequential amendments. Thus the Trade Union Act 1913 still governs political expenditure and the Trade Union (Amalgamations etc.) Act 1964 still governs amalgamations.

1. ABOLITION OF NIRC

[**25**] Immediately on receiving the Royal Assent on 31 July, 1974, TULRA abolished the National Industrial Relations Court, its "jurisdiction, functions and constitution" (s. 1 (3)). That included

—the prohibition of the pre-entry closed shop
—the agency shop
—the approved closed shop
—bargaining units and sole bargaining agencies
—imposed procedure agreements
—cooling off periods
—strike ballots.

[**26**] The members of NIRC may be entitled to redundancy payments (s. 24 (2)).

2. REPEAL OF THE REMAINDER OF THE IRA

[**27**] TULRA, s. 1 (3) and the transitional provisions of ss. 21–23, became operative on 31 July, 1974. The remainder of TULRA was to be brought into force by order (s. 31 (2)) and was so brought into force on 16 September, 1974. Section 1 (1) thereupon repealed the remainder of the IRA, but s. 1 (2) immediately re-enacted parts of it.

[**28**] Those institutions repealed but not re-enacted include

—the general principles
—a worker's "s. 5 rights" to join a union, etc.
—the presumption as to legal enforceability of collective bargains
—the Registrar of Trade Unions and Employers' Associations and the registers
—the guiding principles for trade unions and employers' associations (but *cf.* TULRA ss. 5–7)
—the remaining unfair industrial practices, especially ss. 96–98
—the Commission on Industrial Relations
—the presumption as to strike notice.

3. RE-ENACTMENT OF PARTS OF THE IRA

[**29**] Section 1 (2) expressly re-enacts

—the Code of Practice
—unfair dismissal
—industrial tribunal procedure
—various miscellaneous sections

Other sections of the IRA are repeated more or less verbatim in TULRA without acknowledgment of their source, notably the sections dealing with the accounts and annual returns of unions and employers' associations. Other parts of TULRA, especially some of the definitions, are clearly based on the IRA.

[**30**] Unfair dismissals, industrial tribunal procedure and all but one of the miscellaneous sections re-enacted by s. 1 (2) are dealt with in Chapter Seven, *infra*. The exception is the right of a member of a trade union to nominate who shall receive his provident benefits on death. That is dealt with in Chapter Three, below.

The Code of Practice

[**31**] The original version of the Bill did not include the Code, but the first defeat of the Government was in Committee in the Commons when the Code and the general principles were re-introduced. The principles were later dropped, but the Code remains.

[**32**] The Secretary of State must maintain a Code of Practice giving practical guidance to those engaged in industry "for the purpose of promoting good industrial relations" (para. 1 (1)). The Code introduced under the IRA will continue until revised (paras. 1 (2) and (3)), although some of it is no longer

appropriate. As well as providing practical guidance, the Secretary in revising the Code is enjoined to remember that management has the primary responsibility for the promotion of good industrial relations (para. 1 (4)). As under the IRA the Secretary must consult the TUC and the CBI on the draft of any revised Code (para. 2 (1)), but he is now obliged to publish and "take account of" any advice they give. (para. 2 (2)). Previously he had to publish and take account of advice from the Commission on Industrial Relations.

[**33**] Paragraph 3 repeats, as in the IRA, that failure to comply with the Code is not a wrong in itself, but is evidence of good practice when judging a person's conduct. It has been compared to the Highway Code.

4. TRANSITIONAL ARRANGEMENTS

[**34**] Sections 21–23 make detailed provisions for actions that were pending when the IRA was repealed. Broadly the scheme was:

1. Claims which did not arise from the IRA were unaffected in substance, but the machinery might be different.
2. Unfair dismissals were unaffected in substance, but the machinery might be different.
3. Other claims arising under the IRA were unaffected in substance provided proceedings were begun before 30 April, 1974 (the date on which the Bill was first presented in Parliament) but the machinery might be different.
4. Everything else stopped on the day when the section of the IRA giving rise to the action was repealed (*i.e.*, 31 July or 16 September, 1974). One interesting exception was that the CIR was allowed, if the Secretary of State so permitted, to make and publish reports on various matters then currently under investigation (s. 21 (10)).

[**35**] With the abolition of NIRC other arrangements had to be made for current claims and generally any case actually before NIRC was transferred to the High Court with special provisions to ensure that as far as possible a judgment of the High Court would have the same effect as one of NIRC (especially in relation to enforcement and costs: s. 23 (2) and Sch. 4, para. 5). Some cases were remitted to tribunals.

[**36**] As from 31 July, 1974 appeals from tribunals lie to the High Court (and note TULRA, Sch. 3, para. 15). Other transitional arrangements are made by Schedule 4.

[**37**] There were three extremely important cases before NIRC shortly before its demise, each against the Transport and General Workers Union. The claims were by Heatons Transport (reported to be for £10,000), Craddock Bros. (reported to be for £50,000) and General Aviation Services (who were reported to have a claim worth £2m.). The first two were reportedly withdrawn before NIRC was abolished, but the GAS claim was adjourned by the Court of Appeal until the autumn of 1974. If it is ever heard therefore, it will be by the High Court.

CHAPTER THREE

TRADE UNIONS AND EMPLOYERS' ASSOCIATIONS

[**38**] The IRA introduced new definitions of trade unions and employers' associations and enacted provisions dealing with their status, legality, rules, membership and associated matters. Most of the earlier statutory provisions were in the Trade Union Acts 1871–6 and those were repealed by the IRA. TULRA sweeps aside the IRA's provisions and thus needs to enact its own provisions about all those matters. Thus TULRA

—defines a trade union and an employers' association (s. 28)
—redefines their status (ss. 2 and 3)
—renders them lawful (ss. 2 (5) and 3 (5))
—requires the Registrar of Friendly Societies to maintain lists of them (s. 8)
—removes most of the distinctions between "registered" and "unregistered" organisations (s. 9)
—insists that their rules deal with certain matters (s. 6), and makes amendments to the Trade Union Act 1913 consequential upon the repeal of the IRA (Sch. 3, paras. 2)
—permits the "unscrambling" of funds (s. 20)
—demands that unions and employers' associations keep proper accounts, make annual returns, and ensure that their pension schemes are properly funded (ss. 10–12) and Sch. 2)
—provides for the devolution of their property (s. 4)
—gives a worker certain rights against a trade union (ss. 5 and 7)
—continues the right of nomination of benefits (Sch. 1, para. 31)
—makes consequential amendments of other statutes (Sch. 3, paras. 5, 7. 10 and 12).

1. DESCRIPTION

TRADE UNIONS

[**39**] A trade union is an association of workers which sets out to improve the terms and conditions of employment of its members (its "trade objective"). For most unions an equally important function is to care for its members or their dependants in time of adversity by paying sums of money for instance on death or disablement or during sickness or unemployment (the "provident side") though rules vary from union to union.

[**40**] The trade objective is, however, critical, and it is that which serves to

distinguish a trade union from other bodies that may at first sight appear similar.

[**41**] A trade union may look like a friendly society. The term "friendly society" is applied to various kinds of bodies, the common feature of which is the payment of subscriptions for mutual relief in certain circumstances, like the provident side of a trade union. But a friendly society has no trade objective, nor is it necessarily confined to workers. A trade union may not be registered as a friendly society (TULRA, s. 2 (3)).

[**42**] A trade union (and for that matter a friendly society) may be distinguished from an industrial and provident society. The central feature of an industrial and provident society is that it is a co-operative society. People co-operate together to trade and profit, and any profit is shared by the co-operators by way of dividend. If numbers are small it may be a partnership, but if they are large the society must be registered as a company. A trade union may not be registered as an industrial and provident society (TULRA, s. 2 (3)).

[**43**] Finally, to the extent that it provides cash benefits on the happening of certain contingencies, a trade union is an insurer. It is generally exempt from the requirements applying to industrial insurance companies (but it must not insure the life of a child under ten years of age: s. 6 Industrial Assurance and Friendly Societies Act 1948). It is also exempt from enactments that impose stringent financial requirements on companies that carry on insurance business other than industrial insurance, if the union's insurance business is limited to paying provident benefits and strike pay. Previously there had been some discrimination between registered and unregistered unions (see TULRA, Sch. 3, paras. 5, 7 and 12 and the Acts thereby amended, and note the repeal of the relevant paragraphs in the Insurance Companies Amendment Act 1973: TULRA, Sch. 5).

EMPLOYERS' ASSOCIATIONS

[**44**] An employers' association is a union of employers, which aims to regulate the terms and conditions of employment of the workers employed by its members. Again the trade objective is critical. Most employers' associations will also be concerned for their members' interests as manufacturers or traders as well as for their interests as employers of labour. Some associations may be concerned about resale price maintenance or other restrictive trade practices. But if they do not also concern themselves with the regulation of relations between their members and their members' workers then they are better referred to as trade associations or the like rather than employers' associations.

[**45**] Employers' associations may provide advantages for their members apart from a common policy and collective strength. Often, for example, there is an indemnity fund to assist a strike-bound member. Thus, the association may be an insurer. It is therefore entitled to the same privileges in respect of insurance company law as a trade union: see para. [**43**], above.

2. DEFINITION

[**46**] TULRA introduces new definitions for trade unions and employers' associations.

[**47**] Unions were first made legal by the Trade Union Act 1871 and the definition therein contained though amended in 1876 and 1913 in substance lasted for a century. Its terms were wide enough to include unions of workers (*i.e.* trade unions) and unions of employers (*i.e.* employers' associations). The IRA scrapped that definition and replaced it with four more modern ones for (registered) trade unions and employers' associations and (unregistered) organisations of workers and organisations of employers respectively. TULRA now simplifies that. There is just one definition for trade unions and another for employers' associations. They are based on the IRA's definitions.

TRADE UNIONS

[**48**] A trade union is defined in TULRA, s. 28 (1). It means an organisation of workers whose principal purposes include the regulation of relations with employers, or a federation of such organisations. The organisation may be permanent or temporary, so that it could include a site co-ordinating committee or an *ad hoc* committee set up by workers in a "non-union" factory. However, some stress has been laid on the word "organisation" which, it is said, implies some degree of structure and is therefore something more than an "association" which was the word used in the 1871 Act. The argument does not seem very strong.

[**49**] "Worker" is defined in s. 30 (1) to include employees, independent contractors (other than a professional man in relation to his client) and Crown employees (civil servants).

[**50**] A trade union is an "independent trade union" if it is not employer dominated, nor employer controlled, nor subject to interference by an employer "tending towards such control" (s. 30 (1)). It is important to know whether a union is independent as defined for the purposes of s. 18 (4) (incorporation of collective terms into the individual worker's contract: see Chapter Four), and for the purposes of Sch. 1, paras. 6 and 13 (unfair dismissals: see Chapter Seven).

EMPLOYERS' ASSOCIATIONS

[**51**] An employers' association is now defined in s. 28 (2) as a permanent or temporary organisation of employers whose principal purposes include the regulation of relations with workers or unions, or a federation of such organisations. By s. 30 (1) "employers' association" may include a combination of employers and employers' associations, and of course employers may be individuals or corporations.

[**52**] The same comments apply in relation to the word "organisation" as in the definition of a trade union above.

3. STATUS

[**53**] TULRA makes some changes in the status of industrial organisations. With a few exceptions all trade unions are to be unincorporated associations though with some of the attributes of legal personality. In a few exceptional

cases a trade union may be a body corporate. Employers' associations may be incorporated or unincorporated as they wish.

TRADE UNIONS

"Ordinary" trade unions

[**54**] There is an exceptional kind of trade union called a "special register body". They are discussed below. The status of all other trade unions is as follows.

[**55**] The traditional learning is that there are only two kinds of person known to the law: an *individual,* that is a human being; and a *corporation,* that is an artificial entity. Corporations may be recognised as such by the common law, or may be created by charter or letters patent, or may be formed by or under an Act of Parliament. A company of people not incorporated by one of these modes remains a collection of individuals: in the eyes of the law the company is "they", not "it".

[**56**] Trade unions occupy an intermediate status. The history is well known. The Trade Union Act 1871 legalised but did not incorporate unions. It allowed them to register themselves and so obtain certain advantages. The House of Lords, notably in *Taff Vale Rail. Co.* v. *Amalgamated Society of Railway Servants* (1900), [1901] A.C. 426 and *Bonsor* v. *Musicians' Union,* [1956] A.C. 104 decided that unions registered under the 1871 Act were unincorporated, but had some of the attributes of a body corporate. Unions that were not so registered presumably remained "purely" unincorporated associations of individuals. The IRA made trade unions registered under its scheme into bodies corporate, and whilst it left unincorporated those organisations of workers which did not register it invested them with some of the attributes of legal personality. TULRA now puts all unions other than special register bodies into the one, intermediate category.

[**57**] Any union (other than a special register body) registered under the IRA and so a body corporate ceased to be such on 16 September, 1974 (TULRA, s. 2 (4)). Its property and all rights and liabilities in respect thereof immediately vested in the "appropriate trustees" (s. 19 (2)). They are any trustees specially appointed in writing for the purposes of s. 19, or if none was so appointed, the president and general secretary of the union or its equivalent officers (s. 19 (3) and (5)). A certificate given by the president and general secretary is conclusive evidence of who were the appropriate trustees (s. 19 (4)).

[**58**] Further, a trade union (other than a special register body) may not be registered under the Companies Act, 1948, and any such registration is void (TULRA, s. 2 (2)).

[**59**] So all trade unions (other than special register bodies) are once again unincorporated associations, and s. 2 (1) provides that they shall not be "or be treated as if they were" bodies corporate. However, s. 2 (1) then proceeds to accord to a trade union some of the most important attributes of a body corporate, and a union's status under TULRA is similar to that of a union registered under the 1871 Act or of an unincorporated association of workers under the IRA.

[**60**] The attributes of corporate personality given by TULRA to unincorporated unions are as follows.

(i) *Legal Proceedings*

[**61**] A body corporate may sue and be sued in its corporate name. An unincorporated body of persons cannot normally sue or be sued as a body. All the members may join together to bring or defend the suit as a collection of individuals, but if there is a large number of them it may be impracticable to do so. Otherwise certain appropriate members, say a management committee, may sue or be sued on behalf of themselves and all other members in a representative action under R.S.C., O. 15, r. 12, but there may be technical difficulties with that procedure.

[**62**] Nevertheless, an unincorporated union may sue and be sued in its own name in any civil proceedings, (s. 2 (1) (c)). That is to be read subject to s. 14 which places severe restrictions on suing a trade union in tort (see Chapter Five). It may also be prosecuted in its own name for any crimes committed by it or on its behalf, (s. 2 (1) (*d*)).

(ii) *Property*

[**63**] The property of a body corporate is vested in the corporation itself, but the property of an unincorporated association can only be vested in trustees. That creates problems, for if the trust is for the purposes of the association, it may be void unless those purposes are charitable, and those of a union are not; whilst if the trust is for the union, *i.e.* for the present *and future* members of the association, it may be void for perpetuity or otherwise.

[**64**] Nevertheless, the property of an unincorporated union is vested in trustees on trust for the union (s. 2 (1) (*b*)).

(iii) *Liability*

[**65**] A body corporate being an independent person is liable for its own wrongs and judgment may be executed upon the corporation's own property, which is entirely separate from that of its members. The members of an unincorporated association are liable for wrongs done on their behalf to the full extent of their own personal assets, because the actor is deemed authorised by each member of the association: the law does not recognise the association itself as having a separate existence.

[**66**] Nevertheless, in the case of an unincorporated union any judgment given against it on or after 16 September, 1974 may be enforced against the property of the union (that is, against any property held in trust for it) "in like manner as if the union were a body corporate" (s. 2 (1) (*e*). A judgment against a union sued in its own name may not be enforced against the separate property of its individual members (*cf. Bonsor* v. *Musicians' Union*, [1956] A.C. 104; [1955] 3 All E.R. 518). If the judgment was given before 16 September, 1974 then it may be affected by the transitional provisions of ss. 21–23, outlined in the previous chapter.

(iv) *Contract*

[67] A body corporate being a person in law may make a contract, though being an artificial person it can act only through human agency. An unincorporated association is not even an artificial person, and if a contract is purported to be made on its behalf, it is a contract made on behalf of each and every member. For instance, a contract of membership of such a body is a contract by the new member with each and every other member and not a contract between him and the association.

[68] Nevertheless, an unincorporated trade union may make a contract, (though it can only act through human agents) (s. 2 (1) (*a*)).

Special register unions

[69] A special register *body* is defined in s. 30 (1) as a body corporate (whether incorporated under the Companies Act or by charter or letters patent) whose name was on the special register, instituted under the IRA, on 15 September, 1974. They are incorporated professional associations which do in fact carry on collective bargaining with an employer, although it may be only an incidental function in the case of some of them.

[70] They may or may not be trade unions as defined in TULRA. In order to be placed on the IRA's special register an organisation had to show that its *activities* included the regulation of relations with employers. In order to be a trade union within TULRA the organisation must show that its *principal purposes* include the regulation of such relations.

[71] If therefore the constitution of a special register body (*i.e.* its memorandum of association or charter or whatever) states that one of its purposes is to carry on collective bargaining then it is a trade union. If its constitution does not so state then it is not a trade union.

[72] "Special register union" will hereafter in this book be used to mean a special register body which is a trade union. The expression is not used in TULRA.

[73] A special register union is allowed to be an exception to the rule and to retain its corporate status. It will therefore not need the assistance of s. 2 (1). Otherwise it is like any other trade union: it is entitled to the same privileges and subject to the same obligations. Special register bodies which are not trade unions are outside TULRA altogether: they can claim no privileges thereunder.

[74] It will be noted that a special register body is defined as one which was on the special register on 15 September, 1974. The special register is in any event now closed and TULRA offers no other way of becoming a special register body. It follows that every body corporate whose *principal purposes* included the regulation of relations with employers ought to have ensured that its name was placed on the special register by that date. Otherwise it lost its corporate status on 16 September, 1974 and the procedure outlined above applied (TULRA, s. 2 (4)). The alternative if it wished to retain its corporate status was to alter its constitution and ensure that collective bargaining was not one of its principal purposes. (No company incorporated under the Companies Act could be in that dilemma: IRA s. 157 (2).)

EMPLOYERS' ASSOCIATIONS

[**75**] It is considered to be appropriate for an employers' association to be a body corporate if it so wishes. Section 3 (1) therefore states that it may be either a body corporate or an unincorporated association; but in some circumstances an incorporated association may have to take positive steps to retain its status.

Incorporated employers' associations

[**76**] Where an employers' association is a body corporate, different considerations apply depending on how it achieved that status, whether under the IRA or otherwise.

If the employers' association became incorporated otherwise than under the IRA, there is no problem and it will continue to enjoy that status.

[**77**] If it became incorporated by s. 74 IRA, then by TULRA, s. 3 (3) it will cease to be a body corporate on 15 March, 1975 unless it takes steps to avoid that result. If it wishes to remain a body corporate, it must, by that date, incorporate itself afresh by some other means, and it will probably register under the Companies Act 1948. If it does not take the necessary steps then at midnight on 15 March, 1975 it will cease to be a body corporate and will become an unincorporated association (s. 3 (3)) and its property and any rights or liabilities in respect of its property will be automatically transferred to the appropriate trustees (s. 19 (2)). Those trustees must be specially appointed by writing for the purposes of s. 19, and if none is so appointed the president and general secretary of the association or its equivalent officers will be deemed to be its trustees for this purpose (s. 19 (3) and (5)). A certificate given by the president and general secretary or their equivalent is conclusive evidence as to who are the appropriate trustees (s. 19 (4)).

Unincorporated employers' associations

[**78**] If an employers' association is unincorporated or becomes unincorporated under the above procedure it is nevertheless given by s. 3 (2) the same attributes of corporate personality as those given to an unincorporated trade union by s. 2 (1): see paras. [**60**]–[**68**] above.

[**79**] An employers' association is exempt from the requirements of s. 434 Companies Act 1948, which enacts that associations of more than twenty members formed to carry on a business for the purposes of gain must register under its provisions or be formed in other special ways. "Gain" is wider than "profit" in the usual sense.

4. LEGALITY

[**80**] The legality of most trade unions and employers' associations depends on TULRA, ss. 2 (5) and 3 (5). Were it not for these sections such bodies would almost inevitably be unlawful at common law as being in restraint of trade. They might also be criminal organisations, but that is unlikely.

[**81**] A trade union as defined must have as one of its principal purposes the regulation of relations with employers. It is almost inevitable therefore that

its purposes are in restraint of trade: it aims to restrict the employer's freedom and it also aims to restrict is own members' freedom. But the common law holds unlawful only those agreements that are in *unreasonable* restraint of trade. It is unlikely that the courts will consider unions to be in reasonable restraint of trade, at least if they may by their rule book take industrial action. Therefore most trade unions are unlawful, as being unreasonably in restraint of trade. So too are employers' associations, for similar reasons. "Unlawfulness" in this context merely means that any agreement or trust is void or unenforceable.

[**82**] It is possible, but unlikely, that trade unions or employers' associations could be criminal conspiracies at common law. A criminal conspiracy is an agreement to do something unlawful, but the better view is that "unlawful" here must mean something more than merely void or unenforceable.

[**83**] Successive statutes have given immunity against any such unlawfulness, and so have "legalised" trade unions and employers' associations: first the Trade Union Act 1871, then the IRA, and now TULRA. TULRA makes some changes.

TRADE UNIONS

[**84**] Section 2 (5) enacts immunity for trade unions. It differentiates between special register unions and other trade unions. None of the purposes of an ordinary trade union, just because they are in restraint of trade, is to give rise to any criminal liability nor is it to make any agreement or trust void.

[**85**] In the case of a special register union, s. 2 (5) says that its trade purposes (that is, the regulation of relations with employers) are not to give rise to criminal liability or render any agreement or trust void merely on the ground of restraint of trade. But the lawfulness of any other purpose of a special register union is no concern of TULRA's.

[**86**] Section 2 (5) then adds that no rule of an "ordinary" trade union is to be unlawful or unenforceable on the grounds of restraint of trade, and similarly that in the case of a special register union no rule which relates to its trade purpose is to be so treated. It is thought that the reason for the reference to rules is to meet a point raised in *Edwards* v. *Society of Graphical and Allied Trades*, [1971] Ch. at p. 365; [1970] 3 All E.R. 689. SACHS, L.J. drew a distinction between purposes and rules. The former, he said, were rendered lawful by the 1871 Act, but it did not follow that the latter were. The House of Lords in the earlier case of *Faramus* v. *Film Artistes Association*, [1964] A.C. 925; [1964] 1 All E.R. 25 had rejected the distinction.

[**87**] Section 2 (5) is qualified by s. 5 (5), but that is discussed in connection with membership below.

EMPLOYERS' ASSOCIATIONS

[**88**] Section 3 (5) enacts immunity for employers' associations in the same way as s. 2 (5) enacts it for trade unions.

[**89**] Thus, all the purposes and rules of an unincorporated employers' association may shelter under the umbrella of s. 3 (5) but only the trade purposes

of an incorporated employers' association and any of its rules relating thereto.

[**90**] Apparently therefore the restrictive trade practices of an unincorporated employers' association may thereby escape the common law but not those of an incorporated employers' association. The reason given for this unequal treatment is that an unincorporated employers' association was before the IRA within the definition of a "trade union" under the Trade Union Acts 1871–1964. It was therefore entitled to total immunity from the restraint of trade doctrine. An incorporated employers' association was not within the Acts and so had no immunity, but had instead the advantages of incorporation. TULRA was intended to restore the unincorporated association to its former position and to give the incorporated association some measure of immunity.

5. REGISTRATION

[**91**] TULRA provides that "lists" of unions and employers' associations are to be maintained by the (Chief) Registrar of Friendly Societies (note TULRA, Sch. 3, para. 2 (6)), but it removes most of the differences between a listed organisation and an unlisted one.

THE SCHEME OF REGISTRATION

[**92**] Registration was first introduced by the Trade Union Act 1871. Unions and employers' associations were entitled but not compelled to register with the Registrar of Friendly Societies. A registered organisation enjoyed some (mostly procedural) privileges, but an unregistered organisation was at no serious disadvantage. It seems that most of those who registered did so because it gave them respectability.

[**93**] Registration under the IRA was a much more serious affair. The privileges of a registered organisation were much more substantial but were given only in return for more responsibility and accountability. There was a new Registrar of Trade Unions and Employers' Associations.

[**94**] TULRA abolishes the Registrar of Trade Unions and Employers' Associations, and most of his functions. Those that are left are returned to the Registrar of Friendly Societies (s. 8 (1)). There is in any event little left of the concept of registration. Even the name has disappeared. Instead of being registered, trade unions and employers' associations are to be listed (like historic buildings?). There are two lists, one for unions (including special register unions) and the other for employers' associations (incorporate or unincorporate) (s. 8 (1)).

[**95**] An unlisted union or association is however just as much a trade union or employers' association as a listed one, if it satisfies TULRA's definition.

ADVANTAGES OF REGISTRATION

[**96**] Most of the distinctions between a listed organisation and an unlisted one have disappeared. Thus, TULRA, s. 9 (1) provides that except for tax purposes (s. 9 (3)) any previous Act that refers to a registered organisation

(whether registered under the Act of 1871 or under the IRA) is henceforth to be deemed to refer to a trade union or employers' association as defined in TULRA. Any union or association not registered under the IRA would fall within the IRA's definition of an organisation of workers or an organisation of employers as the case may be, and TULRA, s. 9 (2) provides that except for tax purposes (s. 9 (3)) any prior Act that refers to such an organisation is to be deemed henceforth to refer to a trade union or an employers' association within TULRA's definitions.

[97] The advantages of registration are therefore

1. Only a listed organisation may claim tax relief on its provident income (*i.e.* on the income from its provident funds) (s. 9 (3)). This is the one previously existing difference to survive the assimilation process carried out by sub-ss. 9 (1) and (2).

2. A listed organisation has certain advantages in connection with the transfer of its property on the appointment of new trustees (s. 4 (2)); see paras. [**143**]–[**149**], *post*. This is in form a difference newly created, but the substance was in the 1871 Act.

3. In practical terms it is easier for a listed organisation to prove that it is a trade union or an employers' association as the case may be. It may ask the Registrar for a certificate to that effect (s. 8 (10)) which is evidence that it is within the appropriate definition.

METHOD OF REGISTRATION

[98] There are two routes onto the list: automatic registration and registration by application.

Automatic registration

[99] Section 8 (2) imposes a duty on the Registrar to register an organisation automatically if it falls within any of four categories, unless he is of the opinion that it does not satisfy TULRA's definition of a trade union or an employers' association as the case may be.

[100] The four categories are:

(*a*) an organisation registered under the 1871 Act which was still so registered on 30 September, 1971 (the day before the IRA's registers opened);

(*b*) an organisation which has been formed since 30 September, 1970 and which is made up only of organisations within category (*a*);

(*c*) a union affiliated to the TUC on 15 September, 1974 (so as to "catch" one or two important and reputable unions—like the Union of Post Office Workers—which had never bothered to register under the 1871 Act); and

(*d*) an organisation on one of the permanent registers (but not the special register) under the IRA.

[101] All those are listed willy-nilly, and there is no means whereby an organisation may ask to have its name removed, save on the grounds that it is not within TULRA's definition or that its rules do not comply with TULRA's requirements. The Registrar may of his own initiative remove an organisation on either of those grounds (s. 8 (6); see paras. [**106**] and [**107**], *post*).

[**102**] Special register unions do not fall within any of the four categories, so they must apply to be listed.

Registration by application

[**103**] If any organisation which is not listed wishes to be listed it must apply (s. 8 (3)). The procedure is set out in s. 8 (4): the organisation must complete the prescribed application form, state its name and (main) address, provide a list of its officers, submit a copy of its rules, and pay a fee of £10. (The fee may in future be varied by Regulation.) Thereupon the Registrar must enter the name on the relevant list except in two cases: s. 8 (5). They are first that the Registrar is satisfied that the organisation does not come within the statutory definition (s. 8 (3)), and secondly that its name is too confusing: that is, that its name is:

(*a*) the same as any name still on the 1871 register on 30 September, 1971; or
(*b*) the same as any name ever entered on the IRA's permanent registers (but not the special register); or
(*c*) the same as any name currently on either of TULRA's lists: or
(*d*) so similar to any of the foregoing as to be likely to deceive the public.

(The provisions about a name being "too like" another are not quite so strict if an organisation wants to change its name—see para. [**155**], *post*.)

[**104**] The Registrar has no power to refuse to register on the grounds that the organisations' rules do not comply with TULRA's requirements, but if he so thinks, he may immediately give 28 days' notice of his intention to remove its name from the list (s. 8 (6), para. [**107**] below).

[**105**] If the Registrar refuses to enter a name on the relevant list the organisation may complain to the High Court (s. 8 (7)) and although such applications would normally be heard by the Divisional Court, s. 8 (8) enables the Rules of the Supreme Court to be altered so as to provide for the application to be heard by a single judge, and on appeal with leave by the Court of Appeal.

CANCELLATION OF REGISTRATION

[**106**] There are only two grounds on which an organisation can be removed from the register (s. 8 (6)). The first is that the Registrar is of the opinion that the organisation is not within the statutory definition. The second is that "its rules do not comply with the provisions of this Act". That will usually mean s. 6, but presumably it will also cover rules that conflict with ss. 5 or 7 as well (see paras. [**112**]–[**117**] and [**179**]–[**186**], *post*).

[**107**] In either case the Registrar may act on his own initiative or after an application has been made to him. He must, however, give at least 28 days' notice of his intention to remove a name (s. 8 (6)), and consider objections made to him during that time. In the event of disagreement the organisation may apply to the High Court as above.

PUBLICITY OF LISTS

[**108**] The lists are open to public inspection, free of charge (s. 8 (9)), and a copy of each will be included in the Chief Registrar's Annual Report.

6. RULES

[**109**] Every trade union and every employers' association is obliged by s. 6 (1) to have rules dealing with the matters set out in the remainder of s. 6. Section 6 was the result of an amendment in the House of Lords, carried against the wishes of the Labour Government. It might therefore be amended in due course.

[**110**] TULRA also allows the alteration of rules to unscramble funds put beyond the reach of a judgment creditor for the purposes of the IRA.

[**111**] The Trade Union Act 1913 lays down certain requirements for rules dealing with political expenditure. It was largely untouched by the IRA and TULRA only makes amendments that are consequential on the repeal of the IRA.

RULES UNDER SECTION 6

[**112**] Section 6 (1) requires every trade union and every employers' association as defined in TULRA, whether listed or not, to have rules dealing with the matters set out in s. 6. There appears to be no sanction for breach of s. 6 other than the removal from the Registrar's list, but that, as we have seen, might lead to the loss of tax relief. Such a result could follow if the rules did not comply with some other provision in TULRA: if for instance the rules unduly restricted a member's right of resignation (see para. [**106**], *ante*).

[**113**] It is not proposed to discuss s. 6 in detail, but its requirements fall into three groups:

(*a*) routine rules under sub-ss. 6 (2)-6 (5), dealing with name, address, objects property, funds, benefits and alteration of rules (the 1871 Act applied similar rules to unions registered under it);

(*b*) rules as to election of officers under sub-ss. 6 (6)-6 (9), dealing with the election of a governing body, appointment of officers and other officials, and the holding of elections and ballots (these too were in the 1871 Act in a less sophisticated form);

(*c*) membership rules under sub-ss. 6 (10)–(13) dealing with entitlement to membership discipline procedure and natural justice (these derive from ideas in the IRA, although the common law had been tentatively leading in that direction).

[**114**] Other provisions in TULRA which may directly or indirectly affect the rules are: s. 5 (arbitrary exclusion from membership); s. 7 (resignation); ss. 10–12 (audit and returns); and Schedule 1, para. 31 (nominations) as well as s. 20 (unscrambling of funds). The Trade Union Act 1913 (below) may be relevant too.

[**115**] Section 6 might have required a rule dealing with dissolution of the

organisation, but does not. Section 14 Trade Union Act (Amendment) Act 1876 did; so did the IRA, for registered organisations. The IRA also required a rule dealing with distribution of property on dissolution. Dissolution is considered in paras. [**156**] and [**157**], *post.*

[**116**] Section 4 Trade Union Act 1871 enacted that some rules of a trade union or employers' association should not be "directly enforced" by any court, although the judges gave the section a rather narrow interpretation. That section was repealed by the IRA but that Act in its turn provided that no court should compel an employee to take part in a strike (s. 128 (3)). It also made it an unfair industrial practice for an organisation of workers to discipline a member for refusing to take part in a "political" strike or certain other kinds of industrial action (ss. 65 (7) and (11)).

[**117**] There is no such restriction in TULRA on enforcing rules, and, further, TULRA provides as we saw above, that no rule of an unincorporated organisation and no rule of an incorporated one which relates to its trade objective, is to be held unlawful as being in restraint of trade (ss. 2 (5) and 3 (5)).

UNSCRAMBLING FUNDS

[**118**] TULRA gives to a union (whether listed or not) a power in one particular circumstance to alter its rules even if the rules themselves prohibit alteration. No such power is given to an employers' association.

[**119**] The relevant section is s. 20 and it is designed to allow a union to unscramble funds that had been put out of reach of possible enforcement action under the IRA. It will be remembered that s. 153 (2) (for registered unions and employers' associations) and s. 154 (4) (for unregistered ones) provided that execution could not be levied against any fund of the organisation which was precluded from being used as part of the "fighting fund" to subsidise industrial action.

[**120**] The issue was not very material before 1971: most union agreements were not enforceable contracts, and unions as such could not be sued in tort. Therefore, although union funds were vulnerable to execution, there would rarely be any judgment to enforce. But the introduction of the unfair industrial practice meant that the vulnerability of union funds, particularly provident funds, took on serious proportions, and the way to make them invulnerable was to preclude them from being used as a fighting fund. Some unions therefore introduced a new rule to that effect. But it might be argued that the precluding was temporary and not absolute as long as the precluding rule was liable to be rescinded, therefore some unions at least went one step further and introduced a rule that the precluding rule could not itself be altered.

[**121**] Now the potential liability of a union is more or less what it was before the IRA. TULRA therefore allows unions to unscramble its funds if:

(i) the precluding rule was made between 1 December, 1970 (*i.e.* one year before the first unfair industrial practices became operative) and 30 July, 1974 (both dates inclusive) (s. 20 (1) (*a*)); and

(ii) the rules declare that the precluding rule is unalterable (s. 20 (1) (*b*)); and

(iii) the unscrambling takes place before 31 July, 1978 (s. 20 (2)).

In those circumstances TULRA authorises the revocation or alteration of the precluding rule, notwithstanding the declaration in the rules that it is not to be altered.

[**122**] The precluding rule can only be revoked or amended in accordance with the procedure laid down in the rules for amending or revoking other rules of the union (s. 20 (2)).

POLITICAL FUND RULES

[**123**] Trade unions and employers' associations may be subject to restrictions in spending money for political purposes. A company registered under the Companies Act 1948 must observe the requirements of s. 19 of the Companies Act 1967. A trade union or an unincorporated employers' association must observe the Trade Union Act 1913, as amended. A special register union registered under the Companies Acts must apparently observe both (though that may have been an oversight).

Incorporated organisations subject to the Companies Acts

[**124**] Section 19 (1) Companies Act 1967 requires that any company which spends more than £50 on political purposes or charitable purposes or both must give details of such expenditure in the Directors' report for the year in question. Political purposes are defined in s. 19 (3). Failure to comply renders any director liable to a fine of £200 or six months' imprisonment (s. 22).

Trade unions and unincorporated employers' associations

[**125**] The Trade Union Act 1913 authorised trade unions and employers' associations to spend money on certain political objects subject to the provisions of the Act. Its working was supervised by the Register of Friendly Societies.

[**126**] The IRA made minor amendments to the definitions in the Act and transferred supervision to the Registrar of Trade Unions and Employers' Associations. It also gave a right of appeal from the Registrar's decision. TULRA re-amends those definitions, restores supervision to the Registrar of Friendly Societies, and removes the right of appeal.

[**127**] The Act, as so amended, now applies to trade unions and unincorporated employers' associations (TULRA, Sch. 3, para. 2). If, therefore, they wish to spend money on the political objects covered by the Act they must comply with its terms. But the Act does not prevent them spending money on other political objects—s. 3 (1) Trade Union Act 1913.

[**128**] The political objects envisaged by that Act are broadly the holding of political meetings, the distribution of political literature, the subsidising of the election of a person to Parliament or to a local authority and maintaining him once elected (TUA, s. 3 (3)).

[**129**] If money is to be spent on any of these objects then by s. 3 (1) TUA:

(i) a resolution approving political expenditure passed by a ballot of the members must be in force; and

(ii) rules must be in force, and must be approved by the Registrar, which provide—

(*a*) that payment shall be out of a separate political fund,
(*b*) that any member can contract out of political contributions, and
(*c*) that any member who contracts out shall suffer no discrimination.

If the organisation has no such rules, it must make them; and if there is no such resolution it must pass one. But the resolution must be passed by ballot conducted under the rules of the organisation, and those rules as to the taking of a ballot must be approved as suitable by the Registrar (TUA, s. 4).

[**130**] Once a resolution has been passed it is deemed to be a rule of the organisation, and can be varied or rescinded in accordance with the procedure laid down in the rules for the variation or abrogation of the rules (TUA, s. 3 (4)).

[**131**] If any member has a complaint, and they are usually about contracting out, he may refer the matter to the Registrar, who may make such order as he thinks just, but his decision is final. There is no appeal to a court of law (TUA s. 3 (2).

7. ACCOUNTS AND RETURNS

[**132**] The detailed duties imposed by the IRA on trade unions and employers' associations to keep proper accounts and submit annual returns are retained, and in some respects strengthened by TULRA, despite the fact that s. 1 does not herald their re-enactment. Before the IRA there had been the barest duty under the 1871 Act for registered organisations. The IRA's requirements for members superannuation schemes are also re-enacted.

PROPER ACCOUNTS

[**133**] The duty to keep accounts applies to all trade unions and employers' associations, whether registered or not, except federations: s. 10 (1). The corresponding provision in the IRA was s. 87, but that applied only to registered bodies. Section 10 requires any organisation whether registered or not to keep proper accounts, with a proper system of checking (s. 10 (2)), so as to give a true and fair view of the financial state of the organisation (s. 10 (3)). Accounts may be maintained either at branch level or at head office; they need not be maintained at both, but they must be maintained at one (s. 10 (4)).

[**134**] Failure to do so is made a summary offence on the part of the organisation, with a maximum fine of £100 (s. 12 (1), (5)). The offence is also committed by any and every responsible officer (or if none, by every member of the committee of management) (s. 12 (2)), unless he can show that he honestly and reasonably believed that the duty had been properly delegated, and that the delegate had carried it out or would do so (s. 12 (3)).

[**135**] Falsification of the accounts is made a summary offence with a maximum fine of £400 (s. 12 (4), (5)). Such an act could well amount to the crime of forgery.

ANNUAL RETURN

[**136**] The duty to make annual returns is embodied in TULRA s. 11, and Schedule 2, Part I. It applies to all trade unions and employers associations, whether registered or not, except federations, and except organisations which are not twelve months old (s. 11 (1) and (2)).

[**137**] The annual return must normally be for a calendar year, and be submitted to the Registrar before 1 June (Sch. 2, para. 1, and note Sch. 4, para. 5). It must by paras. 2 and 4 consist of:

—a profit and loss account
—a balance sheet
—any other accounts required by the Registrar
—a copy of the current rules of the organisation
—a note of any change in the officers or head office
—an auditor's report
—any other documents or particulars required by the Registrar.

The Registrar may allow the accounts to relate to a period other than a calendar year, and may require them to be submitted by a date other than 1 June (para. 5). He will normally do so if the organisation is registered under the Companies Act 1948 and is therefore required to make annual returns to the Companies Registry. In that event the Registrar will agree that the documents submitted to the Companies Registry may be submitted in duplicate to him.

[**138**] The accounts must be audited by qualified auditors, and Schedule 2 contains detailed provisions to ensure that the auditors are properly qualified and independent (s. 11 (3) and (6), Sch. 2, paras. 6–22). Anyone may obtain from the organisation in question a copy of its last annual return, including a copy of its rules. The organisation may make a reasonable charge for it (s. 11 (4)). And all annual returns sent to the Registrar are available for inspection by the public (s. 11 (5)).

[**139**] Failure to comply with any of these duties, or the falsification of accounts is an offence under s. 12 (see paras. [**134**] and [**135**] above).

MEMBERS SUPERANNUATION SCHEMES

[**140**] Special provision is made for pension funds, to ensure that they are properly funded. These provisions are found in s. 11 (7) and Schedule 2, Part II. They re-enact the corresponding provisions of the IRA (s. 88 (8) and Sch. 5, Part III) but the rules now apply to any organisation whether registered or not, other than federations and organisations that are not twelve months old, whereas before they applied only to registered organisations.

[**141**] Broadly, the effect of Schedule 2, Part II is that every pension fund, both those at present in operation and any that maybe set up in the future, must be kept separate from other funds of the organisation and must be subjected to the scrutiny of an actuary at least once every five years.

[**142**] Failure to comply with any duty or falsification of accounts is an offence under s. 12 (see paras. [**134**] and [**135**] above).

8. DEVOLUTION OF PROPERTY

[**143**] TULRA makes special provision for the devolution of the property of an unincorporated trade union or an unincorporated employers' association on the appointment or retirement of a trustee provided that the organisation is on the Registrar's list. No problem arises in the case of a special register union or an incorporated employers' association, because, being bodies corporate they have perpetual succession: "a corporation never dies." However in the case of an unincorporated association, its property is vested in trustees, and if no special provision were made the general law of trusts would apply. Thus if a new trustee were appointed or if a trustee retired the "old" body of trustees would all have to join to transfer the title of each item of the trust property to the "new" body of trustees. Section 40 Trustee Act 1925 enacts that there may be an automatic transfer of such property, subject to some exceptions, by virtue of the instrument of appointment or discharge provided that that instrument is a deed. Further, if a trustee wishes to retire without being replaced, he must by s. 39 Trustee Act 1925 do so by deed. That deed suffices for an automatic transfer of the title to the property to the remaining trustees under s. 40.

[**144**] TULRA grants a series of privileges to an unincorporated trade union or employers' association, if it is listed: s. 4 (2). First, ss. 39 and 40 Trustee Act apply even if the trustee is appointed or retires by signed writing instead of by deed (s. 4 (1)). In either case there is an automatic transfer of title, by virtue of the instrument of appointment or discharge.

[**145**] Second, there need not even be signed writing. By s. 4 (3), if the trustee is appointed or discharged by a resolution of the union (or the appropriate committee), then the minute of the resolution is deemed to be the instrument of appointment or discharge.

[**146**] Third, the automatic transfer extends to property to which s. 40 Trustee Act would not normally apply. Normally it would not apply to the following categories of property:

(*a*) mortgages owned by the trustees (because the borrower might be prejudiced for technical conveyancing reasons);

(*b*) leases containing a covenant against assigning without the landlord's consent (lest the automatic transfer render the lease liable to forfeiture); and

(*c*) stocks and shares (because title is transferred only when the transferee is registered in the books of the company).

[**147**] By TULRA, only property in category (*b*) is excluded in the present circumstances; property of kinds (*a*) and (*c*) will be transferred automatically by s. 40 Trustee Act as applied by TULRA. Category (*a*) is unimportant, because here a borrower would suffer no great disadvantage. To allow the automatic transfer of category (*c*) appears to mean that there are strictly two sets of trustees who may both at the same time properly claim to be the exclusive owners of the stocks and shares (*cf.* Companies Act 1948, ss. 26 (2), 75, 117) but the point is probably academic.

[**148**] Fourth, the registrar of a company is bound to register the transfer even if no proper instrument of transfer is produced to him. Section 75 Companies Act would normally require one. But it will usually be impossible for the

trustees to comply in the present case because the shares are transferred to them automatically and not by a transfer. The registrar is nevertheless bound to register them as owners of the shares if there is produced to him a certified copy of the instrument of appointment or discharge (or a certified copy of the resolution deemed to be such) with an attached list (also certified) of the securities concerned. The copies must be certified by the President and General Secretary or the equivalent officers of the organisation (s. 4 (4)–(7)).

[**149**] That illustrates why the privileges are confined to listed organisations. If they were not, then the registrar of each company would have to decide for himself whether or not the organisation was a trade union or employers' association as defined. For if it was within the definition then the transfer of shares would be automatic and he would be in breach of TULRA if he failed to give effect to it. If, on the other hand, it was not within TULRA's definition then the transfer would not be automatic and he would be in breach of the Companies Act if he gave effect to it. It is not appropriate to place him in that dilemma. If however the organisation is listed, it can easily prove that it is within the definition by obtaining a certificate from the Registrar of Friendly Societies (TULRA, s. 8 (10)).

9. AMALGAMATION

[**150**] Section 12 Trade Union Act (Amendment) Act 1876 allowed unions to amalgamate, and the Trade Union (Amalgamations, etc.) Act 1964 was passed to assist them to do so. It was seen as a small step towards counteracting the evils of multi-unionism.

[**151**] The IRA repealed the 1876 Act but made the minimum of alterations to the 1964 Act: it changed the definition of trade union, substituted references to NIRC in place of references to the High Court, and transferred the functions of the Registrar of Friendly Societies to the Registrar of Trade Unions and Employers' Associations. TULRA restores those functions to the High Court and the Registrar of Friendly Societies respectively, and redefines the organisations to which the 1964 Act is to apply.

[**152**] The Act is now to apply to trade unions (as defined in TULRA) and *unincorporated* employers' associations (as therein defined) (Sch. 3, para. 10). Employers' associations which are bodies corporate will be subject to the provisions of their charter or the Companies Act 1948, or other relevant provisions. Again a special register union, perhaps by oversight, may be subject to both sets of requirements.

[**153**] In general terms any organisation to which the Act applies may amalgamate with or transfer its engagements to another similar body (s. 1 (1) TU (A) A). The Registrar must approve the instrument of amalgamation or transfer (s. 1 (4)), and the members of both organisations must approve (s. 1 (1)). Their approval must be by ballot, and before voting they must have been given proper notice of the effect of the proposal (s. 1 (2)). After their approval is given, there is a delay of six weeks before it takes effect (s. 1 (5)). Not later than the expiry of those six weeks any aggrieved member may complain to the Registrar on one or more of four specified grounds (s. 4 (1) and (2)). The Registrar may deal with

the matter himself (s. 4 (3)), or, if he thinks fit, he may refer the matter to the High Court by way of case stated (s. 4 (8)).

10. CHANGE OF NAME

[**154**] In addition to dealing with amalgamations, the Trade Union (Amalgamations, etc.) Act 1964 also allows an organisation whether listed or not to change its name (s. 6) even if its rules make no provision for changing its name. As mentioned above, the Act applies to all trade unions and to unincorporated employers' associations. Special register unions may find that they have to comply with the Companies Act or some other requirement.

[**155**] By virtue of TULRA, Sch. 3, para. 10 (5), if the organisation is listed, the new name does not become operative until the Registrar approves it, and he is not to approve it if it is the same or too like another name on the list. In substance that re-enacts the original provision of the 1964 Act.

11. DISSOLUTION

[**156**] It has already been noted that TULRA does not require a trade union or employers' association to have a rule dealing with its dissolution, though many will have one. A special register union or an incorporated employers' association, whether registered under the Companies Act 1948 or not, may be wound up under the provisions of that Act. So may an unincorporated association formed to carry on a business for gain (which is wider than "making a profit"). That might apply to some employers' associations, but it would hardly cover a trade union.

[**157**] The High Court, however, has inherent jurisdiction to dissolve any unincorporated body for which there is no, or no suitable, provision for winding up. That was seen in the dissolution of SOGAT, the unhappy marriage of NUPB and NATSOPA (*Keys* v. *Boulter* (No. 2), [1972] 2 All E.R. 303).

12. RIGHTS OF MEMBERSHIP

[**158**] TULRA gives every worker a right against a trade union not to be excluded or expelled from membership unreasonably (s. 5). It also gives a member of a trade union a right to resign (s. 7). No such rights are given by TULRA to the members or would-be members of an employers' association.

[**159**] Sections 5 and 7 were the result of amendments carried in the House of Lords against the wishes of the Labour Government. It was also admitted on all sides that such cases of abuse were extremely rare. The Government's view was that the number of cases was too small to justify statutory intervention, though they undertook to consider legislation at a later date.

[**160**] It will be convenient to consider the common law position first for two reasons: (a) s. 5 is expressed to be without prejudice to common law rights (though in practice s. 5 appears to embrace any there may be); and (b) the members or would-be members of an unincorporated employers' association have no statutory rights.

COMMON LAW RIGHTS

[**161**] Before the IRA's guiding principles overtook them, the judges had developed some measure of protection against unjust expulsion from or discipline by bodies like a trade union, and there were signs that they were ready to make some advances towards a right against unfair refusal to accord membership to an applicant, but there were more problems there.

[**162**] It used to be said that the rule book of a union (and the same argument applies to unincorporated employers' associations) was a contract. When a member joined, he made a contract with the union on the terms in the rule book. Since no one can be forced to make a contract, it was difficult for the common law to give a worker a right to join a union on the basis of contract. Likewise with expulsion: if there were an exact performance of the contract, then an expelled member could not complain of breach of contract, no matter how unfair the expulsion might be.

[**163**] Therefore, the Courts began to say that the rule book was a contract, but was not only a contract: it was also, as it were, a constitution. It might therefore give rights over and above those available in contract. LORD DENNING, for ever jealous of the rights of the individual, said this about the rules of an unincorporated association in *Enderby Town Football Club, Ltd.* v. *Football Association*, [1971] Ch. 591 at p. 606, [1971] 1 All E.R. 215 at p. 219:

> "The rules of a body like this are often said to be a contract. So they are in legal theory. But it is a fiction—a fiction created by the lawyers so as to give the courts jurisdiction . . . Putting the fiction aside, the truth is that the rules are nothing more nor less than a legislative code . . . Such regulations, although said to be a contract, are subject to the control of the courts . . ."

He then went on to list four ways in which the courts might exercise that control, even if, by accepting the rules, the member has apparently "signed away his rights". They were on the grounds of

—restraint of trade
—ouster of jurisdiction
—right to work
—natural justice.

Restraint of trade

[**164**] An oppressive rule might be said to interfere unreasonably in a worker's right to dispose of his labour as he wills. If so the rule (if not the whole contract) would be void and unenforceable as between the parties, but it would not give an outsider any right to complain. Thus in principle the argument might assist an aggrieved member or an expelled member, but could not assist anyone refused membership.

[**165**] However, the courts could not go very far along this road in the case of a trade union or an employers' association, because statute prevented it. Section 3 Trade Union Act 1871 provided that the purposes of a trade union or an employers' association should not be void merely because they were in restraint

of trade. It was assumed that "purposes" meant any purposes and therefore included the rules of a union. But in *Faramus* v. *Film Artistes Association* [1964] A.C. 925; [1964] All E.R. 25 it was argued that "purposes" meant main objects, and that therefore not every rule was validated by s. 3. The House of Lords rejected that argument but it was resurrected by SACHS, L.J. in *Edwards* v. *Society of Graphical and Allied Trades*, [1971] Ch. at p. 365; [1970] 3 All E.R. 689. It was a minority view and never represented the law, and TULRA, ss. 2 (5) and 3 (5) puts it beyond doubt: purposes and rules are validated.

[**166**] That appears to end the argument as far as concerns the members of an employers' association are concerned: their rules are not unenforceable merely because they are in restraint of trade.

[**167**] However, s. 5 (5) may help the member of a trade union. It says that nothing in s. 2 (5) is to reduce the common law rights of an expelled member of or a person who wants to join a trade union. For the reasons given above it seems that a person refused membership cannot complain on the grounds of restraint of trade, but s. 5 (5) appears to open the way for a member who was expelled to claim that a rule is unenforceable against him.

Ouster of jurisdiction

[**168**] In the eyes of the common law, it is an essential aspect of every man's freedom that he should have access to the courts for the determination of his rights, and if any agreement purports to prevent him from doing so the agreement is invalid. So, for example, if a union rule book states that the executive council's decision on a question of expulsion is final, it is in fact saying that the ultimate arbiter of an individual's rights is not the court, but the union, and to that extent it ousts the jurisdiction of the courts. That cannot be done, and the rule is void. Notwithstanding the rule, the member may go to court to test the validity of his expulsion.

[**169**] What is usually permissible is for the rules to insist that the member shall first exhaust his domestic remedies, before going to court. That is to say that the member must first make use of any appeals procedure provided by the rules, and only if he is still dissatisfied may he go to court. Faced with such a rule, the court may, but not must, stay a premature application to it: it may refuse to hear the case unless and until the member has tried the union's appeals machinery. However, if the final appeal is to, say, a biennial conference which will not meet again for eighteen months, the court may conclude that it is unreasonable to expect the member to wait that long, and may hear the case even if domestic procedures have not been exhausted. A rule that the member must first exhaust domestic remedies is unlikely to be implied; the rules must say so expressly.

[**170**] Again this head can be of use only to someone who has become a member of the union, and not someone who is refused membership.

Right to work

[**171**] "Every man has a right to work" is a fine political slogan, and it may be a basic human right too, morally speaking; but LORD DENNING has seized on

the phrase in two or three different contexts, and begun to give it some legal shape. It is to be expected that the common law will undergo further development here, but for the moment the cases should be treated with caution.

[172] In *Nagle* v. *Fielden*, [1966] 1 All E.R. 689 a woman trainer wanted a licence from the Jockey Club, who at first refused because she was a woman. The case was compromised, but not before LORD DENNING had declared that a rule which prevented a man (or woman!) earning his living on trivial or capricious grounds was void and could be ignored by the courts: it infringed the right to work. LORD DENNING repeated his views in *Edwards* v. *Society of Graphical and Allied Trades*, [1971] Ch. at p. 365; [1970] 3 All E.R. 689.

[173] It does not take much imagination to see that the "right to work" if developed could be used by an applicant for membership to insist he be not arbitrarily refused membership of a union, or by a non-member to avoid a closed shop arrangement, if the closed shop were considered unreasonable, and in some circumstances by a member to contest arbitrary expulsion from a union. However, it is thought that the right to work is after all only a particular instance of the right to trade. To say that a rule is in restraint of the right to work, is therefore tantamount to saying that it is in restraint of trade.

[174] TULRA, s. 3 (5) would thus appear to circumvent any interference in the rules of an employers' association on the grounds that a rule was in restraint of the right to work. However, in the case of trade unions s. 5 (5) provides that s. 2 (5) is not to prejudice or reduce the common law rights of an expelled member or someone who wishes to join.

Natural justice

[175] It is said that where a tribunal exercises a judicial or similar function, that is, when it decides people's rights, then that tribunal must observe the rules of natural justice, and those rules are that a person whose rights are affected has

—the right to have his case tried by an unbiased tribunal
—the right to have adequate notice of any charges against him
—the right to put his case to the tribunal.

[176] It is not established that a person has a right to be represented by his lawyer before a tribunal. LORD DENNING was of the opinion that the rules must not expressly prohibit it, though it would be in the tribunal's discretion whether to allow it or not. Even if there is no right to be represented, it is clear that a man has a right to be heard, for, according to the reasoning in *R.* v. *Cambridge University* (1723), 1 Stra. 557 even God asked Adam if he had anything to say before he banished him from the Garden of Eden.

[177] The principle is unlikely to assist a person refused membership. It might assist an aggrieved member, but in his case it appears to be covered already by s. 6 (13).

STATUTORY RIGHTS

[178] It is proposed to mention only TULRA, ss. 5 and 7. Other statutes may be relevant in particular cases (*e.g.* the Companies Act 1948, for members of companies; or the Race Relations Act 1968 if there is discrimination on the racial grounds).

Resignation

[**179**] TULRA, s. 7 enacts that every member of a trade union (and that would include a special register union) has a right to resign. He may be required to give reasonable notice (which could be several weeks) and comply with reasonable terms (for instance, he might be asked to pay subscriptions up to the date of resignation).

[**180**] It is thought that the courts would in any event imply a right of resignation, were there no statutory right. That may be relevant for employers' associations.

Exclusion or expulsion

[**181**] Section 5 gives a worker a right not to be unreasonably or arbitrarily excluded from membership of a trade union (including a special register body). There is no such statutory right in connection with employers' associations.

[**182**] A worker is defined in s. 30 (1) to include anyone who works, normally works or seeks to work as an employee, an independent contractor (except a professional man in relation to his client) or a civil servant. His right is a right against exclusion or expulsion only. It is not, for example, a right to complain of unfair discipline (but see ss. 6 (11) and (12)). Further it is not a right to complain of every exclusion or expulsion but only where the exclusion or expulsion is "by way of arbitrary or unreasonable discrimination" (s. 5 (1)).

[**183**] There is no guidance on what might constitute arbitrary or unreasonable discrimination, save that s. 5 (2) declares that neither of the following shall be so regarded: where the worker is of a different description from most of the other members of the union; or where he is not appropriately qualified. Presumably a worker is qualified if he has the necessary "academic, technical or professional qualifications", as in unfair dismissal (*cf.* Sch. 1, para. 6 (9)) whether or not he is a good workman.

[**184**] The right is enforceable in the first instance by application to an industrial tribunal but the tribunal's only remedy is a declaration of the worker's right to be a member s. 5 (3). Although it is supposed to be declaratory only, it may apparently fix a time limit for complying s. 5 (4).

[**185**] If the union does not allow the worker his membership within the time limit (if any) in the declaration, or (if none) within a reasonable time, the worker may then apply to the High Court, which may award compensation or an injunction "or such other relief . . . as the court may think just and expedient" (s. 5 (4)).

[**186**] It may, as NIRC thought in *Langston* v. *Amalgamated Union of Engineering Workers*, [1974] 1 All E.R. 980, be just to make an order and yet be wholly inexpedient.

13. NOMINATIONS

[**187**] TULRA continues a right of nomination that was first introduced for (registered) unions in 1876. It is now available whether the union is listed or not.

[**188**] As a general rule a person may dispose of property on his death only by a will, property executed and attested. Persons under eighteen years of age may not normally make a will. There are some exceptions, and one is found in TULRA, Schedule 1, para. 31 (re-enacting IRA, s. 155).

[**189**] It enables Regulations to be made allowing a member of a union who is sixteen years old or more to nominate someone to receive any provident benefits payable on his death. Further, a union may pay out up to £500 on the death of a member (whether under a nomination or otherwise) without requiring the production of any Probate or Letters of Administration. The limit of £500 may in future be increased (para. 31 (4)).

[**190**] Regulations were made under the IRA: the Industrial Relations (Nominations) Regulations 1971, S.I. 1971 No. 2085. They will continue in force for the time being, as if made under TULRA (Sch. 4, paras. 6 (1) and (2)).

CHAPTER FOUR

COLLECTIVE BARGAINING

[**191**] It should be remembered that the process of collective bargaining may be affected by the incomes policy of the government of the day. Thus successive governments have, from time to time of recent years, imposed limits on the amount of wage increases. They are seen as temporary expedients only. So, once upon a time, was income tax!

[**192**] TULRA in no way affects such measures. But it

—sweeps away the IRA's scheme of legal regulation of the process of collective bargaining (s. 1)
—creates a new presumption of the non-enforceability of collective bargains (s. 18)
—abolishes the Commission on Industrial Relations (s. 1)
—expects a new Conciliation and Arbitration Service
—makes some, generally minor, amendments to other statutes dealing with various aspects of collective bargaining (Sch. 3).

1. THE PROCESS OF BARGAINING

RESTORATION OF THE PRINCIPLE OF FREE COLLECTIVE BARGAINING

[**193**] Most of Part III of the IRA dealing with collective bargaining, namely ss. 37–55 (imposed procedure agreements and sole bargaining agencies), was repealed on the passing of TULRA on 31 July, 1974 (s. 1 (3)). Sections 56 and 57 (disclosure of information) were never operative, but they and the rest of Part III (presumption as to legal enforceability of collective bargains, and deemed agreements) were repealed on 16 September, 1974 when TULRA was brought fully into effect.

[**194**] Thus, TULRA restores the principle of free collective bargaining as traditionally understood. The assumption is that both sides of industry will be collectively organised and that they will settle between them the terms and conditions of employment for the industry or plant or other unit concerned free of outside interference. Each will bargain for what it can get, and bargaining is seen as a continuing process so that either side may seek to renegotiate the agreed terms from time to time as it sees fit. It is also thought proper to leave the parties to settle between themselves any disputes that may arise, whether they be disputes "of right" (that the other is not keeping to his bargain) or disputes "of interest" (that the other will not agree to a proposal).

[**195**] Finally, it is assumed that either side may properly use its collective strength whether in making a bargain or in settling a dispute by threatening or

taking industrial action. Industrial action is considered in the next two chapters.

[**196**] The law then has only a supporting role to play in the process of collective bargaining as a general rule, but there are some exceptions.

EXCEPTIONS TO THE PRINCIPLE

[**197**] In a few exceptional cases the law imposes certain terms on the parties. The more important examples are:

—section 8 of the Terms and Conditions of Employment Act, 1959
—Wages Councils Act 1959 and similar legislation
—The Fair Wages Resolution of the House of Commons, 1946
—Various statutes dealing with nationalised or subsidised industries.

Terms and conditions of Employment Act 1959

[**198**] Section 8 of the Terms and Conditions of Employment Act 1959 is aimed at the "black sheep" employer who pays lower than average wages or otherwise offers poorer than average terms of employment. He will obviously offend the unions. He will also offend those employers who are having to pay more; for he represents unfair competition.

[**199**] The Act provides that a union or an employers' association may report the black sheep to the Secretary of State on the grounds that: (i) there is a collective agreement or award which establishes a normal standard for terms and conditions of employment in the industry concerned, whether nationally or locally; (ii) a substantial proportion of employers and workers in that industry (nationally or locally, as the case may be) are covered by the agreement or award; and (iii) the black sheep is not observing the norm. It should be noted that the black sheep need not be a party to the agreement or award. If the Department of Employment cannot settle the dispute by negotiation, the matter is referred to the Industrial Arbitration Board, and the Board will order the black sheep to observe the norm unless he can prove that the terms he offers are on the whole not less favourable than the norm. The award of the Board is not directly enforceable by the unions or other employers but it has the effect of automatically varying the contracts of employment of the black sheep's workers, who can thereafter sue him if he does not observe the norm.

[**200**] The IRA made two changes in the procedure, apart from giving the Board its present name. One is retained by TULRA; the other is discarded.

[**201**] Before the IRA, the s. 8 procedure was not available in a Wages Council industry (for which, see paras. [**203**] *et seq., infra*). The IRA made it so available and TULRA does not change that. By virtue of the IRA, the procedure was available only to registered trade unions and registered employers' associations, but TULRA restores it to any trade union or employers' association (Sch. 3, para. 8).

[**202**] The functions of the Industrial Arbitration Board are expected to be transferred in due course to the new Conciliation and Arbitration Service, if and when the Service is given statutory authority (see paras. [**248**] *et seq., infra*).

Wages Councils Act 1959

[**203**] The Wages Councils Act 1959 provides statutory machinery for fixing minimum wages in certain industries. The machinery is the setting up of a Wages Council. One may be established by order of the Secretary of State when "no adequate machinery exists for the effective regulation of the remuneration of the workers" concerned. That usually means those industries where trade unions find it difficult to organise, so that voluntary collective bargaining cannot function. There are some fifty Wages Councils established for various industries including the clothing, catering and road haulage industries. The Agricultural Wages Act 1948 establishes a somewhat similar system of Agricultural Wages Boards for workers in agriculture.

[**204**] Wages Councils consist of an equal number of employer representatives and employee representatives plus three independent members, one of whom is chairman. They are appointed by the Secretary of State, although in practice any unions or employers' associations involved in the industry nominate members for the approval of the Secretary. The number of employer and employee representatives depends on the size of the industry.

[**205**] The Council may make proposals about wages, holidays and holiday pay, and the Secretary of State, if he approves, may make an order implementing that proposal. On the making of such an order, the proposed terms are automatically incorporated into the contracts of employment of the workers concerned and are therefore enforceable by them by civil proceedings. An employer who defaults is also liable to criminal prosecution by the Wages Inspectorate. And unions and employers' associations may now use s. 8 Terms and Conditions of Employment Act 1959 to force a lagging employer to comply (see para. [**201**] above). The order lays down a minimum only; there is nothing to stop the workers seeking more, if they can get it.

[**206**] A Wages Council may make recommendations to the Secretary of State about issues of wider concern in the industry, but he need do no more than consider them.

[**207**] Besides protecting the lower paid worker in industries where unions are weak, Wages Councils are supposed to create an environment where voluntary collective bargaining may be established. Thus, it is said, it should be the aim of every Wages Council to commit suicide; for when effective voluntary collective bargaining can be established the Wages Council is superfluous and may be abolished by order of the Secretary of State.

[**208**] The IRA made some amendments to the Wages Council procedure and some of them are retained by TULRA. Those retained are as follows:

1. An organisation of workers may unilaterally ask the Secretary of State to abolish a Wages Council. Before 1971 such an application had to be made jointly by or on behalf of the employers and unions (TULRA, Sch. 3, para. 9 (3)).

2. The grounds of an application for the abolition of a Wages Council are slightly different from the original 1959 Act. This is consequent upon 1; for the original words were inappropriate to cover a unilateral application. The grounds now are that "the existence of a Wages Council is no

longer necessary for the purpose of maintaining a reasonable standard of remuneration . . ." (TULRA, Sch. 3, para. 9 (3)).

3. If an organisation of workers does make a unilateral application to the Secretary to abolish a Wages Council he must consult the Council and the appropriate employers' associations before he begins the procedure for making an order for abolition (TULRA, Sch. 3, para. 9 (8)).

4. A commission of inquiry (see para. [**209**] below) may recommend that a Wages Council be abolished merely on the ground that it is "expedient to do so". Originally one or both of the two conditions set out in s. 6 (2) of the Wages Councils Act had to be satisfied as well, but the IRA deleted those conditions. TULRA is silent.

5. Section 8 of the Terms and Conditions of Employment Act 1959 now applies to Wages Councils industries (see para. [**201**] above).

[**209**] However, some of the amendments made by the IRA have been removed, and the original Wages Councils Act restored. Before setting up or abolishing a Wages Council, the Secretary of State will normally refer the matter to a commission of inquiry for advice. By the IRA the functions of commissions of inquiry were transferred to the Commission on Industrial Relations. That body is abolished by TULRA and the functions are retransferred to commissions of inquiry under the Wages Councils Act. These functions are likely to be transferred in due course to the Conciliation and Arbitration Service (see para. [**248**]) as part of a more thorough going reform of the Wages Councils system. For the time being TULRA restores the original position by: reviving the definition of a commission of inquiry (TULRA, Sch. 3, para. 9 (7)); restoring s. 9 (1) and Schedule 4 of the Wages Councils Act, which provide for the constitution, officers and proceedings of commissions of inquiry (*ibid.*, para. 9 (4)); giving them back their original functions (*ibid.*, para. 9 (2)); and again disqualifying their members under the House of Commons Disqualification Act 1957 (*ibid.*, para. 6 (2)). Sections 22 and 23 of the Wages Councils Act are restored to their original wording (*ibid.*, paras. 9 (5) and (6)).

Fair wages resolution

[**210**] In 1946 the House of Commons passed a resolution concerning the terms on which government departments should make contracts. There had been earlier resolutions to the like effect. The first was in 1891. Of itself a resolution of the House is not law, but every government department will write its terms into their contracts. So will local authorities and most nationalised industries. There are six clauses, the most important of which require the contractor to observe terms and conditions of employment not less favourable than those generally established for that industry; to allow his workers to join trade unions, and to see that any subcontractors also observe the terms of the Resolution.

Other legislation

[**211**] Various Acts of Parliament may impose an obligation on the employer to pay fair wages. They require the employer to observe the same conditions as

are found in the Fair Wages Resolution. Such an obligation may be found in, for example

—Housing Act 1957, s. 92
—Road Traffic Act 1960, s. 152
—Films Act 1960, s. 42
—Independent Broadcasting Act 1973, s. 16.

[**212**] Other statutes achieve a similar result in different ways. For example, the Civil Aviation Act 1949, s. 15, requires workers in the aviation industry to be offered the same terms and conditions of employment as those offered by the nationalised corporations. Thus the public sector can set the standard for the private sector. And the Road Haulage Wages Act 1938, ss. 4 and 5, gives a civil remedy to certain workers in that industry if they are paid "unfair" wages. (Incidentally, TULRA inserts its own definition of trade union into that Act: Sch. 3, para. 4.)

[**213**] Yet again, other Acts (particularly in the nationalised industries) whilst not imposing terms on the parties, place an obligation on management to negotiate with the appropriate trade unions.

2. THE EFFECT OF COLLECTIVE BARGAINS

[**214**] TULRA creates a presumption in the case of most collective bargains that they are not intended to be legally enforceable, thus reversing the presumption created by the IRA. TULRA also makes a new provision laying down strict conditions upon which a "no-strikes" clause may be incorporated in the contract of the individual worker.

THE ENFORCEABILITY OF COLLECTIVE BARGAINS

[**215**] At common law (and the common law may still be relevant) collective agreements between employers and unions are not normally legally enforceable contracts, for the following reasons. One of the requirements of a valid contract in English law is said to be that the parties must intend to enter a legal relationship: they must intend to be bound in law and not "in honour" only.

[**216**] If there is an explicit statement that the parties do or do not intend to be legally bound, there is no problem. If there is no such express statement then the nature of the arrangement may give rise to a presumption. If it is a commercial arrangement there is a presumption that the parties do intend to enter legal relationships, but it is rebuttable, by evidence that they intended only a gentleman's agreement. Conversely, in domestic or social arrangements, the law presumes against an intention to be legally bound, but again that may be rebutted by evidence to the contrary.

[**217**] Now, according to *Ford Motor Co., Ltd.* v. *Amalgamated Union of Engineering and Foundry Workers*, [1969] 2 Q.B. 303; [1969] 2 All E.R. 481 collective bargains do not fall into either category; they are neither "commercial" nor "domestic". Therefore there is no presumption either way at common law: it is a question of what those parties must be taken to have intended when they made that particular agreement. So, the judge said, when Fords

and the unions agreed the "Blue Book" most people at that time thought that collective bargains were not enforceable at law. Thus, on the evidence, Fords and the unions making that agreement in that climate of opinion must have intended not to be bound in law. *Ford* decided that in the case of collective bargains there is no presumption either way; it did not strictly decide that there is a presumption against enforceability, although it almost comes to that.

[**218**] The Boot and Shoe Trust Deed of 1898 was usually quoted as an example of an agreement that was intended to be legally enforceable. If the parties go to the trouble of embodying their arrangements in a formal deed, they presumably intend to be bound.

[**219**] The IRA altered the common law position. It was popularly misconstrued in this context. It did not presume that any collective agreements *were* legally enforceable; it did presume that some collective agreements were *intended to be* legally enforceable. That left open the question whether they were unenforceable on other grounds, for example, because they were too vague to know what precisely had been agreed.

[**220**] TULRA now produces a third set of rules, and which set of rules applies is to be decided by the subject matter of the agreement and the date on which it was made.

[**221**] First a "collective agreement" is defined in s. 30 (1) to mean an agreement or arrangement between a union or unions and an employer or employers about some matter which could properly be the subject of a trade dispute as defined in s. 29 (1). The definition of a trade dispute is discussed in the next chapter. If then the bargain is exclusively about some other matter then it is not a collective agreement as defined and its enforceability will depend on the common law. It will be noted that a collective agreement as defined may be written or oral.

[**222**] If there is a collective agreement as defined then the rules as to its enforceability depend upon the date it was made: TULRA applies unless the agreement was made during the interregnum of the IRA. So s. 18 provides that if the agreement was made before 1 December, 1971 or on or after 16 September, 1974, then the following rules apply:

1. There is a conclusive presumption *against* intention to enter a legally enforceable contract, except in the case of an agreement which falls within paragraphs 2 or 3 below (s. 18 (1)). That goes further than *Ford Motor Co., Ltd.* v. *Amalgamated Union of Engineering and Foundry Workers*: first by creating a presumption against enforceability, whereas *Ford* said that there was no presumption either way in law; secondly, by making the presumption in effect rebuttable only by express written agreement to the contrary.
2. If the agreement is in writing and states that it is to be legally enforceable, then there is a conclusive presumption *in favour of* intention to enter a legally enforceable contract, (s. 18 (2)). That, like s. 34 IRA, leaves open the question whether it is unenforceable on other grounds.
3. An agreement may be part one and part the other, but the "unenforceable" part may be referred to for the purpose of construing the "enforceable" part (s. 18 (3)).

[**223**] Finally, if the agreement was made during the interregnum, that is between 1 December, 1971 and 15 September, 1974, both dates inclusive, then TULRA has nothing at all to say about the agreement itself (but the incorporation of certain of its terms into the individual contract of employment may be restricted by s. 18 (4), paras. [**228**] and [**229**] below). An agreement made during the interregnum will therefore be governed by the IRA in the sense that when the parties actually made the agreement they must be taken to have known of the presumptions contained in s. 34 of that Act. Thus if they made an agreement in writing which did not expressly opt out of legal enforceability (in whole or part) then they must be taken to have intended to enter a legally enforceable contract, (s. 34 (1), IRA); if they made a written agreement that did opt out, or if the agreement was not in writing, then the IRA raised no presumptions and the matter would fall to be decided by the common law as embodied in *Ford Motor Co. Ltd.* v. *Amalgamated Union of Engineering and Foundry Workers.*

[**224**] Section 23 (3) TULRA raises a nice point: an "... obligation ... incurred under any provision of the 1971 Act ..." becomes unenforceable by action on the repeal of the IRA, unless the provision is re-enacted by TULRA, Sch. 1. Where there is an agreement that is presumed to be intended to be legally enforceable by IRA, s. 34, are its obligations incurred under s. 34 or incurred by virtue of the parties' consent? It is thought that the latter is clearly the right view: s. 34 contained rules of evidence only, not rules of substance. Hence if there are any such agreements still in existence, s. 34's presumption stands. The CIR reported a short time ago that very few written agreements had been made since 1 December, 1971 which did not opt out of legal enforceability, and in most of those cases failure to opt out was apparently an oversight!

INCORPORATION INTO THE INDIVIDUAL CONTRACT

[**225**] Whether or not a collective bargain is itself legally enforceable, it, or parts of it, may become incorporated into the contracts of the individual workers covered by it. That is sometimes referred to as the "normative effect" of the collective bargain: it sets the norm for the individual contracts. TULRA places restrictions on the incorporation of "no-strikes" or similar clauses.

[**226**] Apart from TULRA, terms may be incorporated into the individual contract if the employer and the worker concerned have so agreed. Such agreement may be expressed or implied, and if implied, may be implied by conduct or by custom and practice. It is sometimes possible to regard the union as the agent of (all) the workers involved, with authority to *settle* on their behalf the terms of their individual contracts, but that is most unusual. (It will be remembered that the employer is obliged by the Contracts of Employment Act 1972 to notify his workers of any change in their terms of employment. Such "note" is strictly only evidence of the contract, and not the contract itself, but it may help decide whether and what terms have been incorporated into the individual contract.)

[**227**] However, some terms of a collective bargain might by their very nature by considered to be inappropriate to be incorporated into the individual contract: a term, for instance, that the employer will recognise the union

concerned as having sole negotiating rights; or, more to the point, that the union will not call a strike unless and until domestic procedures have been exhausted. It is difficult, but not impossible, to regard such "collective" terms as being incorporated into the individual's contract. In *Rookes* v. *Barnard*, [1964] A.C. 1129; [1964] 1 All E.R. 367 it was conceded by counsel for the defendants that a "no-strikes" clause had been incorporated into the workers' contracts, but there were special circumstances: counsel wanted a decision on the main issue of the tort of intimidation and not the side issue of incorporation.

[**228**] The point has never been finally settled, and TULRA settles it. Section 18 (4) provides that a no-strikes clause in a collective agreement, or any other term in it that "*has the effect of* prohibiting or restricting" a worker's "right" to strike or take other industrial action cannot be incorporated into an individual contract of employment unless five conditions are satisfied; s. 18 (5) adds that one may not contract out of s. 18 (4). The five conditions are that

—the collective agreement is in writing
—the collective agreement expressly authorises incorporation, or provides "that those terms shall be incorporated" (though a collective agreement cannot of itself alter the terms of the worker's contract unless he has agreed in advance or appointed the union his agent to settle)
—the collective agreement is reasonably available for the worker to inspect at work during working hours
—the unions concerned are all "independent" (see s. 30 (1))
—the individual contract does in fact incorporate the no strikes clause, expressly or impliedly.

[**229**] The meaning of s. 18 (4) seems perfectly clear: if a 'no-strikes' clause or a similar restriction on industrial action is to be incorporated into the individual contract, it must be a deliberate act and everyone must be aware of it. However, it is by no means impossible to raise legalistic quibbles about its wording—for instance, what is meant by "the right of workers to engage in a strike"? It is to be hoped that the temptation to quibble will be resisted.

[**230**] Even if a "no-strikes" clause is incorporated in an individual contract, the potentially most serious consequence is avoided by s. 13 (3) (*b*): a breach of contract in contemplation or furtherance of a trade dispute is not to be regarded as an unlawful act for the purpose of establishing liability in tort. That is discussed more fully in the next chapter.

3. THE PEACEFUL SETTLEMENT OF DISPUTES

[**231**] If the parties have made a legal contract, then legal proceedings may be taken to enforce it should it be broken. But that is, to say the least, a very remote possibility, and not only because few collective bargains are contracts.

[**232**] Most disputes will be settled by negotiation between the two sides, or failing that by industrial action. Various agencies have been established over the years to assist the parties in achieving a negotiated settlement, and so avoid the need for industrial action. The more important examples are as follows. TULRA adds to the list.

THE CONCILIATION SERVICE OF THE DEPARTMENT OF EMPLOYMENT

[**233**] This has been called the Department's "fire-fighting role". It is wholly distinct from the statutory role of conciliation officers in connection with unfair dismissal (see para. [**515**]). Officers of the Department offer their services to help settle hundreds if not thousands of disputes every year on a more or less informal basis. Many of the interventions are not even recorded in the statistics. The major drawback in the service is that, being part of the Department, it is under the control of the Secretary of State and it is therefore obliged to conform to the policies of the government of the day. If, for example, there is a dispute about a pay claim in excess of a Government's current "guidelines", the service would have only a restricted role, or even no role at all, to play. However, this fire-fighting role is now being transferred to the new Conciliation and Arbitration Service (see paras. [**248**] *et seq.* below) and the Department's own conciliation service is being wound up. It is expected that the conciliation officers appointed in connection with unfair dismissals will also become part of the staff of the CAS.

[**234**] The Ministry has a great deal of inherent power in this field, but formal authority for its role as conciliator can be found in the Conciliation Act 1896.

CONCILIATION ACT 1896

[**235**] As well as providing formal authority for the fire-fighting role of the Department the Conciliation Act 1896 also provides the basis for the more formal procedures of Committees Investigation, and it also allows for the appointment of a conciliator or an arbitrator. It was enacted at a time when the number of days lost through industrial action gave the politicians cause for concern.

[**236**] Section 2 provides that "where a difference exists or is apprehended" the Secretary of State may

—inquire into the causes
—attempt to mediate
—on the request of either side, appoint a conciliator
—on the request of both sides, appoint an arbitrator.

In theory each of these functions is distinct. Inquiry implies fact finding, without judging; mediation implies an impartial "go-between" who is not directly concerned to achieve any particular result: he is merely an independent chairman; conciliation implies attempting to achieve a settlement by encouraging one side to give way here and the other there, counselling each; and arbitration is of course pronouncing a judgment upon any issues upon which the parties cannot agree. In fact the boundaries are not nearly so clear cut. A mediator for instance will often conciliate. But arbitration is different. Arbitration has not found great favour so far as a means of settling trade disputes in this country —particularly on the union side—but when it does take place it is usually voluntary; thus the Conciliation Act requires the consent of both parties before an arbitrator can be appointed.

[**237**] An important feature of the Act is that the Secretary of State may take the initiative. He does not have to wait for the parties to refer the matter to him before he investigates or attempts to mediate. But he cannot appoint a conciliator or arbitrator unless he is asked. Section 4 of the Act authorises the appointment of permanent conciliation boards "for any district or trade".

[**238**] It is envisaged that most of these functions will now be exercised by the new Conciliation and Arbitration Service (see para. [**248**]), but the Secretary of State will formally retain parallel powers.

INDUSTRIAL COURTS ACT 1919

[**239**] The First World War saw several stops towards industrial co-operation. It was imperative that the unions back the war effort, and a scrics of committees under the chairmanship of Mr. Speaker Whitley led to the establishment of Joint Industrial Councils to settle terms and conditions of employment in several industries; to Whitley Councils established for the same purpose in the non-industrial civil service, and to the establishment of an Industrial Court. That was a misnomer. It is not a court of law, but a panel of arbitrators. It was felt that if such a panel were permanently established it would lead to an increase in the use of arbitration and a decrease in the use of industrial action as a means of settling disputes. The IRA renamed the panel the Industrial Arbitration Board, and that title is retained by TULRA (Sch. 3, para. 3) (and its members are still disqualified under the House of Commons Disqualification Act 1957: *ibid.*, para. 6 (1)).

[**240**] By s. 2, Industrial Courts Act 1919, if one of the parties to an actual or potential trade dispute reports the matter to the Secretary of State and if he cannot settle the dispute by negotiation or otherwise he may adopt one of three methods of arbitration. But there can be arbitration only if both parties consent. The three methods are by reference to

—the Industrial Arbitration Board
—a single arbitrator or a panel or arbitrators appointed by the Secretary of State
—a board of arbitration consisting of nominees of the employers and workers concerned in equal numbers and an independent chairman nominated by the Secretary of State.

[**241**] In addition to its jurisdiction under the Industrial Courts Act, the IAB arbitrates in cases under s. 8 of the Terms and Conditions of Employment Act, under the Fair Wages Resolution and under the "statutory Fair Wages" discussed above (see paras. [**198**], [**210**] and [**211**]).

[**242**] The Industrial Courts Act also provides in s. 4 the authority for Courts of Enquiry. Such Courts are used when the dispute is of a serious kind; when for instance there will be great inconvenience to the public if the dispute is not settled. The Court is a public, formal, fact-finding exercise, and its findings are laid before Parliament. Less serious matters may be referred to Committees of Investigation under the Conciliation Act. If and when the new Conciliation and Arbitration Service is given statutory authority, all the functions of the IAB may be transferred to the CAS and the IAB will be abolished.

THE COMMISSION ON INDUSTRIAL RELATIONS

[**243**] Whilst it is better to settle disputes peacefully rather than by industrial action, it is better still to prevent disputes arising in the first place. That was the thinking of the Donovan Commission (1965–8) which reviewed and made recommendations upon our system of industrial relations. The Donovan Commission was set up when the politicians were worried yet again by the increasingly serious problem of industrial disputes.

[**244**] One of the Commission's recommendations was the establishment of a body which was eventually called the Commission on Industrial Relations. It was brought into being by a Labour Government as a Royal Commission in 1969. It was envisaged as a permanent body composed of persons with a great deal of experience of industrial affairs. Its primary concern was the reform of the system of collective bargaining. It was to suggest improvements in procedural arrangements and make recommendations about union recognition and so forth. It might investigate and attempt to resolve particular disputes referred to it. It might also consider the longer term problems of an industry. It was said to be independent of the government, but acted only on references from the Secretary of State. It had no "teeth". It could bark its reports to the Minister but it could not bite.

[**245**] The Labour Government's intention was to establish the CIR on a statutory basis, but that was not in fact done until the Conservative Government's Industrial Relations Act (ss. 120–123). The CIR's function under that Act was somewhat different. It was still to be an adviser to the Secretary of State (s. 121), but in addition to that role it was given the function of recommending to NIRC solutions to particular problems arising under the IRA's new legal processes, especially whether there should or should not be a sole bargaining agent, or an approved closed shop.

[**246**] The CIR considered several recognition disputes under its pre-1971 voluntary jurisdiction. There were few cases where its advice was wholly accepted. In its more important role of catalyst of industrial relations it was scarcely overworked by the few references made to it by the Secretary of State. Then came the change in government and the Conservative's Industrial Relations Bill. One of the side effects of the TUC's campaign to "Kill the Bill" was that the unions withdrew their co-operation from the CIR and the unionist Commissioners, including the then chairman, resigned. The unions' refusal to co-operate in manning the CIR continued after the Bill became the IRA, though the CIR continued to function without them.

[**247**] The CIR was scarcely then an overwhelming success but the general opinion is that it did quite a lot of valuable work. And with the restoration of a Labour Government, the abolition of NIRC and the repeal of the IRA, the CIR might have continued with success, but the TUC and the new Labour Government considered that its reputation had been debased by its association with NIRC, and that it could not enjoy the full confidence of both sides of industry. Therefore, it had to be replaced by a new Conciliation and Arbitration Service. The CIR itself was formally abolished on 16 September, 1974 (TULRA, s. 1 (1)). The Commissioners may be entitled to redundancy payments: s. 24 (1).

THE CONCILIATION AND ARBITRATION SERVICE

[**248**] The Conciliation and Arbitration Service was established by the Secretary of State at the beginning of September, 1974. It has a Council of ten under the chairmanship of Mr. James Mortimer. The other nine councillors are three trade unionists, three industrialists and three academics. It was set up a couple of weeks before the abolition of the CIR to enable a smooth transfer of "business" to take place, and the CAS has taken over some of the staff of the CIR. The headquarters of the CAS is in London though it will have various regional offices. It is intended to be completely independent of government—an "arm's length body". Its staff are not civil servants, though they have equivalent status.

[**249**] None of this is in TULRA itself. The CAS was established by administrative action. It is intended that it will be given statutory authority later. In the first, non-statutory, stage of its life the CAS has the CIR's original function of seeking to improve industrial relations generally. It has thus assumed the mantle of the CIR. It is also taking over the Department of Employment's advisory and "fire-fighting" role (see para. [**233**], *ante*).

[**250**] Further, it has assumed functions similar to those of the Secretary of State under the Conciliation Act 1896. As well as investigating and offering advice the CAS staff will where appropriate mediate and conciliate. The CAS will with the consent of both parties appoint an arbitrator or a board of arbitrators. It will not itself arbitrate in such cases lest it forfeit the goodwill of one side or the other (or both!). The Secretary of State might still appoint a Committee or Court of Enquiry where appropriate. Conciliation officers concerned with unfair dismissals will become part of the CAS staff.

[**251**] In due course it is intended to give the CAS statutory authority. It will also give guidance on industrial relations generally—which will replace the Code of Practice (see paras. [**31**–[**33**])—and on disclosure of information in particular. Further, the IAB would be absorbed into the CAS and would cease to exist as a separate body. Thus the CAS would inherit jurisdiction over claims under the Fair Wages Resolution, "statutory fair wages" and s. 8 of the Terms and Conditions of Employment Act 1959. The CAS will exercise those functions through a Central Arbitration Committee (CASCA?). CASCA will also adjudicate in recognition disputes, disputes about disclosure of information, and some claims in connection with the reformed Wages Councils (see para. [**209**]). Finally "an official of the CAS" is to assume the functions of the Registrar of Friendly Societies in connection with trade unions (see paras. [**91**]–[**155**]).

[**252**] Thus the scheme is eventually to have one single body charged with the duty of watching over industrial relations: advising, conciliating and where appropriate arranging for arbitration, so achieving peaceful settlements of particular disputes; but a body that is also concerned with longer term improvements to the system which will tend to prevent disputes arising.

CHAPTER FIVE

INDUSTRIAL ACTION

[253] The "right to strike" is a chameleon phrase which takes its meaning from its context. As far as the law is concerned, "right" here means the ability to do the act or acts in question without thereby doing anything unlawful. But effective industrial action will almost inevitably involve some unlawfulness at common law, be it a crime, a tort, or a breach of contract. Successive statutes have therefore intervened to remove liability for certain acts if done "in contemplation or furtherance of a trade dispute", and hence have enabled industrial action to be organised lawfully. Since this is, legally speaking, a privilege or immunity granted by Act of Parliament, it is perhaps more descriptive to speak of a freedom to strike rather than a right to strike.

[254] A distinction must be made between freedom to take part in a strike or other action and freedom to organise it. If a striker incurs any liability it will usually be for breach of his contract of employment, though he may in exceptional cases commit a crime. The liability of the organiser of a strike will usually arise from a tort, or exceptionally a crime.

[255] In many respects TULRA restores the law on industrial action to the state it was in immediately before the IRA. There are however, some important differences. Apart from the section dealing with peaceful picketing, which is discussed in the next chapter, TULRA

—abolishes all unfair industrial practices (though there is still a right to complain of unfair dismissal: see Chapter Seven)
—provides a new definition of a trade dispute (s. 30 (1))
—restores the common law on the legality of taking part in a strike and the effect of strike notices
—re-enacts s. 128 (1), IRA, which makes it clear that no court may by its order compel an employee to work (s. 16)
—effectively re-enacts the provisions of the Trades Disputes Acts 1906–65 giving immunity from actions in tort to an individual who organises industrial action but with some variations and additions (s. 13)
—restores immunity to unions and employers' associations from actions in tort, but with some limitations (s. 14)
—restricts the availability of an *ex parte* injunction (s. 17)

1. ABOLITION OF UNFAIR INDUSTRIAL PRACTICES

[256] The IRA removed jurisdiction over industrial disputes from the ordinary courts and gave it to a new specialist court, NIRC. It did that by widening the statutory immunities against common law liability, by creating instead a new statutory liability, the unfair industrial practice, and by giving NIRC exclusive jurisdiction over the relevant unfair industrial practices.

[**257**] NIRC was abolished on 31 July, 1974 upon the passing of TULRA, s. 1 (3) and with it went the machinery for complaining of those unfair industrial practices. With the repeal of the remainder of the IRA on 16 September, 1974, the concept of the unfair industrial practice has disappeared.

2. STATUTORY IMMUNITY

[**258**] By abolishing the unfair industrial practice, TULRA returns to the old system of potential common law liability, negatived by statutory immunity. Immunity is granted for certain acts done "in contemplation or furtherance of a trade dispute". TULRA thus revives the traditional "golden formula" for immunity, but with a new definition of "trade dispute" in s. 29. The new definition is based partly on that contained in s. 5 Trades Disputes Act 1906 and partly on the definition of an "industrial dispute" in the IRA. It also contains some new elements designed to deal with issues raised in recent cases. Perhaps it should be emphasised that where statutory immunity is available, it is available to any person, not just a union official, and it is available whether the industrial action is official or unofficial, constitutional or unconstitutional.

TRADE DISPUTE

[**259**] Section 29 defines a trade dispute as a dispute between certain categories of people which is connected with a certain type of subject matter. The overall notion is that a "trade dispute" is to be contrasted with a "political dispute", but the precise line is by no means easy to draw. ROSKILL, L.J. in *Sherard* v. *Amalgamated Union of Engineering Workers,* [1973] I.C.R. 421 thought the phrase "political strike" "... should be used, at any rate in a court of law, with considerable caution, for it does not lend itself to precise or accurate definition". It is usually said that a strike against the government as such is a political dispute; but if the government is the employer of some of the workers involved, it may be difficult to say whether the strike is against the government as the government, or the government as employer. So in *Sherard's* case, a one-day strike was called by the AUEW against the then government's wages freeze. On the face of it that was a "political strike". But the AUEW had members in the government's employ whose wages had been frozen, and it could be argued therefore that the union was supporting its members who were in dispute with their employer for refusing to pay more. The Court of Appeal therefore accepted that there could be a trade dispute (or strictly an "industrial dispute" within the IRA).

Dispute

[**260**] A trade dispute must be a dispute. First then, "dispute" is a wide word and would cover any real difference of opinion. As LORD DENNING put it in *Beetham* v. *Trinidad Cement, Ltd.* [1960] A.C. 132; [1960] 1 All E.R. 274 in this characteristically forceful metaphor:

"By definition a trade dispute exists wherever a difference exists and a difference can exist long before the parties become locked in combat . . . It is sufficient that they should be sparring for an opening."

Parties

[**261**] Secondly, the dispute must be between employers and workers or workers and workers. "Worker" is defined generally in s. 30 (1) (repeating in effect IRA, ss. 167 (1) and (4)) to include employees, independent contractors (other than a professional man in relation to his client), and crown employees (other than the armed services) but not policemen. Section 30 (2) brings in doctors, dentists, opticians and others engaged in the Health Service (*cf.* IRA, s. 167 (2)).

[**262**] "Employer" is not as such defined in TULRA, except that s. 30 (2) provides that where appropriate various Health Service authorities are to be deemed employers.

[**263**] For the purposes of s. 29 "employers" includes "employers' association" and "workers" includes "trade union": s. 29 (4). The definition of "industrial dispute" in the IRA also allowed that industrial organisations could be parties. The aim is to cover cases like *Torquay Hotel Co., Ltd.* v. *Cousins*, [1969] 2 Ch. 106; [1969] 1 All E.R. 522 where the court held that the dispute was between the employer and the union as such, and not between the employer and any workers.

[**264**] Disputes between employers and employers are not and never have been trade disputes as defined (*cf. Larkin* v. *Long*, [1915] A.C. 814). As for disputes between employers and workers, s. 29 (2) provides that there can be a trade dispute between a Minister and workers, even if he is technically not their employer provided that the Minister is involved in either of the ways specified in s. 29 (2). That would cover disputes arising from a Whitley Council, a Wages Council or some other similar body.

[**265**] Also in connection with disputes between employers and workers, s. 25 (6) settles doubts that have been raised from time to time about whether a trade dispute must be between an employer and *his* workers. The better view was that it need not, and s. 25 (6) confirms that. The workers must however be engaged in the dispute as workers, and not in any other capacity. NIRC so held in relation to an "industrial dispute" under the IRA (*Midland Cold Storage, Ltd.* v. *Turner*, [1972] 3 All E.R. 773; [1972] I.C.R. 230).

[**266**] But the most important aspect of TULRA's definition of a trade dispute is the re-introduction of disputes between workers and workers, which the IRA had excluded. LORD DENNING related the history of the phrase in *Cory Lighterage, Ltd.* v. *Transport and General Workers Union*, [1973] 2 All E.R. 558; [1973] I.C.R. 339. Its significance may be seen in relation to three kinds of disputes: closed shop disputes, demarcation disputes and recognition disputes. If union men do not want to work with a non-union man, is their dispute with him, or with the employer for employing him? A trio of cases around 1920 indicates the possible differences of approach (*Valentine* v. *Hyde*, [1919] 2 Ch. 129; *Hodges* v. *Webb*, [1920] 2 Ch. 70 and *White* v. *Riley*, [1921] 1 Ch. 1). It will depend on the circumstances of each case, but clearly the em-

ployer is not necessarily involved in every closed shop dispute. So too if one group of workers disagrees with another group about who does what, the employer may or may not become a party to the dispute. And lastly whilst a recognition dispute will usually involve the employer, there have been cases, like *J. T. Stratford & Son, Ltd.* v. *Lindley*, [1965] A.C. 307; [1964] 3 All E.R. 102, where the courts have said that the "real" dispute stemmed from inter-union rivalry. All these disputes would now fall within s. 29 as being disputes between workers and workers, or their unions.

Connected with

[**267**] Assuming that the dispute is between the appropriate parties, it must also be shown to be a dispute "connected with" the appropriate subject matter. "Connected with", a phrase common to the Acts of 1906 and 1974, implies a looser tie than the IRA's "relates *wholly or mainly* to", but whether the courts will so interpret it remains to be seen (*cf. J. T. Stratford & Son, Ltd.* v. *Lindley*, [1965] A.C. 307; [1964] 3 All E.R. 102). "Relates to" seems to be used as a synonym for "is connected with" in ss. 29 (2) and (3).

Subject matter

[**268**] The matters which may be the subject of a trade dispute are set out in paragraphs (*a*) to (*g*) of s. 29 (1). They bear some resemblance to the matters which could be the subject of an "industrial dispute" within the IRA, but there are some additions. Thus a trade dispute must be connected with one or more of the following:

(*a*) The terms of the contract or the physical conditions of the working environment. That is common to the Acts of 1906, 1971 and 1974.

(*b*) The engagement, non-engagement, termination or suspension of employment of a worker. The 1906 Act said "employment or non-employment", and the IRA used the present wording, save that TULRA adds after "termination or suspension of employment" the words "or the duties of employment". That is to meet the point raised in *Cory Lighterage* v. *Transport and General Workers Union*, [1973] 2 All E.R. 558; [1973] I.C.R. 339 where the Court of Appeal expressed the view (*obiter*) that "suspension of employment" meant suspension without pay and did not extend to suspension on full pay. It is now clear that either can give rise to a trade dispute.

(*c*) Demarcation disputes. "Allocation of work . . . as between workers" is common to TULRA and the IRA, but TULRA inserts "or the duties of employment" to guard against a possible restrictive interpretation.

(*d*) Discipline. That as such is new, but previously some matters of discipline could have come under other heads depending on the nature of the discipline: terms of employment, termination or suspension of employment, etc. The IRA included "procedures relating to discipline", which is not quite the same.

(*e*) Membership or non-membership of a union. That again is new as such, although it is thought it could properly be regarded as covered by "terms and conditions of employment" (*cf. White* v. *Riley*, [1921] 1 Ch. 1).

(*f*) Facilities for union officials. That was introduced by the IRA.

(*g*) Negotiating and consultative machinery, and procedures relating to anything in paragraphs (*a*) to (*f*) including in particular recognition disputes. That more or less represents a compendium of IRA, s. 166 (5). The better view is that a recognition dispute is in any event connected with the terms and conditions of employment of the workers who wish to be represented, but it has never been finally settled.

[**269**] One innovation that has attracted a great deal of attention is s. 29 (3), which enacts that a dispute may be a trade dispute even though it relates to matters occurring outside Great Britain. An amendment in the House of Lords added the proviso that if a person wishes to claim statutory immunity for his acts done in this country on the grounds that they were done in connection with such an overseas dispute, he must first show that the outcome of the overseas dispute is "likely to" affect him in one of the ways specified in paragraphs (*a*) to (*g*) above.

[**270**] The reason for the new subsection is the ever-increasing importance of the multi-national company. Another piece of internationalism is found in s. 30 (6): it is immaterial for the purposes of TULRA that the proper law of the contract under which a person is employed is not the law of the United Kingdom.

CONTEMPLATION OR FURTHERANCE

[**271**] TULRA introduces a gloss on the word "contemplation". The accepted interpretation of "contemplation or furtherance" is to be found in the opinion of LORD SHAW in *Conway* v. *Wade*, [1909] A.C. 506 at p. 522:

> ". . . the contemplation of such a dispute must be the contemplation of something impending or likely to occur . . . [The words] do not cover the case of coercive interference in which the intervener may have it in his own mind that if he does not get his own way he will thereupon take ways and means to bring a trade dispute into existence. To 'contemplate a trade dispute' is to have before the mind some objective event or situation . . . but does not mean a contemplation, meditation or resolve in regard to something as yet wholly within the mind and of a subjective character. . . . With regard to the term 'furtherance' of a trade dispute, I think this must apply to a trade dispute already in existence and that the act done must be in the course of it and for the purpose of promoting the interests of either part or both parties to it."

So a person must act with the predominant purpose of promoting some legitimate trade objective, and not from an ulterior motive. Thus, in *Conway* v. *Wade* itself, Wade, it was found, was motivated by a personal grudge against Conway, and so was not within the "golden formula". Further, subject to s. 29 (5), it has to be shown that the dispute was actually existing or was objectively imminent.

[**272**] Section 29 (5) extends the meaning of "in contemplation". It enacts that if an act threat or demand would have lead to a trade dispute, but for the fact that the other side gave way, the act threat or demand is nevertheless to be deemed done in contemplation of a trade dispute. It is thought that this rather curious provision was designed to meet the point in the rather curious case of *Cory Lighterage* v. *Transport and General Workers Union*, [1973] 2 All E.R. 558; [1973] I.C.R. 339. Mr. Shute deliberately disqualified himself from membership of the TGWU knowing that his fellow workers would therefore refuse to work with him, as indeed happened. The employer suspended him on full pay at the union's insistence. The Court of Appeal held that there was no industrial dispute within the IRA: none between Shute and the employer because Shute had wanted to be sent home; none between the union and the employer because the employer had agreed with the union's demand. Nor, said the Court (and this is the most difficult part of the decision) was any such dispute in contemplation at that stage. *Cory* is to be regarded as decided on its own special facts, but should a similar situation arise again, s. 29 (5) would apply. However, it is thought that there would now be a trade dispute on those facts even without s. 29 (5), for there clearly was a dispute between Shute and the union. Disputes between workers and workers were not industrial disputes within the IRA, but may be trade disputes within TULRA.

3. LIABILITY IN CONTRACT

[**273**] We must now consider how far industrial action may give rise to liability in contract. Many strikes are in breach of a collective procedure agreement (so-called "unconstitutional strikes"), but few such agreements are legally enforceable contracts (see Chapter Four). Therefore for practical purposes we may confine the discussion to breaches of the individual contract of employment.

STRIKES

[**274**] TULRA has repealed and has not re-enacted s. 147 IRA which dealt with the interpretation and effect of strike notices. It has thus restored the common law position which is somewhat confused. There is a nice academic argument about the legality of strike action at common law, but it is of little practical importance.

[**275**] The lawfulness or otherwise of strike action at common law will depend upon whether and what notice was given that a strike would take place, whether the stoppage is of fixed or indefinite duration, and whether there is a total or partial withdrawal of labour.

[**276**] It is a term of the contract of employment that the worker be ready and willing to work. If, therefore, the contract is still in being and the worker refuses to work, whether it be called a strike, a withdrawal of labour or whatever, there is on the face of it a breach of contract. On the other hand any worker may terminate his contract of employment by giving notice of the proper length in accordance with the terms of the contract express or implied, subject to a minimum of one week if the Contracts of Employment Act applies. If therefore all the workers taking part in the strike have lawfully terminated

their contracts, the strike is lawful; if they have broken their contracts the strike is unlawful.

[**277**] It follows that workers are in breach of contract, and so are acting unlawfully, if they partially withdraw their labour, when, for instance, they "black" the goods of a particular customer by refusing to handle them contrary to their employer's instructions, or when they refuse to work with a certain fellow employee contrary to the employer's orders.

[**278**] So too it follows that a one-day strike or any other such "limited" strike action is a breach of contract. The workers have not terminated their contracts. On the contrary they clearly regard it as still in being, but they decline to carry out their obligations for the stated period. Such action is therefore unlawful at common law.

[**279**] If however there is a total, indefinite stoppage, the lawfulness of the strike will normally depend on whether or not proper notice was given of the strike:

(*a*) If no notice was given, or if notice was given but it was shorter than that required to terminate the contract of employment, then in either case it is clear that the contract has not been properly terminated and therefore the refusal to work is a breach of contract, and hence the strike is unlawful.

(*b*) If proper notice was given, and it was express notice to terminate the contract, then the contract has not been broken and the strike is lawful.

(*c*) The position is less clear, however, if notice of the appropriate length is given, but the notice is not expressed to be notice of termination. Before 1963 it was regarded, it seems, as implied notice to terminate. However, DONOVAN, L.J. in Court of Appeal in *Rookes* v. *Barnard*, [1963] 1 Q.B. 623; [1962] 2 All E.R. 579 suggested that this approach was wrong. Strikers, he said, do not want to give up their jobs, they merely want to be paid more, or secure some other advantage. Therefore it would be wrong to interpret a "neutral" notice of this sort as being a notice of *intent to terminate* the contract. In his opinion a strike after such notice was in breach of contract. LORD DEVLIN in the House of Lords ([1964] A.C. 1129; [1964] 1 All E.R. 367) took a similar view and so did LORD DENNING in the subsequent case of *J. T. Stratford & Son, Ltd.* v. *Lindley*, [1965] A.C. 307; [1964] 3 All E.R. 102.

[**280**] Thus the orthodox view is that at common law a strike is a breach of contract, unless proper notice has been given expressly terminating the contract. And further it is arguable that to give such a notice is of itself an anticipatory breach of contract.

[**281**] Another view was put by LORD DENNING who had second thoughts in *Morgan* v. *Fry*, [1968] 2 Q.B. 710; [1968] 3 All E.R. 452 for, said he, if a strike is a breach of contract, there is no right to strike. On the other hand, the law had for sixty years recognised a right to strike. He resolved the dilemma by saying that a strike after due notice operated to suspend the contract of employment, because there was a term, implied by law, to that effect in the contract of employment. That is a neat solution but it remains to be seen whether it will find general acceptance. The other judges in the case decided on different

grounds: DAVIES, L.J. said that a strike notice was notice of termination plus an offer to work on new terms, but that is difficult to reconcile with the views expressed in *Rookes* v. *Barnard*, that a "neutral" strike notice is not to be construed as notice of termination. RUSSELL, L.J. said that a strike was a breach of contract, but that did not necessarily mean that a threat of a strike would always constitute the tort of intimidation as in *Rookes* v. *Barnard*.

[**282**] It is possible to argue that a majority of the Court of Appeal in *Morgan* v. *Fry*, [1968] 2 Q.B. 710; [1968] 3 All E.R. 452 (*i.e.* LORD DENNING and DAVIES, L.J.) held that a strike after due notice was lawful at common law, but in view of the different bases for that decision the case cannot be regarded as satisfactory.

[**283**] Sometimes the contract of employment may incorporate a "no-strikes" clause. In view of TULRA, s. 18 (4), it will be the exception rather than the rule (see para. [**228**]), but a strike in breach of such a clause will obviously be unlawful.

OTHER FORMS OF INDUSTRIAL ACTION

[**284**] There are many other ways in which workers may bring pressure to bear on an employer. Most if not all involve a breach of the contract of employment, or some other unlawfulness.

[**285**] If for instance a man works to rule, by observing punctiliously every detailed duty of his contract, he can hardly be said to be breaking his contract, but as was seen in *Secretary of State for Employment* v. *Associated Society of Locomotive Engineers and Firemen* (*No. 2*), [1972] I.C.R. 19; [1972] 2 All E.R. 949 "work to rule" is often a euphemism for breaking rules. The Court held in that case that the workers acted in breach of contract when they "bent" the rules by giving them an unreasonable interpretation and then purported to work to the bent rules, so frustrating the commercial operation of the railways.

[**286**] Likewise a go-slow is a breach of contract, because by deliberately working more slowly than is usual, the worker is in breach of his implied obligation to give reasonable service. A ban on overtime may involve a breach of contract; it depends whether under the contract of employment overtime was voluntary or obligatory.

[**287**] A sit-in, where workers occupy their employer's premises without working, may involve the tort of trespass. The worker has, by virtue of his contract of employment, an implied permission to enter his employer's premises. If the contract has been terminated the worker no longer has a right to enter and is therefore a trespasser. Similar principles apply in the case of a work-in, where the workers not only occupy the employer's premises but also continue to work. Both the sit-in and the work-in may involve a breach of contract if the workers refuse to obey the employer's lawful instructions.

[**288**] Indirect action in the form of "blacking" (or a "secondary boycott") will usually involve a breach of contract as explained previously.

[**289**] The employer, too, has many ways in which he may bring pressure to bear on his workers, from a withdrawal of privileges to a lock-out. The lawfulness of his action will usually depend on whether or not he is in breach of contract, upon similar principles to those explained above.

CONSEQUENCES

[**290**] As we have already seen, one important consequence of holding that a strike, even after due notice, is in breach of contract is that there is no legal right to strike. Other consequences are as follows.

[**291**] If a strike is a breach of contract, the employer has certain remedies. First, if a strike is a breach of contract, it is such a serious breach as will entitle the employer to dismiss the strikers without notice. Secondly, the employer may sue each individual striker for damages for breach of contract, but in normal circumstances it would not be worthwhile (*National Coal Board* v. *Galley*, [1958] 1 All E.R. 91; [1958] 1 W.L.R. 16). An employer may not obtain an injunction to restrain a threatened strike, nor may he obtain an order to compel strikers to return to work: TULRA, s. 16 (re-enacting IRA, s. 12 (1)). Quite apart from statute, it is unlikely that any court would make such an order (see para. [**369**]).

[**292**] Potentially the most important result of holding that a strike or other industrial action is in breach of contract is in connection with the so-called trade torts discussed below. To break a contract may be regarded as the doing of an unlawful act or the use of unlawful means for the purpose of those torts. However, s. 13 (3) (*b*), TULRA enacts, and this is an entirely new provision, that a breach of contract in contemplation or furtherance of a trade dispute is not to be so regarded.

[**293**] On the other hand, if a striker expressly terminates his contract, he may forfeit accrued rights, say to a pension, which depend on a certain length of service. When the strike is settled he makes a new contract with his employer and has no accrued length of service. Of course, as between the employer and himself it may be agreed that he shall be deemed to be re-instated to his old position, but that cannot affect third parties, for example the trustees of a pension fund who, subject to the terms of any trust deed, would be entitled and indeed bound to insist on the true position. But in practical terms the most important rights which depend on continuity of employment are the statutory provisions about unfair dismissal, redundancy payments and the length of notice. And statute provides that, for those purposes, continuity of employment is not broken by strikes and lockouts whether in breach or on termination of the contract of employment.

4. LIABILITY IN TORT

[**294**] We now turn to consider what if any tortious liability is likely to be incurred in connection with industrial action.

[**295**] In the first place, s. 14, TULRA, imposes severe restrictions upon bringing actions in tort against a trade union as such or against an employers' association as such. That is discussed later (see paras. [**371**] *et seq.*, *infra*).

[**296**] Secondly, s. 13, TULRA, gives protection to the individual organiser of industrial action by providing that certain acts done in contemplation or furtherance of a trade dispute shall not be actionable in tort. The protection so given is more or less the same as that available immediately before the passing of the IRA. The original Bill gave wider immunity, but a House of Lords

amendment produced the present version. Section 13 aims to provide some immunity against the so-called trade torts; inducing a breach of contract, intimidation and conspiracy. The first causes most problems—it can be seen as a trinity of torts, usually labelled "directly inducing a breach of contract", "directly procuring a breach of contract" and "indirectly procuring a breach of contract", but at the same time it shows signs of developing into an amorphous tort of "interference with contract." Section 13 also protects against the tort (if it exists!) of "interference with trade".

[**297**] The defence of s. 13 then is only available if there is a trade dispute. In the case of some of the torts there is also the defence of "justification" at common law, which is available whether there is a trade dispute or not, but as will be seen (para. [**360**] *et seq.*, *infra*), it is of little relevance to industrial action.

[**298**] Enough has been said to indicate that the law of the trade torts is extremely complex, but it is thought that all the torts, other than conspiracy, fit into an overall pattern. They involve essentially three parties, and, instead of harming the plaintiff directly, I use you to harm him. Thus:

> 1. If you deliberately harm the plaintiff by an unlawful act, you are liable to him. But I may be liable too, if I deliberately instigated your unlawful act. If I persuade you to commit a tort against him, I am joint tortfeasor. If I persuade you to break your contract with him, I am liable to him in tort under *Lumley* v. *Gye* (1853), 2 E. & B. 216. The nature of the liability is persuasion to unlawfulness.
>
> 2. If you deliberately harm the plaintiff, but you do nothing unlawful to him, you are not liable. If I am to be liable to him, then, it must be on the grounds that I have done something unlawful myself. *Rookes* v. *Barnard*, [1964] A.C. 1129; [1964] 1 All E.R. 367, says I am liable if I deliberately and unlawfully coerced you into harming him. But it is possible that it is the deliberate unlawfulness on my part that is critical, rather than its coercive nature. The nature of the liability is unlawful coercion, but it could become unlawful persuasion.
>
> 3. Finally, I may not seek your co-operation at all. I may act against you, so causing loss to the plaintiff. I have, as it were, killed, or at least hit, two birds with one stone. I have used you as my involuntary agent to harm the plaintiff. If I have done no wrong to you, I am not liable to him. If I have done wrong to you, I may be liable to him too.

As a theory however this is highly speculative at present, and should be treated with caution.

INTERFERENCE WITH TRADE

Mere interference

[**299**] Any form of industrial action by workers is likely to interfere with their employer's trade, but it is *not* a tort, without more, deliberately to interfere with the trade, business or employment of another person, or with the right of another person to dispose of his capital or his labour as he wills. However, s. 13 (2) takes the precaution of declaring "for the avoidance of doubt" that it shall not be actionable in tort to do any of those things in contemplation or furtherance of a trade dispute. The reason for s. 13 (2) is as follows.

[**300**] A great debate took place at the end of the last century about the nature of tortious liability. One school of thought held that it was tortious deliberately to cause loss to another without good reason. According to that school, the motive of the defendant was all important: if he was spiteful (that is, if he had no legitimate reason to harm the other) he was liable; but if he could excuse himself by showing that his motive was the pursuit of his own legitimate objectives (selfishness?), he was not liable. The other school of thought said motive was irrelevant for the purpose of establishing liability in tort (apart from conspiracy which is anomalous): the question was, what had the defendant done, not why had he done it; had he committed a recognised wrong in law or not? If not then he was not liable, no matter how unfair or spiteful he might be.

[**301**] Eventually, the latter school of thought prevailed. The vital case was *Allen* v. *Flood*, [1898] A.C. 1. Allen called a strike of some boilermakers to bring pressure to bear on the employer to dismiss two shipwrights. On the facts proved, Allen could be liable only on the ground that he had deliberately interfered with the shipwrights' employment without lawful excuse. The House of Lords held that he was not liable. He had done nothing wrongful in itself and apart from conspiracy a bad motive could not make unlawful that which was otherwise lawful. However, a differently constituted House of Lords in *Quinn* v. *Leathem*, [1901] A.C. 495 cast doubts on the proposition and to avoid difficulties the Trade Disputes Act 1906 declared that to interfere with trade, etc., was not unlawful if done in a trade dispute. Subsequent case law has vindicated *Allen* v. *Flood* and removed the doubts raised by *Quinn* v. *Leathem* so that merely to interfere with trade is not unlawful even outside a trade dispute, but the relevant section of the Trades Disputes Act was repeated in the IRA and now appears as s. 13 (2), TULRA, "for the avoidance of doubt".

Unlawful interference

[**302**] It is sometimes said that there is a tort of interference with trade by unlawful means. But it is clear from *Allen* v. *Flood*, [1898] A.C. 1 that unlawful means is equivalent to a tort or a breach of contract: a civil wrong. Therefore, to ask if the defendant has "interfered with trade by unlawful means" is only another way of asking if the defendant has committed a tort or a breach of contract, but with this difference: he may deliberately commit a wrong against A, and thereby "interfere with the trade" of B.

[**303**] The defendant's wrongful act, as he intended, causes loss to B through A. A is the apparent object of the wrong, but B is the real, though indirect, object. For instance, I lock you up (false imprisonment) in order to prevent you going to work for the plaintiff, or I call a lightning strike of your workers (inducing a breach of contract) to prevent your delivering goods to him.

[**304**] Here motive is important, but it does not make unlawful an act that is otherwise lawful; it merely serves to indicate an additional plaintiff in respect of an undoubted unlawful act. It is thought that this is the true ground of liability for what is labelled directly or indirectly procuring a breach of contract and for interfering in contract (see paras. [**315**] *et seq., post*).

[**305**] If the tort of unlawful interference eventually becomes recognised as

such, s. 13 (2), TULRA, ought to afford a defence. B's only cause of action is "(unlawful) interference with trade", and s. 13 (2) on the face of it protects a defendant within the golden formula. Section 13 (3) may also offer a defence, in particular circumstances, by showing that means that are apparently unlawful are not to be regarded as unlawful, as explained below.

[**306**] All this may seem an arid academic argument, but it may well prove a way for the courts to discover new liabilities should they wish to do so. The foundations have already been laid: "I have always understood", said LORD DENNING in *Torquay Hotel Co., Ltd.* v. *Cousins*, [1969] 2 Ch. 106, "that if one person deliberately interferes with the trade or business of another and does so by unlawful means, that is, *by an act which he is not at liberty to commit,* then he is acting unlawfully. . . .". (Italics supplied.)

[**307**] This is dangerous ground. Before *Allen* v. *Flood,* [1898] A.C. 1 there might have been a tort of *unjustified* interference with trade, or unfair competition, with the judges deciding what was fair, reasonable and justified. *Allen* v. *Flood* was heard by the House of Lords twice, on the second occasion with nine Lords present and eight Queen's Bench judges to offer their advice. The House as has been said decided that apart from conspiracy motive was not relevant for the purpose of establishing liability in tort: I could be as unfair as I like, provided I did no legal wrong of which you could complain.

[**308**] So *Allen* v. *Flood* looks at the person "on the receiving end" and asks was it a wrong *to him.* LORD DENNING looks at the actor, and asks was it a wrong *by him.* The two do not coincide. I do wrong if I commit a crime, or a breach of statute, or a contempt of court, but none of those is necessarily a wrong *to you.* It is respectfully submitted that *Allen* v. *Flood* is the sounder principle. LORD DENNING's definition seems to make acts more unlawful by virtue of being less direct.

[**309**] Which way the common law will move, or whether it will move at all, it is impossible to be sure, but the indications are that it is moving towards the concept of equating unfairness with unlawfulness. And that raises all the old arguments as to whether the judges are the best people to decide what is fair and reasonable in the industrial setting.

INDUCING A BREACH OF CONTRACT

Direct inducement

[**310**] It is a tort knowingly to persuade another to break his contract with the plaintiff to the plaintiff's loss. The tort was established by *Lumley* v. *Gye* (1858), 2 E. & B. 216, but has undergone considerable judicial development since then. The facts of *Lumley* v. *Gye* were as follows: Johanna Wagner contracted to sing for Lumley and no one else, but Gye deliberately persuaded her to break her contract and sing for him instead. He was held liable in tort to his rival.

[**311**] The defendant must act deliberately. The early statements required that he should *intend* to cause a breach of contract, but in *Emerald Construction Co., Ltd.* v. *Lowthian,* [1966] 1 All E.R. 1013; [1966] 1 W.L.R. 691 the Court of Appeal held that recklessness would be sufficient. Recklessness means that the defendant must foresee the possible consequences of his act; he must foresee the possibility of a breach of contract, though he cares not whether a breach results

or not. Unfortunately some of the expressions used in *Emerald Construction* could apply to a negligent defendant, but negligence is something radically different: it is *not foreseeing* the consequences when you ought to, and the better view is that negligence is not enough to establish liability for this tort.

[**312**] We have seen that almost every form of industrial action can involve a breach of contract by the workers, and if it does the organiser will commit a tort by persuading them to take that action. Section 13 (1) (*a*) may offer a defence. It is a defence to an action for persuading a breach of a contract *of employment*. And by s. 30 (1) that means a contract of service or apprenticeship. Section 13 (1) (*a*) therefore affords no defence for persuading other types of workers to break their contracts (say, independent contractors, who have a contract "for services"). Nor does it extend to commercial contracts, so that it does not apply to persuading a customer or supplier to break his contract with the employer. Nor does it apply to persuading an agent to break his fiduciary duty to his principal (*Prudential Assurance Co. Ltd.* v. *Lorenz* (1971), 11 K.I.R. 78.

[**313**] The word "only" must be remembered: if, for instance, I persuade you to break your contract of employment by telling you lies about your employer, s. 13 (1) (*a*) protects me against an action for persuading you to break your contract, but not against an action for defamation.

[**314**] Section 13 (3) (*b*) may be noted. Its real purpose is probably to do with "indirect procurement" and conspiracy, but it is certainly arguable that it accidentally affords protection to an action for persuading a person to break any contract, whether of employment or not, provided always that the golden formula applies. It is unlikely that the Courts in their present "expansionist" mood will accept the argument. It depends on the nature of the liability in *Lumley* v. *Gye* (1853) 2 E. & B. 216. It is suggested that the better view is that my liability depends upon my having persuaded you to commit an unlawful act against the plaintiff by breaking your contract with him. It is not enough that I have persuaded you to cause loss to the plaintiff. It must be shown, for the tort under discussion, that you have done an unlawful act to him. But s. 13 (3) (*b*) says that a breach of contract in contemplation or furtherance of a trade dispute is not to be regarded as ". . . the doing of an unlawful act . . . for the purpose of establishing liability in tort". Therefore, I have persuaded you to do something "not unlawful", just as if I have persuaded you to terminate your contract lawfully, or to refuse to enter a contract. In view of the attitude of the court in *Torquay Hotel Co., Ltd.* v. *Cousins*, [1969] 2 Ch. 106; [1969] 1 All E.R. 522 the likelihood of that argument succeeding is remote, but it ought to succeed! The case is discussed in paras. [**334**] *et seq., post.*

Direct and indirect procurement

[**315**] "Blacking" and breaches of commercial contracts cause more intricate problems.

[**316**] If I persuade you to break your contract, I am liable. But suppose, without persuading you, I nevertheless deliberately cause you to break your contract: I put you in breach of contract. Suppose I lock you up, or poison you, so that you cannot go to work, can your employer sue me for putting you in breach of contract? The difference between procurement and persuasion in

this context lies in your freewill. If I persuade, you choose whether to break your contract or not. If I lock you up you have no choice: you are an involuntary agent. The quality of your act is essentially different. If you deliberately (though perhaps reluctantly) break your contract you are clearly acting unlawfully. If on the other hand you are my involuntary puppet, there may be no breach of contract at all. In some circumstances the contract may be frustrated. But even if there is a breach of contract you were helpless to prevent it. I alone caused the breach but I am not liable on your contract. It is thought therefore that "procuring a breach of contract" though superficially similar to "inducing a person to break a contract" is truly a different type of case altogether. It is suggested that "procuring a breach of contract" is a species of the tort of "(unlawfully) interfering with trade" (see paras. [**302**–[**309**], *ante*). If that is true the breach of your contract with the plaintiff is only the occasion of the loss, not an essential ingredient in establishing liability. I could be liable even if the contract were not broken (if, for instance, it was frustrated) or if there were no contract at all (if, for example, I deliberately prevented you from making a contract).

[**317**] However, it must be emphasised that the courts at present treat "inducing" and "procuring" as one and the same: they ask merely whether I have deliberately caused your breach of contract and so occasioned loss to the plaintiff.

Direct procurement

[**318**] The label "direct procurement" of a breach of contract is applied to a three-party situation, where you have a contract with the plaintiff and in order to harm him I act deliberately upon you and cause you to be in breach of your contract.

[**319**] First, suppose I do a wrongful act to you. If I commit a tort against you (and locking you up, or giving you a dose of some noxious potion, would be a trespass to your person), you can sue me and s. 13 will not help me. But it may protect me from liability to the other party to your contract.

[**320**] If procuring a breach of contract is regarded as a species of *Lumley* v. *Gye* (1853), 2 E. & B. 216 and that is the orthodox view, then s. 13 (1) (*a*) gives me a defence if I put you in breach of a contract of employment, but not if the contract was of another sort. If on the other hand the liability is considered to be a species of interfering with trade, s. 13 (2) should give me a defence whatever the sort of contract, always assuming a trade dispute.

[**321**] If instead of committing a tort against you I deliberately break my contract with you, that too would be a wrongful act on my part, unless there is a trade dispute; for if I break my contract in contemplation or furtherance of a trade dispute that is deemed not unlawful for the purposes of establishing liability in tort (s. 13 (3) (*b*)). For example, in *D. C. Thomson & Co., Ltd.* v. *Deakin*, [1952] Ch. 646; [1952] 2 All E.R. 361 Thomsons contracted for supplies of paper from Bowaters. Bowaters' drivers were unwilling to deliver it. Bowaters were aware of that fact, and did not ask them to deliver. Thus there was no breach of contract of employment, but there was a breach of the commercial contract between Bowaters and Thomsons. The question was raised what might have been the position if Bowaters had ordered the drivers to deliver. If the drivers had refused, they would have broken their contracts of employ-

ment. Could it be said that the drivers were liable to Thomsons for the tort of procuring Bowaters to break the commercial contract by the unlawful means of breaking their own contracts of employment? Section 13 (3) (*b*) now answers no, but that is not necessarily the end of the question (see para. [**323**]).

[**322**] Whether anything other than a tort or breach of contract is to be regarded as an unlawful act for this purpose depends on how one defines "unlawful means". That was discussed under "unlawful interference", paras. [**302**] *et seq., ante.*

[**323**] Next, suppose I put you in "breach" of your contract, but by doing to you an act that is lawful in itself or one that is deemed lawful. Suppose for instance Bowaters' drivers had all lawfully terminated their contracts in order to prevent Bowaters from delivering paper to Thomsons.

[**324**] The manner in which the tort is categorised here become crucial: if "procuring a breach" is a species of *Lumley* v. *Gye* Bowaters' drivers would in theory be liable. But if the tort is a species of interference with trade, then they are not liable, because they have used no unlawful means, as explained above. In the former case, s. 13 (1) (*a*) would provide a defence to procuring a breach of a contract *of employment* (so that would not avail Bowaters' drivers); in the latter, there would be no need of a defence.

[**325**] Yet again it must be said that the courts have not drawn any distinction between "inducing" and "procuring" and the orthodox opinion at the moment is that "procuring" is part of *Lumley* v. *Gye*. In the present situation though, it is mighty close to saying that I am liable for breaking your contract—a contract to which I am not party. That would have startling results in other areas of the law.

[**326**] One final small point may be added. The common law regarded a master as having a property right in his servant. If therefore I commit a tort against a domestic servant, so depriving the master of his services, I may be liable to the master under the *actio per quod servitium amisit*. That, it seems, applies only to domestic or menial servants. Nothing in s. 13 is material.

Indirect procurement

[**327**] Indirect procurement is the label given to the situation where you, as before, have a contract with the plaintiff, and, as before, I am aiming at him. But here, instead of acting directly against you, I act against you indirectly. The typical case is that of "blacking" or the secondary boycott. I instigate your workers to break their contracts of employment with you so putting you into breach of your contract with the plaintiff.

[**328**] So in *J. T. Stratford & Son, Ltd.* v. *Lindley*, [1965] A.C. 307; [1964] 3 All E.R. 102 the union was in dispute with Stratford. Stratfords hired out barges. The contract of hire obliged the hirers to return the barges to Stratfords at the end of the hiring. The hirers employed lightermen to operate the barges. The lightermen were members of the union. The union told the lightermen not to return the barges to Stratfords at the end of the period of hire. The lightermen followed the union's instructions, thereby breaking their contract of employment, and the union officials had therefore committed a tort against the hirers of inducing the lightermen to break their contracts of employment. But further the hirers had thereby been put into breach of the commercial contract (of hire) because of the clause requiring the hirers to return the barges at the end

of the period of hire. The union officials had indirectly but deliberately caused that breach, and were held to have committed a tort against Stratfords. There was no statutory defence because it was held that on the facts there was no genuine trade dispute.

[**329**] As before, there are two ways of analysing this tort. The orthodox way is to regard it as an extension of *Lumley* v. *Gye* (1853) 2 E. & B. 216. So one looks at the contract of hire, and says that the defendants have deliberately caused a breach of that, but have done so indirectly, through the lightermen. It is now clear that the defendant in an action for indirect procurement is liable only if he uses unlawful means in achieving that end: *Torquay Hotel Co., Ltd.* v. *Cousins*, [1969] 2 Ch. 106; [1969] 1 All E.R. 522. In *J. T. Stratford & Son, Ltd.* v. *Lindley* the defendants had used unlawful means. They had committed a tort against the hirers, the tort of (directly) inducing the lightermen to break their contracts of employment.

[**330**] If there were a trade dispute then s. 13 (1) (*a*) would provide an indirect defence to the indirect tort in this way; the defendant has (indirectly) procured a breach of the commercial contract in contemplation or furtherance of a trade dispute. But that is not a contract of employment so s. 13 (1) (*a*) gives no immediate immunity. However, because the alleged tort is indirect, it must be shown that the defendant used unlawful means to achieve his end. But what are the means used? The tort of (directly) persuading the workers to break their contracts of employment. Are those unlawful means? No, because the direct tort is rendered "not actionable" by s. 13 (1) (*a*). Section 13 (3) (*a*) then operates to say that anything "not actionable" is deemed "not unlawful" for the purpose of establishing liability in tort. Therefore the defendant has indirectly induced a breach of the commercial contract, but has not used unlawful means, and so has committed no tort. That argument holds good only if the workers are employed under a contract *of employment* (see para. [**312**], *ante*). It held good under the Trades Disputes Act 1906, although there were some judicial doubts expressed. Before s. 13 (3) (*a*) it was not beyond doubt that the means used were lawful because they were "not actionable". Some judges though that the means were unlawful even though not actionable.

[**331**] The alternative analysis is to call *J. T. Stratford & Son, Ltd.* v. *Lindley* the tort of interference with trade. If that is correct, s. 13 (2) should provide a defence in a trade dispute whatever the type of contract or even if there is no contract.

[**332**] Whichever analysis is adopted there is still the problem of what constitutes unlawful means. That has been discussed under "unlawful interference", paras. [**302**] *et seq., ante.*

[**333**] TULRA intervenes to this extent, that s. 13 (3) provides that (*a*) a tort rendered "not actionable" by s. 13 (1) or (2), and (*b*) a breach of contract done within the golden formula are not to be regarded as unlawful means.

INTERFERENCE WITH CONTRACT

[**334**] It is thought that the better view is that interference with a contract is not an independent tort, but there are indications that it may become so. Thus, LORD DENNING in *Torquay Hotel Co., Ltd.* v. *Cousins*, [1969] 2 Ch.

106; [1969] 1 All E.R. 522 said of *Lumley* v. *Gye* (1853), 2 E. & B. 216: "The time has come when the principle should be further extended to cover 'deliberate and direct interference with the execution of the contract without that causing any breach' ".

[**335**] The facts of the case were as follows: The TGWU were in dispute with the Imperial Hotel at Torquay. For reasons that do not here concern us it was held that there was no trade dispute for the purposes of the golden formula. The Imperial used to obtain oil for its central heating from Esso under a standing contract. The contract provided that Esso should not be liable for failure to deliver due to industrial action. Esso's drivers were members of the TGWU. The TGWU told Esso and the drivers that the Imperial was "black" and that no oil should be delivered. No oil was delivered. The Imperial sued the TGWU organisers.

[**336**] The majority of the Court of Appeal said that Esso had broken their contract with the Imperial (although the exclusion clause exempted Esso from liability!) and the union officials were liable for inducing the breach. That decision is open to much criticism on the facts, but much more important, LORD DENNING decided on the wider ground that any deliberate, direct, and unjustified interference in the execution of a contract, even without causing a breach, gave rise to liability in tort.

[**337**] It is respectfully submitted that, as so stated, the principle is both too wide and too narrow. It is in essence a principle that might have existed before *Allen* v. *Flood*, [1898] A.C. 1 (see paras. [**300**] and [**301**]). In order to conform with the weighty authority of that case, it seems that the principle should be that any deliberate *unlawful* and unjustified interference gives rise to liability. But there seems no reason why it should be confined to direct interference; nor to interference in a contract. It is perhaps best seen as another aspect of the tort of unlawful interference in trade: thus if in *Torquay Hotel* the union officials had committed a tort against Esso with the intention and effect of causing loss to Imperial they should be liable to Imperial. Whether or not they had committed a tort against Esso depends on whether the drivers were in breach of their contracts of employment (*cf. D. C. Thomson & Co., Ltd.* v. *Deakin*, [1952] Ch. 646; [1952] 2 All E.R. 361). But whether Esso were in breach of contract or not is irrelevant.

[**338**] If, however, deliberate interference in a contract is an independent tort, then s. 13 gives no protection against it, and it will often be unlawful to organise industrial action. The original version of the Bill extended immunity to "interference" but the House of Lords removed such immunity.

INTIMIDATION

[**339**] It is a tort deliberately to coerce another by means of an unlawful threat into harming the plaintiff. An unlawful threat is a threat of an unlawful act. Thus a threat to take strike action can amount to the tort of intimidation if the strike involves breaches of the contract of employment. *Rookes* v. *Barnard*, [1964] A.C. 1129; [1964] 1 All E.R. 367 so held, and it also held that the 1906 Act did not give complete immunity. The Trade Disputes Act 1965 supplied the missing immunity and that now appears as s. 13 (1) (*b*), TULRA.

[**340**] It is said that the tort can be committed in a two-party situation, but it will not occur often; for if I threaten to commit an unlawful act against you, you may be able to prevent my carrying out my threat by a *quia timet* injunction without resorting to the tort of intimidation. Furthermore, if you are to succeed in suing me for intimidation, you must show that the threat has caused you loss and that is improbable. What is likely to cause your loss is my carrying out the threat, but then you would sue me for doing the unlawful act, not for threatening it.

[**341**] However, the potential plaintiff in a three-party situation does not have an adequate remedy apart from the tort of intimidation; for in that situation I tell you that if you do not harm him I shall make you, by doing an unlawful act to you. If you accept the inevitable and accede to my demand the plaintiff may have no remedy unless he can complain of my unlawful threat. So it was in *Rookes* v. *Barnard*: Rookes did not belong to the union. The other men in the shop did, and were unwilling to work with him. They decided to strike if he were not removed. The strike was unconstitutional and it was conceded by counsel (who wanted a decision on the major issue, of course) that the no-strikes clause in the procedure agreement was incorporated in the contracts of employment. The strike was therefore in breach of those contracts. Barnard and Fistal (who were fellow employees) and Silverthorne (who was a full time union official) informed the employers, who therefore lawfully dismissed Rookes. Rookes had no cause of action against the employers, but it was held he could succeed against Barnard and the others because their deliberate and unlawful threat had caused him loss. The employees had threatened to break their contracts and Silverthorne was a co-conspirator.

[**342**] "Threat" in this context means no more than informing the other person of what you intend to do should he not comply with your wishes with intent to persuade him to comply. The House of Lords in *Rookes* v. *Barnard* emphasised that the threat must be coercive; that is to say that the other must have no real choice but to submit.

[**343**] If it is to be actionable, the threat must be a threat of an unlawful act. A tort is certainly an unlawful act for that purpose, and *Rookes* v. *Barnard* held that a breach of contract was also. Whether anything else suffices depends on how one views "unlawful means" for the purposes of "unlawful interference with trade" (see paras. [**306**] *et seq.*). *Rookes* v. *Barnard* decided intimidation was an independent tort and not merely a species of interference with trade. But if it becomes unlawful actually to interfere in a person's trade by an act that is not a civil wrong, it will be unlawful to threaten to do so.

[**344**] Section 13 offers various defences. Where the threat is a threat to *organise* industrial action it may well be intimidation as being a threat of the tort of inducing persons to break their contracts of employment. The better view is that immunity was given in that case even by the 1906 Act: the tort of inducing was rendered "not actionable" by s. 3, TDA, and therefore, said some, it was not an unlawful act, and a threat to do it was not an unlawful threat. Others said that the inducing was still unlawful even though not actionable, and therefore the tort of intimidation was still committed. To guard against the latter interpretation the TDA 1965 enacted that threatening to induce a person to break a contract of employment was not actionable if done within the

golden formula. Both routes to immunity are preserved by TULRA: the former by s. 13 (1) (*a*) (strengthened now by s. 13 (3) (*a*)), and the latter by s. 13 (1) (*b*).

[**345**] It will be noticed that the protection is limited to contracts *of employment*.

[**346**] Where the threat is a threat to *take* industrial action, it may amount to intimidation as being a threat to break a contract. The 1906 Act gave no protection, but the 1965 Act did. That is now in s. 13 (1) (*b*): it is not actionable in contemplation or furtherance of a trade dispute to threaten that a contract *of employment* will be broken. TULRA adds a second defence: a breach of contract within the golden formula is not an unlawful act for that purpose (s. 13 (3) (*b*)).

[**347**] If interference with contract falling short of a breach is unlawful, (see paras. [**334**] *et seq.*), then a threat of it would give rise to an action for intimidation. The only way in which s. 13 can protect is if the liability be considered a species of unlawful interference with trade. Section 13 (2) would then apply to make the interference "not actionable" and s. 13 (3) (*a*) would make it "not unlawful" for the purposes of intimidation. If it is insisted that interference with contract is a separate tort, then s. 13 will not protect against any intimidation arising therefrom. The original version of the Bill would have given protection, but the House of Lords removed the relevant phrases.

CONSPIRACY

[**348**] It is usually said that conspiracy consists of a combination of two or more persons either to effect an unlawful purpose (often called "conspiracy to injure") or to effect a lawful purpose by unlawful means. Criminal liability may be incurred by the mere agreement. Civil liability depends on some overt act having been done in pursuance of the agreement to the plaintiff's detriment.

[**349**] Conspiracy is anomalous in that liability may depend on numbers and motive. What is lawful in one, may be unlawful in two, and the unlawfulness may depend not on the nature of the act, but on the motive behind it. The reason for the anomaly apparently lies in its historical origin, being derived from the jurisdiction of the Court of Star Chamber. Logically civil conspiracy should have disappeared after *Allen* v. *Flood*, [1898] A.C. 1 but unfortunately *Quinn* v. *Leathem*, [1901] A.C. 495 gave it new life.

Conspiracy to injure

[**350**] The tort is committed when two or more persons acting with the predominant purpose of damaging the plaintiff agree upon and do some act which causes him loss.

[**351**] "To injure" means to cause *wrongful* harm, and an act done by an individual is not made wrongful by a bad motive. It is otherwise with conspiracy: a bad motive of itself makes the act wrongful. Thus the motive of the defendants is critical. If their object is to inflict loss on the plaintiff, they commit a tort; if their purpose is to pursue their own legitimate objectives, they do not. (And if their purpose is partly one and partly something else, the question

is what is the predominant motive.) Suppose you and I take a dislike to Smith, and decide to ruin him by calling a strike of his workers. If we do so act and achieve our object we commit the tort of conspiracy to injure because we are acting from pure spite. If on the other hand we, as union officials, think that Smith pays too low a wage, and we call a strike to force him to pay more, then we do not commit the tort of conspiracy even if we ruin Smith, because we were pursuing our legitimate trade objectives.

[352] If some conspirators act against the plaintiff from a bad motive and some act from a legitimate motive only the former are liable

[353] The better view is that it is for the plaintiff to prove that the object of the conspirators was to inflict loss on him, and if he cannot so prove he does not succeed. But the contrary view has some support; namely, that if the conspirators deliberately do an act that they know will harm the plaintiff and it does so harm him, then they are liable unless they can prove that they were pursuing their own legitimate objectives.

[354] There is no clear definition of legitimate objectives. It will depend on what the judge considers to be appropriate. Normal trade union objectives are legitimate. Thus, in *Crofter Hand Woven Harris Tweed Co., Ltd.* v. *Veitch.* [1942] A.C. 435; [1942] 1 All E.R. 142 the TGWU asked the employers for increased wages. They said they could not afford the increases because that would lead to price increases and rival manufacturers would then undercut them. The TGWU officials caused supplies to the rival manufacturers to be cut off. The House of Lords held there was no actionable conspiracy: the officials were acting with the predominant purpose of pursuing their legitimate trade objectives; they were not merely out to ruin the rival manufacturers. Furthermore the Courts have said that legitimate objectives are not only such advantages as can be valued in money terms: so, for instance, it was held legitimate for the Musicians' Union to attempt to stamp out a colour bar in a club where their members played. *Scala Ballroom (Wolverhampton), Ltd.* v. *Ratcliffe,* [1958] 3 All E.R. 220; [1958] 1 W.L.R. 1057.

[355] Section 13 (4), TULRA, despite its apparent relevance, does not in fact apply: s. 13 (4) provides a defence only if the defendants are acting in contemplation or furtherance of a trade dispute. If they are genuinely so acting, then they are pursuing their own legitimate objectives. If they are, then they do not commit an actionable conspiracy to injure. If on the other hand their objective is to harm the plaintiff, so that they are liable in conspiracy, it cannot be said that they are acting in contemplation or furtherance of a trade dispute, so that s. 13 (4) does not apply (see *Rookes* v. *Barnard,* [1964] A.C. 1129; [1964] 1 All E.R. 367).

Conspiracy to use unlawful means

[356] If two or more agree to do something of itself unlawful and do so act thereby causing loss to the plaintiff, then, whatever their motive they are liable for the tort of conspiracy. Here the act is unlawful even in one. So a conspiracy to commit a crime or tort will be actionable. And, it has been held, a conspiracy to act in contravention of a statute, but not a conspiracy to carry out an agreement in restraint of trade at common law.

[**357**] A conspiracy to break contracts is probably a conspiracy to use unlawful means, especially in view of *Rookes* v. *Barnard*, but it is by no means certain.

[**358**] Statutory protection may now be available in a trade dispute. *Rookes* v. *Barnard* held that s. 1, TDA 1906, did not apply at all to conspiracies to use unlawful means. Section 13 (4), TULRA, re-enacts that section but with a tiny but significant difference: the words "in tort" are added after the word "actionable" on both occasions. So now in the first place a conspiracy is "not actionable in tort" in certain conditions. Any other civil proceedings (say under the Restrictive Trade Practices Act?) would not be prohibited. But more important, in the second place, actions in tort may be brought only for conspiracies to commit a tort. It is therefore not now actionable to conspire to break contracts in a trade dispute (if it ever was!), nor to conspire to act in breach of a statute which gives no civil remedy, nor even to conspire to commit a crime which has no civil counterpart.

[**359**] Section 13 (3) (*b*) gives additional protection by declaring that a breach of contract in contemplation or furtherance of a trade dispute is not in any event an unlawful act for the present purpose.

APPENDIX: THE DEFENCE OF JUSTIFICATION

[**360**] There is a general defence of justification at common law in the case of some of the torts discussed above, but it may not be of much use in trade disputes.

[**361**] We have to look, yet again, at *Allen* v. *Flood*, [1898] A.C. 1. Before *Allen* v. *Flood* it might have been a tort deliberately to inflict loss on another without lawful excuse, but the defendant could justify himself by showing that he was pursuing his own legitimate objectives. In that context justification had a wide meaning: that the defendant acted with a good motive.

[**362**] However, *Allen* v. *Flood* said that the defendant incurred liability only if he did a *wrongful* act, and a bad motive could not of itself make an act wrongful. The corollary is that a good motive cannot of itself make an act rightful. So the defence of justification shrank into meaning that the defendant could show that his apparently wrongful act was not really wrongful at all: he had a right to do it. But as we have also seen in some of the more recent cases there seems to be an inclination to return towards the idea that unfairness is unlawfulness. It follows that if that is to happen, the defence of justification must expand again and that tendency can be detected particularly in some of LORD DENNING's judgments.

[**363**] But for the present the defence of justification comes to this, as stated by SIMONDS, J. in *Camden Nominees, Ltd.* v. *Forcey*, [1940] Ch. 352; [1940] 2 All E.R. 1 where Miss Forcey organised a rent strike, so committing the tort of inducing the tenants to break the terms of their leases:

> "Advice which is intended to have persuasive effect is not distinguishable from inducement and there is no reason to suppose that the giving of such advice is justifiable except by those persons in whom the law recognises a duty to give it".

The law would recognise such a duty in very few cases: for example, parent and child, perhaps, or doctor and patient, say where a doctor tells a patient for the sake of his health to leave his job at once.

[**364**] There is apparently only one case where the defence of justification has succeeded, *Brimelow* v. *Casson*, [1924] 1 Ch. 302 where the defendant persuaded chorus girls to leave their troupe because they were paid so little they had to supplement their earnings by prostitution. But the union official had no legal duty to persuade them to leave, and SIMONDS, J. in *Camden Nominees* v. *Forcey* suggested that *Brimelow* v. *Casson* was not really a case of justification at all.

[**365**] There is strong authority for the proposition that normal trade union activity cannot be justified by claiming that it is to advance the legitimate interests of the workers, or even those of the employers: *South Wales Miners' Federation* v. *Glamorgan Coal Co.*, [1903] 2 K.B. 545, where a series of one-day stoppages was called in the mines with the idea of restricting output and so keeping up the price of coal. However, LORD DENNING, taking a wider view of the ambit of liability, has also taken a wider view of the ambit of the defence of justification in, for instance, *Morgan* v. *Fry*, [1968] 2 Q.B. 710; [1968] 3 All E.R. 432 and *Cory Lighterage* v. *Transport and General Workers Union*, [1973] 2 All E.R. 558; [1973] I.C.R. 339.

[**366**] The defence, such as it is, is certainly available against the tort of including a breach of contract, and probably against the tort of intimidation. It is built in, as it were, into the definition of conspiracy to injure, but there it has its wider connotation of acting with a good motive.

[**367**] There is a troublesome dictum that crops up from time to time from *Read* v. *Friendly Society of Operative Stonemasons of England, Ireland and Wales*, [1902] 2 K.B. 732 to the effect that one can never justify the use of unlawful means, and it is sometimes argued that therefore justification can play no part in "indirect procurement" or other torts that involve the use of unlawful means. But if justification means demonstrating that you have a duty to do the act in question, then justification could apply to such torts if you could show that the apparently unlawful means were in fact lawful. The dictum is probably a hang over from the law prior to *Allen* v. *Flood*, [1898] A.C. 1.

5. RESTRICTION ON CIVIL PROCEEDINGS

[**368**] So far we have been discussing what civil liability may be incurred in law for taking industrial action, and we have seen that the golden formula may be a defence. However, even where liability does exist, the plaintiff's remedies may be restricted by TULRA, ss. 14, 16 and 17.

INJUNCTIONS AGAINST EMPLOYEES

[**369**] Section 16 has already been noted. A court may not compel an employee to work by granting an order for specific performance or an injunction. Strictly, s. 16 applies only to an employee and not to any other worker, but a court is unlikely to grant such an order in the case of any contract for personal services. Both orders are derived from the jurisdiction of Equity, and the refusal of the courts to grant such orders in these circumstances is sometimes

justified on the grounds that to do so would be akin to enforcing slavery which is unconscionable, and sometimes on the ground that it is in fact impossible to make a man work so that the court could not enforce its order and Equity does nothing in vain.

[**370**] Section 16 does not apply to an employer, but normally the court would not order an employer to take back a worker, it may however do so if there are "special" (but as yet undefined) circumstances: see *Hill* v. *C. A. Parsons & Co., Ltd.*, [1972] Ch. 305; [1971] 3 All E.R. 1345.

ACTIONS IN TORT AGAINST TRADE UNIONS AND EMPLOYERS' ASSOCIATIONS

[**371**] Section 14 (1) TULRA, re-enacting the effect of s. 4, TDA 1906, provides that as a general rule industrial organisations have total immunity from suit in tort. There are two exceptions, one of which is new.

The general rule

[**372**] Section 14 (1) (*a*) disallows actions in tort against an unincorporated union or employers' association in respect of any act done by or on behalf of that body, whether the action is against the body in its own name, or against its trustees or is a representative action. That in substance was s. 4 (1), TDA 1906.

[**373**] Section 14 (1) (*b*) gives similar protection for the first time to incorporated trade unions (*i.e.* special register unions—see para. [**72**]) and incorporated employers' associations. Previously such bodies had to choose between the advantages of incorporation and the protection of s. 4, TDA 1906. But, since such bodies may have other functions, protection is given only against torts committed whilst they are exercising their functions as trade unions or employers' associations respectively: that is "in connection with the regulation or relations between employers or employers' associations and workers or trade unions".

[**374**] Section 14 (1) (*c*) closes a loophole that some said existed in s. 4, TDA 1906. That Act gave immunity in respect of any tort "alleged to have been committed . . ." Did the section therefore prohibit an injunction in respect of any tort alleged *to be about to be* committed? Section 14 (1) (*c*) now makes it clear that no action will lie in such circumstances.

Exceptions

[**375**] No action will lie against the organisation for any tort whatever committed in contemplation or furtherance of a trade dispute, but if a tort is committed outside the golden formula an action may lie:

(i) For any negligence, nuisance or breach of duty resulting in personal injury (s. 14 (2) (*a*) and (3)). That is new, as such, but some actions which fall easily under this head might previously have been squeezed under the next: see s. 9 Trade Union Act 1871. The example usually given is of a union official negligently injuring someone whilst driving a car that belongs to the union. It could be said that this was an action that touched and concerned union property on the basis of casual delegation or otherwise.

(ii) For any breach of duty in respect of property (s. 14 (2) (*b*)). That is to the same effect as s. 4 (2), TDA 1906, which preserved the liability of trustees of a union in respect of union property under s. 9, Trade Union Act 1871. Section 9 however applied only to unions registered under that Act, whereas s. 14 (2) (*b*), TULRA, applies to all unions. Section 14 (2) (*b*) would allow, for instance, actions for nuisance and actions under the Occupiers Liability Act 1957. As pointed out in paras. [**61**] and [**62**] above, such an action may now be commenced against any organisation in its own name. It need not be against the trustees, but it may be.

It is only in these two exceptional cases that a union or employers' association may be sued in tort. Whether it is liable or not will depend on the usual rules of vicarious liability: did its servant commit a tort in the course of his employment, or was its agent acting within the scope of his authority?

[**376**] It scarcely needs saying that this is a complete reversal of the policy of the IRA which made the organisation liable rather than the individual, as far as possible (see *Heatons Transport* (*St. Helens*), *Ltd.* v. *Transport and General Workers Union*, [1973] A.C. 15; [1972] 3 All E.R. 101.

EX PARTE INJUNCTIONS

[**377**] Section 17 TULRA, places some limits on the availability of an *ex parte* injunction in a trade dispute. IRA, Sch. 3, para. 22 (3) placed similar limits on the availability of interim relief in NIRC.

[**378**] The limitation applies only where the defendant claims "or in the opinion of the court would be likely to claim" that he acted within the golden formula. In that event, the court may not grant an injunction without hearing the defendant's argument unless it is satisfied that all steps which were reasonable in the circumstances have been taken to give the defendant notice of the application and to give him an opportunity of being heard.

[**379**] The purpose is fairly obvious. An interlocutory injunction may be granted *ex parte*, that is on the basis of the plaintiff's evidence alone, if the circumstances demand urgency: R.S.C., O. 29, r. 1. But in the industrial situation an injunction temporarily restraining a strike or other action, even for a few days, could destroy its effectiveness. Should it be later shown that the threatened industrial action was in fact lawful (remembering that in the first instance the judge has heard only the plaintiff's evidence) and therefore should not have been restrained, the law's "abstentionist" position would have been compromised. Thus, if interim relief is to be given at all, the judge should at least hear both parties.

[**380**] If the defendant refuses to appear or if it is otherwise unreasonable to wait for him, the plaintiff may have his order against the organisers of the industrial action. It will be remembered that s. 16 prohibits an order against strikers themselves and s. 14 prohibits an order against a union in these circumstances.

6. CRIMINAL LIABILITY

[**381**] As a general rule the criminal law plays only a small part in the law of industrial action, apart from picketing which is discussed in the next chapter, and TULRA affects it only indirectly. Criminal sanctions against industrial action may be introduced in times of emergency, especially in wartime. They have also appeared in times of economic emergency in peacetime, lately for instance under the Counter Inflation (Temporary Provisions) Act 1972. But these are recognised as exceptions to the general rule.

[**382**] Much industrial action could fall foul of the common law crime of conspiracy: an agreement of two or more to do anything unlawful, but that is avoided by s. 3 Conspiracy and Protection of Property Act 1875, which provides that a conspiracy to do an act in contemplation or furtherance of a trade dispute is not a crime unless the act itself is a crime. TULRA restores the words "trade dispute" in that section in place of "industrial dispute" in TULRA (ss. 29 (7), 30 (1)).

[**383**] One general crime is however created by s. 5, CPPA 1875. It is a crime deliberately to break a contract of employment where the accused knew or ought to have known that by so doing (whether alone or with others) he was likely to endanger human life or limb or risk the damage or destruction of valuable propertly. Most strikes are now regarded as involving a breach of the contract of employment, and this section is a potential weapon against many of them. It is however little used. It might be mentioned that s. 4, CPPA 1875, and s. 31 of the Electricity (Supply) Act 1919 (which made it criminal for gas, water or electricity workers to strike in breach of contract) were repealed by the IRA and have naturally not been revived by TULRA.

[**384**] Otherwise, certain special categories of "worker" may incur criminal liability by taking industrial action: especially the armed services, the merchant navy (save that a merchant seaman may strike by terminating his contract in a trade dispute—see TULRA, Sch. 3, para. 14—on 48 hours' notice if his ship is in a safe berth in the UK) and the police.

[**385**] To organise a criminal strike is itself a crime, and further by the curious Aliens Restriction Amendment Act 1919 an alien commits an offence if he organises industrial action unless he has been *bona fide* engaged in that industry for at least two years.

7. EMERGENCY PROCEDURES

[**386**] It might perhaps be noted for the sake of completeness that the two emergency procedures introduced by the IRA are no more. They were the 'cooling off period' and the 'strike ballot'. Now, therefore, if a strike looks likely to cause a major disruption of the economy the government may proclaim a state of emergency under the Emergency Powers Act 1920 and govern by Orders in Council. Troops may be used to maintain essential supplies and services under the Emergency Powers Act 1964.

CHAPTER SIX
PICKETING

[**387**] The right to picket is now embodied in TULRA, s. 15. In substance it revives s. 2, Trade Disputes Act 1906, but with a prohibition against picketing a person's home. That restriction was first introduced by the IRA. The IRA adopted a negative formula: picketing should not of itself be a crime or a tort (s. 134). TULRA returns to a positive statement: "It shall be lawful . . ." But the right does not amount to much. Section 15 gives a right to be in a certain place, but strictly it gives no right to do anything once you are there. The right, such as it is, is only exercisable upon the conditions set out in s. 15, and furthermore the equivalent section in the Trade Disputes Act has been restrictively interpreted by the courts.

[**388**] The Consultative Document issued before TULRA was introduced as a Bill proposed a right to obstruct the highway to give pickets an opportunity to persuade those entering or leaving the premises picketed, but that was missing from the Bill itself, because it was thought too controversial in the delicate political situation. It may appear in a future Bill.

A RIGHT OF ATTENDANCE

[**389**] Section 15 gives a conditional right of attendance. It probably does nothing more. But were it not for s. 15 the attendance of even one peaceful picket could be regarded as the offence of obstructing the highway. Pickets might also be held to have committed the torts of trespass to the highway or nuisance. There might also be the offence of watching the besetting under s. 7, Conspiracy and Protection of Property Act 1875, but that section only makes criminal what would be at least tortious without it. Section 15 protects against those liabilities provided picketing is at the proper place for the proper purposes.

[**390**] But, limited as it is, s. 15 *apparently* gives a positive right to attend. Section 134 IRA clearly did not: *Kavanagh* v. *Hiscock*, [1974] 1 Q.B. 600; [1974] 2 All E.R. 177. However, the difference in wording is probably not material, except perhaps for political reasons. It seems fairly clear from *Kavanagh* v. *Hiscock* that the Divisional Court considered that the duty of the police to prevent a breach of the peace would override any right a picket may have to obstruct the highway. In any event, as will be seen in a moment, once a breach of the peace is likely the attendance ceases to be for a peaceful purpose so that there is no longer a right to attend.

THE PLACE OF ATTENDANCE

[**391**] Pickets may attend "at or near" any place where any person (presumably a person they wish to persuade) "happens to be". They may not however attend at or near his residence unless he lives "on the job". In that case they may attend at or near the *workplace* even though it happens to be the place where the person resides. But, it is said, "at or near" does not mean "in or on" so that if pickets step inside the relevant premises they apparently step outside s. 15, and may be liable for the tort of trespass.

[**392**] It seems that s. 15 permits attendance only on the public highway, and not even on a private road leading to the workplace, though it is difficult to justify that construction on the wording of the section.

THE PURPOSE OF ATTENDANCE

[**393**] Protection is given by s. 15 only to pickets who are acting in contemplation or furtherance of a trade dispute. The meaning of that phrase was discussed in the previous chapter. If pickets act with any other motive, they are not protected by s. 15.

[**394**] Even if he is within the golden formula a picket may properly attend only for peaceful purposes: "for the purpose only of peacefully obtaining or communicating information or peacefully persuading any person to work or abstain from working." To say that a picket may attend for the purposes of peaceful persuation does not mean that he may attend provided he has a peaceful intent. Rather it means that a picket may attend in order that peaceful picketing may take place. A picket may have a totally peaceful intention, yet nevertheless he may have no right to attend under s. 15 if the circumstances are such that "there is a real danger that something more than mere (peaceful) picketing" may occur. That was said by LORD PARKER in the well known case of *Piddington* v. *Bates*, [1961] 3 All E.R. 660; [1961] 1 W.L.R. 162 which illustrates the point: Piddington wanted to join two other pickets at the rear entrance of the Free Press. But the police constable said that two were enough. Piddington, claiming "I know my rights!" gently pushed past the policeman and was gently arrested. He evidently did not know his rights. He was found guilty of obstructing a policeman in the execution of his duty. The policeman, it was found, reasonably believed that a breach of the peace was likely to occur, and had a duty to prevent it.

[**395**] So a picket may attend only in order that peaceful picketing may take place. If there is a "real danger" that something more is likely to occur there is no right of attendance.

Peaceful picketing

[**396**] In the first place it should be remembered that "peaceful picketing" has a restricted meaning. It means only the giving and receiving of information or persuading a person to work or not to work. It covers picketing workers, but is scarcely apt to cover the picketing of suppliers or customers except to inform them. It certainly does not cover physically preventing anyone from entering

the workplace, be he worker or not, no matter how non-violent the pickets. So in *Broome* v. *Director of Public Prosecutions*, [1974] 1 All E.R. 314; [1974] I.C.R. 84. Broome was held to be acting unlawfully when he stood in front of a lorry to stop it entering a site, even though his intention was only to delay it whilst he spoke to the driver. The case was decided under the IRA but the result is the same under TULRA.

Criminal offences

[397] Secondly, even assuming the aim is to persuade workers entering or leaving the workplace, there is a right to attend under s. 15 in order that *peaceful* picketing may take place but there is no right to attend if a criminal offence is likely to be committed for that is "something more" than peaceful picketing. The criminal offence may be anything from using threatening words and behaviour or any other conduct likely to cause a breach of the peace through assault to riot or affray. There are also five specific offences under s. 7, CPPA 1875, including criminal intimidation and criminal watching and besetting, but in *Ward Lock Co., Ltd.* v. *Operative Printers Assistants' Society* (1906), 22 T.L.R. 327 it was held that that section

> ". . . legalises nothing, and it renders nothing wrongful that was not so before. Its object is solely to visit certain selected classes of acts which were previously wrongful, *i.e.* were at least civil torts with penal consequences capable of being summarily inflicted."

[398] The police will normally intervene to prevent a *tort* only if it constitutes a threat to the peace or is otherwise a criminal offence. Section 7, CPPA 1875 could give rise to such a situation. If for example pickets strayed outside s. 15, then they might well commit the tort of nuisance against the picketed employer. That would then be an unlawful watching and besetting and hence an offence under s. 7.

[399] If a policeman reasonably apprehends that an offence is likely to be committed he has a duty to prevent it. If the pickets resist him they commit the offence of obstructing a police officer in the execution of his duty. But in any event, once "something more" than mere picketing is likely, the attendance of the pickets is not for peaceful purposes only. Hence their attendance is outside s. 15, and hence they have no right to obstruct the highway. Therefore, they commit the offence of obstructing the highway, and the police have the right and the duty to move them on. If they refuse to move on then again they commit the offence of obstructing a policeman in the execution of his duty. Further, even a picket who only stands by and watches could in some circumstances be guilty of the crime of conspiracy.

[400] This list of crimes should not be regarded as by any means complete A picket's lot, like that of the police involved, is not a happy one!

[401] To repeat, s. 15 authorises attendance in order that peaceful picketing may take place but nothing more. It follows that if in the circumstances it is impossible for it to take place, there is no right for anyone at all to attend.

[402] So in *Kavanagh* v. *Hiscock*, [1974] 1 Q.B. 600; [1974] 2 All E.R. 177 there were forty or fifty pickets outside a site entrance awaiting the departure of the workers. A police cordon moved back all but the four "official" pickets.

Subsequently the police moved those four too, thus leaving no one "on duty". Thereupon, Kavanagh tried to push through the cordon in order to station himself at the entrance and in so doing assaulted P.C. Hiscock, Kavanagh claimed a right to attend, but the IRA gave him none. The decision would not be different under TULRA, for the Court accepted the evidence of the police that if any picket had been allowed at the entrance some offence was likely to have been committed.

[**403**] If then a breach of the peace is likely there is no right to attend, and it is immaterial whether the breach of the peace is likely to be caused by the pickets themselves, by the persons picketed, or even by bystanders.

[**404**] It should be noted that s. 15 itself places no limitation on the number of the pickets, but the effect of the case law is that pickets may attend only in reasonable numbers.

[**405**] Thus mass picketing is almost inevitably illegal: the mere presence of a large number of persons can give rise to the apprehension of a breach of the peace. And in practice the pickets in such cases may well be intent on physically preventing persons entering the premises. On either count there is something more than peaceful picketing so that there is no right to attend and hence an illegal obstruction of the highway.

[**406**] So in practice the "right" given by s. 15 is a right to attend at such time and in such place and in such numbers as will in the reasonable opinion of the police create no real danger of any breach of the peace. The problem is that therefore no picket can be sure of his rights. It is only safe to act with police permission. And in fact the police may well be consulted by a union before a picket line is established.

Civil liability

[**407**] As long as they remain within s. 15, pickets incur no liability for the torts of nuisance or trespass to the highway, but once there is "something more", if, for example, their conduct is not peaceful picketing as defined, then they render themselves liable for those torts. Again mass picketing may of itself be something more than mere picketing and so constitute an actionable nuisance.

[**408**] There is always the possibility of the tort of assault—causing another reasonably to apprehend physical violence to his person. There are other possibilities too, such as defamation by reason of chanted slogans or by placards. (The trade torts create some problems, see paras. [**409**]–[**413**], *infra*.) So if there is the likelihood of "something more" than mere picketing, there is an actionable nuisance at least. The picket is therefore a wrongful watching a besetting, and hence an offence under s. 7, CPPA 1875, as explained in para. [**397**].

A RIGHT TO PERSUADE?

[**409**] Assuming that pickets are attending for the purpose of peaceful persuasion in such circumstances as to give rise to no likelihood of any breach of the peace, what next? Does s. 15 give them any right to persuade? It is thought not, but the section is arguably ambiguous.

[**410**] Clearly there is no right to stop anyone and make him listen: *Broome* v. *Director of Public Prosecutions*, [1974] 1 All E.R. 314; [1974] I.C.R. 84; but if he chooses to stop may the picket incur liability by persuading him, or is the persuasion rendered rightful by s. 15?

[**411**] It is true that Lord Reid in *Broome* apparently said that a picket had a right to attend and persuade, but none of the other Lords went so far, and Lord Reid's dictum was restrictively interpreted in *Kavanagh* v. *Hiscock*. It appears, therefore, that s. 15 merely authorises attendance in order that peaceful persuasion may take place, and says nothing about the lawfulness or otherwise of the persuasion, even though that makes the "right" to picket "somewhat barren" or even "meaningless".

[**412**] The issue would become important if for instance pickets persuade self employed building workers ("on the lump") to join a strike without lawfully terminating their contracts. They have persuaded a person not to work within s. 15, but they have also induced a person to break his contract, and s. 13 gives no immunity because the contracts are not contracts of employment. If s. 15 gives a right to persuade then the pickets are not liable; if not, they are liable.

[**413**] Even if, contrary to what is suggested above, s. 15 does give a right to persuade, it would apply to peaceful picketing as therein defined. Thus, it would not on the face of it protect against persuading a lorry driver not to deliver supplies in breach of his contract of employment with the supplier (though that would be protected by s. 13) nor any liability that might arise from the consequent breach of the commercial contract for supplies (which, on those facts, ought also to fall within s. 13—see Chapter Five).

CHAPTER SEVEN

UNFAIR DISMISSAL

[**414**] TULRA re-enacts with some amendments those provisions of the IRA dealing with unfair dismissals. In particular ss. 22–33, IRA are now substantially re-enacted in TULRA, Schedule 1, Part II. If the effective date of termination (see para. [**467**]) fell before 16 September, 1974, then the IRA is to continue to apply save that appeals from an industrial tribunal will go to the High Court (TULRA, Sch. 4, para. 2). If the effective date of termination is on or after 16 September, 1974, then TULRA will apply to the dismissal (Sch. 4, para. 1).

[**415**] With some important exceptions, therefore, every employee has a right, as against his employer, not to be unfairly dismissed from employment, and if he is unfairly dismissed by his employer he may complain to an industrial tribunal (Sch. 1, para. 4). The tribunal may recommend that he be re-instated or re-engaged or award him compensation (Sch. 1, para. 17).

[**416**] The major changes introduced by TULRA are that

—the qualifying period of 104 weeks' continuous employment has been reduced: as from 16 September, 1974 the period is 52 weeks, and as from 16 March, 1975 the period is 26 weeks (Sch. 1, para. 10)

—the definition of "dismissal" now expressly includes "constructive dismissal" (Sch. 1, para. 5 (2))

—there are changes in connection with the fairness or otherwise of dismissal for union activities, especially in a closed shop (Sch. 1, 6 (4)–(6))

—it is now made clear that the onus of proof is on the employer to show that the dismissal was fair, and not on the employee to show that it was unfair (Sch. 1, para. 6 (8))

—the time limit for applications is extended from 4 weeks to 3 months (Sch. 1, para. 21 (4))

—the maximum compensation is increased from 40 weeks' pay (or £4160) to 50 weeks' pay (or £5200) (Sch. 1, para. 20 (1))

—the tribunal may recommend re-instatement or re-engagement instead of just the latter (Sch. 1, para. 17 (2))

—designated procedure agreements are to be approved by the Secretary of State rather than NIRC (Sch. 1, para. 31 (1))

—the employer may no longer seek a contribution or indemnity from a union if he dismisses an employee because of union pressure (*cf.* Sch. 1, para. 15)

—an appeal from the tribunal's decision on a point of law lies to the High Court and not to NIRC (*cf.* Sch. 3, para. 15).

[**417**] It is possible that the whole of the law on unfair dismissals will soon be revised and codified with the other statutory rights of an individual.

[**418**] In determining a claim of unfair dismissal the relevant questions are: Did the employee have the right not to be unfairly dismissed? Was he dismissed? Was the dismissal unfair? What is the remedy?

1. WHO HAS THE RIGHT?

"EMPLOYEE"

[**419**] By Schedule 1, para. 4, every employee in every relevant employment has a right as against his employer not to be unfairly dismissed. The claimant must therefore show that he is an employee as defined. Section 30 defines an employee as an individual who works or has worked under a contract of employment, otherwise than in police service, and "contract of employment" means a contract of service or apprenticeship. In other words only a servant or apprentice has the right and not an independent contractor.

[**420**] Civil servants are not employees as defined, because technically they do not have a contract of employment. However they are given a right against unfair dismissal by virtue of Schedule 1, para. 33 (re-enacting IRA, s. 162). Para. 33 (2) states that "Crown employment" means employment under or for the purposes of a government department, otherwise than in the armed services, and "Crown employee" is defined accordingly. And by para. 33 (1) the Act is to apply to Crown employment in the same way as it applies to other employment.

[**421**] It may perhaps be conveniently mentioned here that para. 27 (re-enacting s. 148, IRA) makes special provisions for teachers in voluntary aided schools. They are employees, clearly, and they are employed by the governors of the school. They may however, in the circumstances described in para. 27, be deemed employees of the local education authority.

EXCLUDED CLASSES

[**422**] In principle then every employee as so defined has the right but there are some exceptions. In the first place there are certain classes of employment that are excluded by Schedule 1, para. 9. These are

—small businesses (less than four employees)
—employment by spouse or close relatives (defined in para. 9 (4)
—dock workers, as defined
—share fishermen, as defined
—teachers in Scotland, as defined
—part-time workers (normally less than 21 hours per week)
—overseas employment, as defined in paras. 9 (2) and (3).

The Secretary of State may by order vary or add to these classes (para. 11 (2)). No such order has yet been made.

[**423**] Generally speaking, any employee in any of these excluded classes of employment is debarred from making a claim for unfair dismissal, but there is one exception: an employee in a "small business", as defined in para. 9 (1) (*a*),

may claim if the reason for his dismissal is what the Act calls an "inadmissible reason" (para. 11 (1)). An inadmissible reason is one which relates to certain union activities (see paras. [**480**]–[**496**]). So whilst such employees have no general right not to be unfairly dismissed, they may have a right not to be dismissed for union activities.

DISQUALIFIED EMPLOYEES

[**424**] In the first place then an employee may be disqualified by the nature of his employment.

[**425**] In the second place he may be disqualified by his personal circumstances. These call for a little more comment. They are

—the recent employee
—the retired employee
—the fixed-term employee
—the protected employee.

The recent employee

[**426**] In order to qualify fully for the right not to be unfairly dismissed, an employee must complete a minimum number of weeks of continuous employment (para. 10 (*a*)). The minimum period under the IRA was 104 weeks' continuous employment, but TULRA reduces it. As from 16 September, 1974 the period is 52 weeks, and as from 16 March, 1975 the period is to be reduced still further to 26 weeks. In all cases the relevant period is to be computed by counting backwards from the "effective date of termination". The length of continuous employment necessary will depend on the effective date of termination, and not on the date of presentation of the claim. If the effective date of termination falls before 16 September 1974 the employee must show 104 weeks; if it falls between 16 September, 1974 and 15 March, 1975 (both dates inclusive) he must show 52 weeks, and if it falls on or after 16 March, 1975, 26 weeks.

[**427**] "Continuous employment" is a technical term. It means the same as in Schedule 1 of the Contracts of Employment Act 1972 (TULRA, Sch. 1, para. 30 (1)). Reference should be made to that Act for the precise rules, but there are two separate questions to be answered. First, was there continuity of employment? Employment may be deemed to be continuous throughout certain periods when the employee is not in fact at work; or it may be deemed continuous despite a change in employer. Second, for how many weeks is the employee deemed employed? The fact that there has been continuity of employment from week 1 to week 26 does not mean that there has been 26 weeks' continuous employment! Some actual absences from work, though they do not break the continuity of employment may nevertheless *not* be counted towards the total of weeks continuously employed. There is a presumption that employment was continuous until the contrary is proved (para. 30 (2)).

[**428**] The "effective date of termination" is defined in para. 5 (5). It is discussed in paras. [**467**] *et seq., post.*

[**429**] The Secretary of State may make regulations which deem employment to be continuous in certain circumstances even though the continuity was in fact broken (Sch. 1, paras. 30 (3) and (4)). These are cases where the employee has been dismissed but is re-engaged following the presentation of a claim either under the Act or under a designated procedure agreement (see "protected employee", paras. [**442**] *et seq., post*), or following the activities of a conciliation officer, even if no formal complaint is made under the Act. Regulations were made under the corresponding provisions of the IRA (Industrial Relations (Continuity of Employment) Regulations 1972, S.I. 1972 No. 55) and they continue as if made under TULRA, Sch. 4, paras. 6 (1) and (2).

[**430**] Even if he has not completed the minimum qualifying period of continuous employment the employee still has a limited right to complain of unfair dismissal. He has the right to complain if he was dismissed because of union activities: if the reason for dismissal is an "inadmissible reason" as defined (para. 11 (1)): see paras. [**480**]–[**496**], *post*.

The retired employee

[**431**] It is deemed not unfair to dismiss a person who is too old. By Schedule 1, para. 10 (*b*) a person who has reached the normal retiring age for the job on or before the "effective date of termination" of his employment cannot present a claim under the Act. "Effective date of termination" is explained under "dismissal" in paras. [**467**], *et seq., post*.

[**432**] In any event a man loses the right to present a claim when he reaches 65, and a woman when she reaches 60; this will be relevant where there is no "normal" retiring age for the job, or when the "normal" age is higher than 65 and 60 respectively.

[**433**] Again, para. 11 (1) makes one exception. A retired employee may still present a claim if the reason for his enforced retirement was that he engaged in union activities, so that he was dismissed for an "inadmissible reason" as defined: see paras. [**480**]–[**496**], *post*.

Fixed term employees

[**434**] An employee's right to complain of unfair dismissal may be limited by para. 12 (re-enacting IRA, s. 30) if he is employed on a fixed-term contract of two years or more.

[**435**] A fixed-term contract is one in which the maximum duration is certain, in the sense that one can calculate at its commencement the actual calendar date upon which it must eventually expire. It does not matter that it may be terminated before that date whether by notice or otherwise.

[**436**] It will be seen in a moment that TULRA defines dismissal as including the expiry of a fixed-term contract without its being renewed under the same contract, and it is important to emphasise that para. 12 deals only with the situation where dismissal occurs in that way. If the employee is dismissed in any other fashion, para. 12 does not prejudice his right to claim.

[**437**] There are two separate situations; the temporary provisions and the permanent provisions.

The temporary provisions, para. 12 (a)

[**438**] An employee (other than an apprentice) may not complain of unfair dismissal if

—he had a fixed-term contract to two years or more
—the contract was made before 28 February, 1972
—the "dismissal" was the expiry of the fixed term.

The relevance of 28 February, 1972 is that it was on that date that a right not to be unfairly dismissed was first introduced by the IRA. Paragraph 12 (*a*) is temporary in that it applies only to contracts entered into before that date and the number of such contracts is naturally decreasing. It will be observed that para. 12 (*a*) does not prevent an apprentice from presenting a claim even if his contract was made before that date.

The permanent provisions, para. 12 (b)

[**439**] An employee may sign away some of his rights against unfair dismissal if he has a fixed term contract of two years or more. This is one occasion where it is permissible to contract out of TULRA: para. 32 (2) (*b*).

[**440**] Paragraph 12 (*b*) provides that an employee may not complain of unfair dismissal if

—he has a fixed term contract of two years or more
—the "dismissal" was the expiry of that term
—he has agreed in writing to forego his claim
—he so agreed before the expiry of his fixed-term contract.

Unlike para 12 (*a*), para 12 (*b*) makes no distinction between apprentices and other employees. Nor does it matter when the contract was made. Paragraph 12 (*b*) may therefore apply to apprentices whatever the date of their contract. However, it can in practice apply to any other employee only if his contract was made on or after 28 February, 1972. If it was made before that date, para. 12 (*a*) has already excluded the relevant right so that the employee has nothing to sign away.

[**441**] The waiver must be in writing and it must be made before the expiry of the fixed term. It may be part of the original agreement, but it need not be.

The protected employee

[**442**] An employee may be contracted out of TULRA's provisions for unfair dismissal if he is adequately protected by a collective bargain made between his union and his employer. If there is such a collective agreement it would not be appropriate for the employee to have two claims, one statutory and one under the domestic agreement, but neither would it be appropriate to "let the employer off" with anything less satisfactory than the statutory arrangements. The Act therefore allows collective contracting out of the unfair dismissals provisions, but only under a designated "dismissal procedures agreement" which satisfies certain tests (Sch. 1, paras. 13 (3), 32 (2) (*c*)).

[**443**] A "dismissals procedure agreement" is defined in s. 30 (1) as an agreement in writing. The definition also requires that it be made by one or more *independent* trade unions and one or more employers or employers associations. And para. 13 (2) (*a*) makes it clear that every trade union concerned must be independent. "Independent" is defined in s. 30 (1): the union must not be dominated or controlled by an employer, nor subject to interference by an employer "tending towards control".

[**444**] If a dismissals procedure agreement is to qualify for the present purposes it must satisfy the other conditions listed in para. 13 (2): it must be clear to whom the agreement applies; it must offer remedies for unfair dismissal; those remedies must be available to all the employees concerned without discrimination (so that union members must not have any advantages over non-members in representation at any hearing, in rights of appeal or otherwise); the remedies must on the whole be as beneficial as those offered by the Act, though they need not be precisely the same; and there must be a final right of appeal to an independent referee in the event of a deadlock.

[**445**] Finally, all the parties to the procedure agreement must agree to the contracting out (para. 13 (1)).

[**446**] The procedure is straightforward. All the parties jointly refer the question to the Secretary of State: para. (13 (1). If he is satisfied that the agreement meets all the conditions in para. 13 (2) he may (not must) make an order, the effect of which is to substitute the provisions of the agreement for those of the Act (para. 13 (3)). These paragraphs follow closely the wording of s. 31, IRA, but under that Act the agreement was to be referred to NIRC, not to the Secretary of State.

[**447**] An order designating a dismissals procedure agreement may be revoked by the Secretary of State upon the application of any one of the parties to it (para. 14 (1)). The Secretary of State must revoke the order if he is satisfied that either of two conditions is satisfied, but apparently he has no power to revoke an order otherwise. The two conditions are set out in para. 14 (2): either that all the parties to the agreement want the order to be revoked or that it no longer fulfils the conditions of para. 13 (2). The revocation order may contain transitional provisions (para. 14 (3)).

2. DISMISSAL

[**448**] The claimant, having shown that he is an employee as defined and that he does have the right not to be unfairly dismissed, must next prove that he was dismissed from employment. "Dismissal" for this purpose is defined in Schedule 1, para. 5. It means (as in the IRA)

—termination by the employer with or without notice
—expiry of a fixed-term contract without renewal.

But TULRA adds a new para. 5 (2) (*c*):

—"constructive dismissal".

KINDS OF DISMISSAL

Dismissal on notice

[**449**] If the employer wishes to dismiss his employee he must give him proper notice unless there are grounds for summary dismissal (see paras. [**457**], [**458**], *post*. The length of notice necessary is ascertained by what the parties expressly or impliedly agreed or by reference to the Contracts of Employment Act 1972. The Act lays down minima; the parties may agree more. The period so ascertained is sometimes called the obligatory period of notice. The employer may give notice longer than the obligatory period, but he may not lawfully give less. If he gives less he is liable to an action for damages for breach of contract at common law (for "wrongful dismissal"), whether or not he is liable under TULRA for unfair dismissal.

[**450**] All this is straightforward, but there are two points to be noted. One is the date on which dismissal is deemed to occur. That is discussed in paras. [**467**]–[**472**]. The other point to note is the special case of the employee who serves a counter-notice.

Counter-notice

[**451**] Schedule 1, paras. 5 (3) and (4) provide that an employee under notice may in certain circumstances himself terminate his contract of employment but yet be deemed dismissed by his employer for the purposes of unfair dismissal. The reason is this: an employee who is sacked will want to look for another job, and the law encourages him to do so. Suppose he finds a new job whilst still serving out his notice with his first employer, and suppose further the new employer insists that he start at once. If he serves out his notice, he does not get the new job; if he does not serve out his notice it is he, not the first employer, who has terminated the contract of employment, and, but for para. 5 (3), he would lose any claim for compensation for unfair dismissal.

[**452**] Paragraphs 5 (3) and (4) cater for two situations: where the employer gives the obligatory period of notice but no more; and "any other case", which in the circumstances must mean where the employer gives notice that is longer than the obligatory period.

[**453**] If the employer gives the obligatory notice, but no more, the employee may at any time during that period himself give notice to terminate the contract sooner. The employee's notice must be in writing. Although it is the employee who has in fact terminated the contract, para. 5 (3) deems the employee to have been dismissed by the employer. It further provides that the reasons for the dismissal shall be deemed to be the reasons for which the employer served notice in the first place. The paragraph does not lay down any minimum period for the employee's counter-notice, nor does it require the employee to have any particular reason for serving a counter notice. Effectively, therefore, it gives the employee an option whether to serve out his notice or not, provided he gives his counter-notice in writing.

[**454**] If the employer gives longer notice than the obligatory period a similar procedure applies, but in this case the employee must be careful when he serves his counter-notice. The employer's notice is regarded as split into two parts: the

obligatory period and the surplus. The obligatory period is counted backwards from the date on which the actual notice expires, and the employee must serve his counter-notice during the obligatory period. So suppose the employer is obliged to give four weeks' notice, but in fact gives six weeks' notice on 1 June. The notice expires on 12 July. The "obligatory period" is four weeks, counting back from 12 July, *i.e.* the obligatory period is 15 June to 12 July, and the employee if he wishes to take advantage of para. 5 (3) must serve his notice between those two dates.

[456] Mr. Heyd-Smith served his counter-notice too soon: he served it during the period of the employer's notice but before the obligatory period. It was held that he had resigned: *Oldham, Ltd.* v. *Heyd-Smith* (1973), 16 K.I.R. 177.

Dismissal without notice

[457] In some circumstances the employer may lawfully terminate the contract without notice. That is called summary dismissal. The circumstances are that the employee has been guilty of a serious breach of contract: "repudiatory conduct". The orthodox legal analysis is that the employee has by his conduct shown that he no longer intends to be bound by the contract, but that of itself does not terminate the contract. Rather it gives the employer an option: either he may waive the breach and treat the contract as still on foot (without prejudice to any claim for damages for breach of contract if he wishes to press it), or he may "accept the breach" as terminating the contract. In strict theory it is the employee who by his conduct terminates the contract if (but only if) the employer subsequently "accepts the breach". In practice, at least for the present purposes the contract is regarded as terminated by the employer's act of summarily dismissing the employee (that is, his act of "accepting the breach"): but *cf.* paras. **[462]** *et seq., infra*

[458] If the employer has grounds for summary dismissal he may, of course, choose to dismiss on notice, but in this case he may give shorter notice than would otherwise be necessary.

Expiry of a fixed term

[459] There is a dismissal as defined if a fixed-term contract expires "without being renewed under the same contract". Clearly, therefore, if the employee is not offered any further employment at all there is a dismissal for the purposes of unfair dismissal.

[460] The position may become more complicated if he stays on. The fact that his employment continues does not of course mean that the original contract continues. One occasionally hears of a managing director who has been with a firm all his life, starting as a tea boy and working up. He may have thirty years' continuous employment with that firm, but he will have had a succession of different contracts. So with Schedule 1, para. 5 (2) (*b*) the question is not whether the employment is renewed but whether the contract is renewed. If then the employee is given what is clearly a different contract, there is a technical dismissal within the Act. If on the other hand the parties have agreed to vary the original contract by extending its duration, but otherwise the terms and conditions of employment remain exactly the same, then the original contract has been renewed and there has been no dismissal. There is great scope for semantic argument about the area between! It seems that the original contract may be varied in other ways, and still remain the same contract, but if the variations are substantial in their effect then the result is to be regarded as a different contract. It may be relevant to decide that issue not only in order to determine whether there has been a dismissal within the Act, but also to determine whether the employee has a fixed-term contract of two years or more so as to be able to contract out of the Act's provisions. So in *British Broadcasting Corporation* v. *Ioannou*, [1974] I.R.L.R. 77 Mr. Ioannou had been employed on a three-year contract, then for another two years and then for a final year, so that he had six years' continuous employment. NIRC was prepared to regard the original contract as having been extended for a further two years, so making a five-year fixed-term contract. It did not matter that there had been some variation in the terms of the contract upon renewal. However, said the court, important changes had been made in the agreement for the final year, so that it could not be regarded as the same contract as before. During the final twelve months therefore Mr. Ioannou was employed on a fixed-term contract of one year only, and could not validly sign away his right to compensation for unfair dismissal under s. 30, IRA (now TULRA, Sch. 1, para. 12).

[**461**] According to an industrial tribunal not every extension is a renewal:

> ". . . a fixed-term contract is renewed when there is an agreement for a further term, whether it is for a fixed term or for a general hiring terminable by notice. An extension of the period to allow negotiations to be carried on cannot properly be described as a renewal". (*West* v. *South Western Regional Hospital Board* (1973), 8 I.T.R. 581.)

But if an employee continues to work beyond the date of expiry of his fixed term it is thought that in the absence of some agreement, express or implied, that the extension is conditional only (as in *West*'s case), the law will infer that his contract has been renewed from week to week or from month to month or for some other period, depending upon the frequency of the payment of his wages.

Constructive dismissal

[**462**] Constructive dismissal is a phrase used to describe the situation where the employer in breach of contract makes it impossible for the employee to continue in his employ; where he, as it were, drives the employee out. For example, the employer insists on transferring the employee to another factory hundreds of miles away, when the employee is by his contract not obliged to move there. That, according to the admissible evidence, is what happened in *Sutcliffe* v. *Hawker Siddeley Aviation, Ltd* (1974), 16 K.I.R. 85. The orthodox legal analysis of the situation is the converse of summary dismissal: the employer is guilty of a serious breach of contract ("repudiatory conduct"), and the employee is entitled either to waive the breach and continue the contract, or to accept that the breach has terminated the contract. In one sense the employer terminates the contract, because it is his conduct that terminates the contract;

but it does so if, but only if, the employee decides to exercise his option to treat the contract as repudiated. In that sense, therefore, it is the employee who terminates the contract by so deciding. The situation is a sort of "summary resignation".

[**463**] The IRA did not specifically include "constructive dismissal" as being a form of "dismissal" for the purposes of unfair dismissal. The omission was apparently deliberate, despite the fact that it is written into the Redundancy Payments Act 1965. However, in *Sutcliffe*'s case, SIR JOHN DONALDSON in NIRC said that "constructive dismissal" was clearly covered by the words of the Act, presumably regarding it as a termination by the employer. TULRA confirms the effect of that decision, but Schedule 1, para. 5 (2) (*c*) seems to contemplate that the employee terminates the contract.

[**464**] Constructive dismissal has always constituted "dismissal" for the purposes of the Redundancy Payments Act, but there is one important difference. Constructive dismissal for the purposes of that Act is where the employee justifiably terminates his contract *without notice*. For the purposes of TULRA, an employee is dismissed if he terminates his contract *with or without* notice, as long as the circumstances are such that he would have been justified in terminating it without notice.

[**465**] In some situations the employers' breach of contract may be so far reaching or fundamental that it is quite impossible for the contract to continue. This is usually but not inevitably said to be the case when the employer wrongfully dismisses the employee, that is, dismisses him in breach of contract.

[**466**] Such action ought to entitle the employee to an option either to "accept the breach" as putting an end to the contract or to ignore the breach and continue with the contract. But if the employer has made it clear that he will not in any circumstances have the man as an employee, it is quite impossible for the contract to continue, and therefore the employee has no option but to accept that the breach has in fact terminated the contract (*Sanders* v. *Ernest A. Neale Ltd.*, [1974] 3 All E.R. 327; [1974] I.C.R. 565).

TIME OF DISMISSAL

[**467**] One other problem on dismissal is when exactly is the employee dismissed? For most purposes the relevant date is "the effective date of termination", which is defined in Schedule 1, para. 5 (5) as follows:

—if the employee was given notice, the date on which the notice expired
—if he was not given notice, the date on which dismissal actually occurred
—if he was on a fixed-term contract, the date on which the term expired.

[**468**] In every case, therefore, the effective date of termination means what it says: it is the date on which employment actually ceases. So if an employer gives no notice when he should give notice, the effective date of termination is the date of summary dismissal and not on the date when notice would have expired, if it had been given. So too, if the employer gives less notice than he should: the employee is dismissed when the actual notice expires, and not when proper notice would have expired. It makes no difference if the employer pays wages in lieu of notice, for they are regarded only as damages for breach of contract—the employer may be admitting he is wrong in terminating the contract prematurely, but he does effectively terminate it prematurely.

[**469**] There is, however, an occasion for hair-splitting if the employer gives notice but indicates that the employee need not serve it out. If the employee does not in fact go to work, there are two possibilities: either the contract is still in being during the period of notice, but the man is on paid leave or for some other reason the employer is not insisting on his right to have the man work; or the employee has by his conduct agreed to a premature termination of his contract.

[**470**] In the former case the man is dismissed by his employer and the effective date of termination is the date on which the notice expires. In the latter case there is no "dismissal" as defined. The contract has been terminated by mutual agreement, and not by the unilateral act of either party. Fortunately, the courts are reluctant to find that there has been a consensual variation in these circumstances, unless the evidence is clear (*Lees* v. *Arthur Greaves* (*Lees*), *Ltd.*, [1974] 2 All E.R. 393).

[**471**] The effective date of termination is relevant in deciding whether the employee has a sufficient number of weeks' continuous employment to qualify for the right against unfair dismissal, for it is on that date that his continuous employment ends. It is also relevant in deciding what is the requisite qualifying period: depending when the effective date of termination falls, the employee may have to show 104, 52 or 26 weeks' continuous employment. The time limit on making a complaint to an industrial tribunal also runs from the effective date of termination.

[**472**] The "date of dismissal" may be different. It is important to know the "date of dismissal" in order to determine the fairness of a dismissal in connection with industrial action (see paras. [**503**] *et seq.*, *infra*). It is defined in para. 8 (3): if the contract was terminated by notice, whether given by the employer or the employee, then the date of dismissal is the date on which notice was *given*. Otherwise the date of dismissal is the same as the effective date of termination.

3. FAIR OR UNFAIR?

[**473**] If the employee is qualified to present a claim, and if he has proved that he was dismissed, as defined above, then the next question is, Was he dismissed fairly or unfairly? It may perhaps be emphasised that this question is completely different from the question whether the dismissal was wrongful, that is in breach of contract. The reason for the dismissal must be shown to be acceptable in principle and fair in fact.

ACCEPTABLE IN PRINCIPLE

[**474**] The onus is on the employer to show why he dismissed the employee. If he had several reasons, he must show what was the principle reason. Further, he must show that it was one of five kinds of reasons that the Act considers acceptable (Sch. 1, para. 6 (1)).

[**475**] Four of the five kinds of acceptable reasons are set out in para. 6 (2), as explained in para. 6 (9), and they come to this:

—that the employee could not do the job (whether because he was physically or mentally incapable of the work, or did not hold the appropriate qualifications)

—that the employee was guilty of misconduct

—that the employee was redundant (as defined in the Redundancy Payments Act 1965)

—that it would be a breach of a Statute to continue to employ him in that job.

The fifth kind of reason is set out in para. 6 (1) (*b*):

—that it was some other substantial reason such as would justify the dismissal of that sort of employee (which is not to say that it would justify the actual dismissal in question).

If the employer fails to show why he dismissed the employee or if the reason given is not one of these five types, then the inference is that the dismissal is unfair, but the Act does not say so.

[**476**] The tribunals have scarcely begun to indicate what might be "some other substantial reason" for this purpose, but there is one very substantial reason upon which the employer cannot rely. He may not say that industrial action or the threat of it forced him to dismiss the man: para. 15. To that extent TULRA repeats the provisions of the IRA, but there is a significant difference: the IRA in such circumstances allowed the employee to recover full compensation against the employer, but then gave the employer a right of contribution or indemnity from the union which took or threatened industrial action. TULRA allows the employee to recover in full from the employer (para. 19 (5)) but gives him no statutory right of contribution or indemnity against anyone. The employer would therefore have to look to the law of tort for a remedy, but he is likely to be met with a defence under s. 13.

[**477**] The IRA gave the employee no direct right against the union (*Langston* v. *Amalgamated Union of Engineering Workers*, [1974] 1 All E.R. 980; [1974] I.C.R. 180. It is a nice point whether an employee could now have an action against the union organisers in tort—on the grounds that they have induced the employer to commit an unlawful (?) act, akin to the liability under *Lumley* v. *Gye* (1853), 2 E & B. 216. Section 13 would give no defence if there were any such cause of action, but in most cases the employee would have received adequate compensation from his employer.

FAIR IN FACT

[**478**] If the employer does show an acceptable reason for dismissal, then the question of fairness is still open: para. 6 (3). The general rule is that it is up to the employer to satisfy the Tribunal not only that he had a reason that in principle was a good reason for dismissal, but that on the facts of that particular case it was reasonable for that employer to dismiss that employee for that reason (para. 6 (8)). TULRA here makes it clear that the employer must justify the actual dismissal. The IRA did not specifically say so, and there was an academic argument about what would be the situation if the evidence was evenly balanced and the Tribunal could not decide whether the dismissal was fair or unfair.

[**479**] Save in the special cases discussed below, TULRA like the IRA gives no details of what should be considered fair and reasonable, other than that it should be judged with "regard to equity and the substantial merits of the case".

In other words each case is to be considered individually without overdue concern for precedent. In this context the tribunals have found the Code of Practice helpful as a guide: see for instance paras. 130, 131, 132 and especially 133 of the Code. Its use in this context was one of the main reasons why the Code was retained by TULRA (see paras. [**31**]–[**33**]). There are six special cases which call for comment:

—dismissal for union activities
—dismissal in a closed shop
—dismissal for redundancy
—dismissal by lockout
—dismissal for industrial action
—dismissal on racial grounds.

Dismissal for union activities

[**480**] Here TULRA makes some changes in the law consequent upon the repeal of s. 5, IRA. The IRA drew distinctions between registered trade unions and unregistered organisations of workers. TULRA will have none of that, but instead TULRA draws a new distinction: between unions that are "independent trade unions" and those that are not. An "independent trade union" is defined in s. 30 (1). It is based on a similar definition in the IRA in that a union is not "independent" if it is employer dominated or employer controlled. But TULRA goes further: a union is not independent if it is likely to be tamed by an employer's interference "tending towards such control". Interference may consist of providing financial or other material support or it may be "by any other means whatsoever".

[**481**] The definition aims to exclude the "house union" or staff association that in effect is run by a company for its own employees only and is therefore considered by the TUC not to be a real union at all.

[**482**] On the fairness or otherwise of dismissal for union activities, TULRA lays down the following general rules in Schedule 1, para. 6 (4); they may be subject to some qualification where there is a closed shop (see para. [**485**] *et seq.*) (para. 32 (2) (*a*)):

1. It is unfair to dismiss an employee on the grounds that he is a member of an *independent* trade union, or proposes to join one.
2. It is unfair to dismiss an employee for taking an active part in an independent trade union "at the appropriate time" or proposing to do so.
3. It is unfair to dismiss an employee for refusing to join or remain in a non-independent trade union or proposing to do so.

Any reason which is unfair by these tests or by the test of para. 6 (5) (see below) is deemed an "inadmissible reason" (para. 6 (6)) and it will be recalled that some employees who are normally debarred from claiming for unfair dismissal may nevertheless present a claim if the ground of dismissal is an inadmissible reason (para. 11 (1)). They are employees in small businesses (para. 9 (1) (*a*)), employees with less than 26 (or 52) weeks' continuous employment (para. 10 (*a*)), and employees who are compulsorily retired (para. 10 (*b*)). An inadmissible reason may also be relevant in considering dismissal for redundancy and dismissal for industrial action (see paras. [**497**] and [**503**], respectively).

[**483**] The "appropriate time" for union activities is not defined, but presumably it means in the employee's own time, or with the employer's consent in the employer's time. Section 5 (5), IRA which so defined it has gone, but the same result would follow from a reasonable construction of the contract of employment.

[**484**] It will be observed that TULRA speaks of an employee "proposing" to do something. This sounds less definite than the equivalent phrase in the IRA which was "had indicated his intention". Whether the tribunals will make anything of the change in wording remains to be seen. For the present at least these provisions represent all that remains of a worker's "s. 5 rights" against his employer under the IRA. In particular an employee may now complain only of unfair *dismissal* whereas previously he could also complain of any other discrimination.

Dismissal in a closed shop

[**485**] TULRA is somewhat obscure on this point, and it is not possible to say with any certainty how the tribunals and the courts will interpret it. The relevant paragraphs are Schedule 1, para. 6 (5) and the definition of "union membership agreement" in s. 30 (1).

[**486**] The original version of the Bill proposed that if there were a closed shop, it would be fair to dismiss an employee who refused to join unless he conscientiously objected on religious grounds to joining any union. Then came the notorious "Lever amendments", when it will be remembered that Opposition amendments were defeated in the House of Commons by the casting vote of the Speaker in one case, and of his deputy in the other. It was then discovered that Mr. Harold Lever had been wrongly "nodded through" the division lobbies and his vote against the amendments should not have been counted. The Bill had therefore to be fetched back from the Lords to be corrected by the inclusion of the relevant amendments. The Labour Government has pledged itself to remove the effect of the amendments, but unless and until that happens there is the problem of trying to decide what they mean.

[**487**] The intention apparently was that as a general rule it should be fair to dismiss an employee who refuses to join a closed shop, but that in three exceptional cases it would be unfair to do so, so that in those cases the employee would be entitled to compensation. The three cases are

—that the employee conscientiously objects on religious grounds to joining any union
—that the employee objects "on any reasonable grounds" to joining a particular union
—that the employee is a member of another "appropriate" union.

It is not clear that the intention has been carried into effect in TULRA, especially with regard to the third exception.

[**488**] A closed shop in this context is a "union membership agreement", as defined in s. 30 (1). It means an express or tacit agreement or arrangement or understanding whereby in practice all the employees of a certain class are required, as a condition of employment, to join the union or one of the unions

party to the arrangement "or . . . another appropriate independent trade union".

[**489**] TULRA offers no criteria for judging the appropriateness or otherwise of another union, being content to leave the problem to be solved by litigation. But quite apart from that, the definition is ambiguous. It is not clear whether or not the option of joining another appropriate union *must* be offered to the employee. The natural reading is that the option must be offered to the employee before the arrangement can satisfy the definition of a "union membership agreement". If that is right, then few if any closed shops will fall within the definition because closed shops do not usually offer that option. Assuming that to be the correct reading TULRA does not say that all closed shops must henceforth offer the option. All it says is that if a closed shop does not offer the option it does not fall within the definitionin s. 30 (1). It could be argued that the advantage of getting within the definition will encourage unions to offer the relevant option in their closed shops, but that is highly unlikely. The CIR reported that closed shops had continued to be enforced contrary to the IRA. There is no reason to suppose that TULRA will have any greater effect.

[**490**] If the arrangement falls within the definition, para. 6 (5) lays down special rules for deciding the fairness or unfairness of a dismissal.

[**491**] If the arrangement does not fall within the definition, then para. 6 (5) will not apply in relation to it, and the fairness of dismissing a non-member will be judged with regard to equity and the substantial merits of the case, disregarding any union pressure, under the general rules of paras. 6 (8) and 15, see paras. [**476**] and [**478**].

[**492**] Paragraph 6 (5) can be made to apply to the usual closed shop arrangement straining slightly the language of the definition in s. 30 (1) and saying that the definition does not always require the arrangement to offer the employee the option of joining another appropriate union. It would involve reading s. 30 as requiring the arrangement to give an option to join ". . . another [*if any*] appropriate independent trade union" or some such words. A case could be made out for that on the grounds that it is sometimes wholly inappropriate to have another union involved. Even under the regime of the IRA that was found to be so with Equity and the National Union of Seamen respectively. Particularly if a narrow view were taken of the appropriateness of joining another union, the usual closed shop arrangement could fall within the definition and para. 6 (5) would then apply. However, the third exception referred to above would not as such exist, but it could be regarded as a species of the more general second exception.

[**493**] If there is a union membership agreement as defined, then by para. 6 (5) it is fair to dismiss an employee who refuses or proposes to refuse to be a member of the union or one of the unions concerned unless he falls within one of two exceptions. If he falls within either, then it is unfair to dismiss him.

[**494**] The first exception is that he "genuinely objects on grounds of religious belief" to joining any union. That is fairly clear, if restrictive.

[**495**] The other exception, if it survives, promises to be another fertile source of litigation. It is that the employee objects "on any reasonable grounds" to joining a particular trade union. Again TULRA offers no criteria of reasonableness, and again it is impossible to predict what the tribunals will make of

the phrase. The underlying conflict is, as always, between the freedom of the individual and the security of the workgroup. One's predelictions on that (political?) issue will colour one's view of the reasonableness of enforcing a closed shop.

[**496**] Any reason which by the application of para. 6 (5) is deemed unfair is an inadmissible reason (para. 6 (6)) with the results indicated in para. [**482**] *supra*.

Dismissal for redundancy

[**497**] The dismissal of a man for redundancy is normally fair, but it becomes unfair if it is shown that:

1. another or others in his "position" (defined in s. 30 (1)) were not made redundant; and
2. *either* he was victimised because of his union activities (an "inadmissible reason": see paras. [**480**]–[**496**]),

   or (i) there was a customary arrangement, such as "last in, first out";
   (ii) that arrangement was not followed; and
   (iii) there were no special reasons why it was not followed. Special reasons are not defined.

That is now Schedule 1, para. 6 (7). It is substantially what the IRA said, but whereas the IRA referred to s. 5 rights, TULRA refers to an inadmissible reason.

[**498**] Under the Redundancy Payments Act 1965 a person who is dismissed is, for the purposes of that Act, presumed to be redundant until the contrary is shown. That presumption does not apply in proceedings for unfair dismissal (para. 23).

[**499**] Paragraph 29 empowers the Secretary of State to make regulations to cover the situation of a man who is entitled both to compensation for unfair dismissal and to a redundancy payment so as to prevent his being paid twice. That is a repetition of s. 150, IRA. No such regulations were made under that section.

Dismissal by lockout

[**500**] TULRA, like the IRA, makes a special provision for dismissal by way of lockout, because in the absence of special provisions a lockout would constitute a "dismissal" as defined above for the purposes of unfair dismissal. The tribunal would then be required to decide whether the reasons for the lockout were fair or unfair. It would be inappropriate for the tribunal to be called on to decide the fairness of industrial action.

[**501**] So para. 7 (1) provides that if there is a dismissal by way of a lockout, then it is not an unfair dismissal if the employee is offered re-engagement (not necessarily re-instatement) at the end of the lockout. The offer may be made by the same employer, or his successor or associate (as defined in s. 30 (3), (4) and (5)), and the job offered may be the same "position" (as defined) or another which would be "reasonably suitable" (para. 7 (3)). The tribunal would decide

what was reasonably suitable. The offer need not be made immediately at the end of the lockout, if it is made as from "the date of resumption of work" which means the date as from which the majority of "comparable employees" (as defined) were offered re-engagement (paras. 7 (1) and (4)).

[**502**] If then an employee is offered re-engagement, the dismissal is not unfair. If he is not taken back, then the question of fairness is still open. Instead of asking why the employee was dismissed, whether the reason was acceptable in principle and fair in fact, we must ask why the employee was not taken back, and whether that was acceptable in principle and fair in fact, and that is to be judged on the principles discussed above: paras. [**473**]–[**479**] (para. 7 (2)).

Dismissal for industrial action

[**503**] Similarly TULRA makes special provision for deciding the fairness or otherwise of an employer's action in dismissing employees who are taking industrial action lest a tribunal be asked to decide whether the strike or other action is fair or not. Schedule 1, para. 8 is the relevant paragraph, repeating s. 26, IRA.

[**504**] Paragraph 8 will apply only if the employee is actually taking part in industrial action on the "date of dismissal". It will not apply therefore if such action is merely threatened; nor will it apply if such action has ceased. Fairness in those cases would be judged by the general rules outlined above.

[**505**] The date of dismissal is defined in para. 8 (3). If the employee is dismissed after notice, the date of dismissal is the date on which notice is *given*. Otherwise it is the same as the "effective date of termination". That is explained in para. [**467**], *ante*.

[**506**] There are two cases in which it may be unfair to dismiss for taking industrial action, otherwise such a dismissal is fair (para. 8 (2)).

[**507**] The first case where it may be unfair to dismiss for taking industrial action is where the employer does not dismiss all those taking industrial action, even if he dismisses all but one. In that situation the dismissal is unfair if the employee can prove that he was victimised for union activities (an "inadmissible reason": see paras. [**480**]–[**496**]) (para. (2) (*a*)).

[**508**] The second situation where dismissal for taking industrial action may be unfair is where the employer discriminates in taking men back after the industrial action. Whether the employer dismisses all or some only of the employees who take part in the industrial action, he should nevertheless offer to re-engage all or none of those dismissed; for if the claimant can show that he was not offered re-engagement, and at least one of his fellows was, the dismissal may be unfair. It will be unfair if the reason for the discrimination was the claimant's union activities ("an inadmissible reason": see paras. [**480**]–[**496**]) (para. 8 (2) (*b*)). Re-engagement here means the same as it does in para. 7 (see "Dismissal by lockout", para. [**500**], *ante* (para. 8 (3)).

[**509**] TULRA differs from the IRA in replacing "s. 5 rights" with "an inadmissible reason". It also replaces "other irregular industrial action short of a strike" with "other industrial action". The former had to involve a breach of contract, the latter usually will, but need not.

Dismissal on racial grounds

[**510**] The Race Relations Act 1968 makes it unlawful to discriminate against a person on the grounds of his colour, race or ethnic or national origins in various situations. One such situation is in dismissal from employment. If therefore an employer dismisses a man on racial grounds he may be liable both for unfair dismissal under TULRA and for unlawful discrimination under the Race Relations Act. Paragraph 28 seeks to prevent duplication of proceedings.

[**511**] If the dismissal appears to be an unfair dismissal, and if the employee was qualified to present a claim on that ground to an industrial tribunal when his employment was terminated, then no action is to be taken under the Race Relations Act unless and until an industrial tribunal has decided that the dismissal was unfair and that one of the reasons (but not necessarily the principal reason) for the dismissal was racial.

4. COMPLAINT TO A TRIBUNAL

[**512**] If the employee has grounds for claiming unfair dismissal he may complain to an industrial tribunal (Schedule 1, paras. 4, 16 and 17). The procedure follows closely the procedure established by the IRA.

TIME LIMIT

[**513**] The employee must present his claim within three months (para. 21 (4)). The period begins to run from and including the "effective date of termination" (see para. [**467**], *ante*). The tribunal may extend the time limit if it was "not reasonably practicable" to present the claim within the three months.

[**514**] That represents a change from the IRA. Under the IRA the time limit was four weeks, and it could be extended only if it was "not practicable" to comply. It is thought that the inclusion of the word "reasonably" makes little if any difference, and that the tribunals will continue to apply the time limit quite strictly.

PROCEDURE

[**515**] The Secretary of State may make Regulations laying down detailed procedure for dealing with applications (para. 21 (1)) and in particular the regulations must require the complaint to be notified of a conciliation officer appointed under para. 26 (para. 21 (3)). The conciliation officer must, in the circumstances indicated in para. 26, attempt to negotiate a settlement, and such a settlement is valid even if it amounts to "contracting out" of the Act (para. 32 (2) (*e*)). A conciliation officer may negotiate a settlement even if no formal complaint is presented to the tribunal (paras. 26 (4) and 32 (2) (*d*); and see paras. 30 (3) and (4)).

[**516**] The existing Regulations will continue to apply for the present. Thus the Regulations made under the IRA (Industrial Tribunals (Industrial Relations) Regulations 1972, S.I. 1972 No. 38) are deemed made under para. 21 by Schedule 4, paras. 6 (1) (2) and (3). (Procedure for matters arising under the Industrial

Training Act 1964 will still be governed by the Regulations made (or deemed made) under s. 46 Redundancy Payments Act 1965, namely the Industrial Tribunals (England and Wales) Regulations, S.I. 1965 No. 1101, 1967 No. 301, 1970 No. 941 and 1971 No. 1660: TULRA, Sch. 4, para. 6 (4).

REMEDIES

[517] If the matter is not settled by conciliation, the complaint will be heard by an industrial tribunal. Where the dismissal was in the interests of national security the tribunal must dismiss the claim (para. 18). Otherwise the tribunal will decide if the claim is well founded.

Re-instatement or re-engagement

[518] If the tribunal is satisfied that the claim is proved, then it must recommend that the employee be re-engaged or re-instated (or engaged by a successor or associate of the former employer) provided that it would be both fair and practicable for him to be taken back. The tribunal may recommend only, it may not compel. There is of course an element of discretion inherent in deciding what is fair and practicable, but if the tribunal decides that it is fair and practicable, it must make the recommendation, stating what terms it considers to be reasonable. Re-instatement is different from re-engagement. Re-instatement means that the employee is restored to his former position so that as between himself and his employer it is as though he had never been dismissed. Re-engagement means that he is taken back into the employ of his former employer, but there has been an actual break in his employment from the time he was dismissed until he is taken back. Potentially the most serious consequence of that would be to break the continuity of his employment for various statutory purposes. However, the Industrial Relations (Continuity of Employment) Regulations 1972, S.I. 1972 No. 55, will in these circumstances deem the employment to be continuous, but, it should be noted, only for those statutory purposes (*cf.* TULRA, Sch. 1, paras. 30 (3) and (4) and Sch. 4, paras. 6 (1) and (2)).

[519] Under the IRA the tribunal had no power to recommend re-instatement.

Compensation

[520] If the tribunal does not make a recommendation for re-instatement or re-engagement (because it would be unfair or impracticable) it must award compensation (para. 17 (3) (*a*)). It has no discretion as to the making of the order, but it does have a discretion as to the amount (para. 19). If the tribunal has made such a recommendation, but it is not complied with "for whatever reason", then again the tribunal must award compensation, (para. 17 (3) (*b*)). The amount of compensation may be increased if the employer unreasonably refuses to comply with the recommendation, or decreased if the employee unreasonably refuses to comply (para. 19 (4)). Otherwise the tribunal awards such sum as it considers will fairly compensate the employee (para. 19 (1)). If the employee is partly to blame for his own dismissal the compensation may be reduced (para. 19 (3)). Further, under the general law, the employee must take reasonable steps to minimise or mitigate his loss, and if he fails to do so, his compensation may be reduced on the ground (para. 19 (2)).

[**521**] The maximum compensation which may be awarded has now been increased to £5200 or two years' (*i.e.* 104 weeks') pay whichever is the less (para. 20 (1)). A "week's pay" for this purpose is to be determined by the Industrial Relations (Week's Pay) Regulations 1972, S.I. 1972 No. 56 (TULRA, Sch. 1, para. 20 (2) and Sch. 4, paras. 6 (1) and (2)). The maximum may be increased by order of the Secretary of State (para. 20 (3)). No order has yet been made.

APPEALS

[**522**] NIRC has been abolished and henceforth an appeal on a point of law only will lie to the High Court. (Tribunals and Inquiries Act 1971, s. 13; TULRA, Sch. 3, para. 15.) The transitional arrangements have been mentioned in Chapter Two above.

THE TRADE UNION AND LABOUR RELATIONS ACT 1974

(1974 c. 52)

ARRANGEMENT OF SECTIONS

An Act to repeal the Industrial Relations Act 1971; *to make provisions with respect to the law relating to trade unions, employers associations, workers and employers, including the law relating to unfair dismissal, and with respect to the jurisdiction and procedure of industrial tribunals; and for connected purposes* [31st July 1974]

Repeal of Industrial Relations Act 1971

1. Repeal of Industrial Relations Act 1971 and re-enactment of certain provisions

(1) The Industrial Relations Act 1971 is hereby repealed.

(2) Nevertheless, Schedule 1 to this Act shall have effect for re-enacting, with amendments consequential on the following sections of this Act and other amendments, the under-mentioned provisions of that Act, that is to say—

(*a*) Part I of that Schedule so re-enacts sections 2 to 4 (code of practice);
(*b*) Part II of that Schedule so re-enacts sections 22 to 33 (unfair dismissal);
(*c*) Part III of that Schedule so re-enacts sections 100, 106, 116, 118 and 159 and Schedule 6 (jurisdiction and procedure of industrial tribunals and other provisions with respect to those tribunals); and
(*d*) Part IV so re-enacts sections 146, 148, 149, 150, 151, 155, 161 and 162 (conciliation officers, and miscellaneous and supplementary provisions).

(3) The repeal by this section of the following provisions of the 1971 Act, that is to say, sections 7 (2) and (3), 11 to 18, 31, 32, 37 to 55, 76, 77, 99, 101 to 105, 111, 112, 114, 115, 129, 136, 138, to 145 and 160 and Schedule 1 (jurisdiction, functions and constitution of the National Industrial Relations Court) shall take effect on the passing of this Act and on the passing of this Act that Court is hereby abolished. [**523**]

Status and regulation of trade unions and employers' associations

2. Status of trade unions

(1) A trade union which is not a special register body shall not be, or be treated as if it were, a body corporate, but—

(*a*) it shall be capable of making contracts;

(*b*) all property belonging to the trade union shall be vested in trustees in trust for the union;

(*c*) subject to section 14 below, it shall be capable of suing and being sued in its own name, whether in proceedings relating to property or founded on contract or tort or any other cause of action whatsoever;

(*d*) proceedings for any offence alleged to have been committed by it or on its behalf may be brought against it in its own name; and

(*e*) any judgment, order or award made in proceedings of any description brought against the trade union on or after the commencement of this section shall be enforceable, by way of execution, diligence, punishment for contempt or otherwise, against any property held in trust for the trade union to the like extent and in the like manner as if the union were a body corporate.

(2) A trade union which is not a special register body shall not be registered as a company under the Companies Act 1948 and accordingly any registration of any such union under that Act (whenever effected) shall be void.

(3) No trade union shall be registered under the Friendly Societies Act 1896 or the Industrial and Provident Societies Act 1965 and accordingly any registration of a trade union under either of those Acts (whenever effected) shall be void.

(4) A trade union (other than a special register body) which, immediately before the commencement of this section, was a body corporate shall, on that commencement, cease to be a body corporate and the provisions of section 19 below (as well as this section and section 4 below) shall apply to the trade union on and after that commencement.

(5) The purposes of any trade union which is not a special register body and, in so far as they relate to the regulation of relations between employers and employers' associations and workers, the purposes of any trade union which is such a body, shall not, by reason only that they are in restraint of trade, be unlawful so as—

(*a*) to make any member of the trade union liable to criminal proceedings for conspiracy or otherwise, or

(*b*) to make any agreement or trust void or voidable;

nor shall any rule of a trade union which is not a special register body or, in so far as it so relates, any rule of any other trade union be unlawful or unenforceable by reason only that it is in restraint of trade. [**524**]

3. Status of employers' associations

(1) An employers' association may be either a body corporate or an unincorporated association.

(2) Where an employers' association is unincorporated—

(*a*) it shall be capable of making contracts;

(*b*) all property belonging to the employers' association shall be vested in trustees in trust for the association;

(*c*) subject to section 14 below, it shall be capable of suing and being sued in its own name, whether in proceedings relating to property or founded on contract or tort or any other cause of action whatsoever;

(*d*) proceedings for any offence alleged to have been committed by it or on its behalf may be brought against it in its own name; and

e) any judgment, order or award made in proceedings of any description brought against the employers' association on or after the commencement of this section shall be enforceable, by way of execution, diligence, punishment for contempt or otherwise, against any property held in trust for the employers' association to the like extent and in the like manner as if the association were a body corporate.

(3) Any employers' association which became a body corporate by virtue of section 74 of the 1971 Act shall cease to be a body corporate by virtue of that section at the expiration of the period of six months beginning with the commencement of this section and the provisions of section 19 below (as well as this section and section 4 below) shall apply to it on and after the expiration of that period, unless before the expiration of that period it has again become a body corporate.

(4) Nothing in section 434 of the Companies Act 1948 (associations of over twenty members for certain purposes must be incorporated or otherwise formed in special ways) shall be taken to prevent the formation of an employers' association which is neither registered as a company under that Act nor otherwise incorporated.

(5) The purposes of an unincorporated employers' association and, in so far as they relate to the regulation of relations between employers and workers or trade unions, the purposes of an employers' association which is a body corporate, shall not, by reason only that they are in restraint of trade, be unlawful so as—

(*a*) to make any member of the association liable to criminal proceedings for conspiracy or otherwise; or

(*b*) to make any agreement or trust void or voidable;

nor shall any rule of an unincorporated employers' association or, in so far as it so relates, any rule of an employers' association which is a body corporate be unlawful or unenforceable by reason only that it is in restraint of trade. [525]

4. Supplementary provisions about property of trade unions and unincorporated employers' associations

(1) Sections 39 and 40 of the Trustee Act 1925 and sections 38 and 39 of the Trustee Act (Northern Ireland) 1958 (vesting of property on retirement of trustee or appointment of new trustee) shall, in their application to trustees in whom any property is vested in trust for a trade union or an unincorporated employers' association to which this subsection applies, each have effect as if for any reference to a deed there were substituted a reference to an instrument in writing and as if in subsection (4) of section 40 of the said Act of 1925 and of section 39 of the said Act of 1958 paragraphs (*a*) and (*c*) were omitted.

(2) Subsection (1) above applies to a trade union (other than a special register body) and to an unincorporated employers' association whose name is (in either case) for the time being entered in the list of trade unions or of employers' associations under section 8 below.

(3) An instrument in writing appointing a new trustee of a trade union or unincorporated employers' association to which subsection (1) above applies is referred to in this section as an "instrument of appointment" and an instrument in writing discharging a trustee of such a union or association is referred to as an "instrument of discharge"; and for the purposes of this section (and the sections of the Acts of 1925 and 1958 applied by subsection (1) above), where a trustee of such a union or association is appointed or discharged by a resolution taken by or on behalf of the union or association, the written record of the resolution shall be treated as if it were the instrument in writing appointing or, as the case may be, discharging that trustee.

(4) Where by any enactment or instrument the transfer of securities of any description is required to be effected or recorded by means of entries in a register then, if—

(*a*) there is produced to the person who is authorised or required to keep the register, a copy of an instrument of appointment or of an instrument of discharge which contains or has attached to it a list identifying the securities of that description held in trust for the union or association to which the instrument relates at the date of the appointment or discharge; and

(*b*) it appears to that person that any of the securities so identified are included in the register kept by him,

he shall, notwithstanding anything in section 75 or 117 of the Companies Act 1948 or any other enactment or instrument regulating the keeping of the register, make such entries as may be necessary to give effect to the instrument of appointment or of discharge.

(5) A document which purports to be a copy of an instrument of appointment or of an instrument of discharge containing or having attached to it such a list and to be certified to be a copy of such an instrument in accordance with subsection (6) below shall be taken to be a copy of such an instrument unless the contrary is proved.

(6) The certificate referred to in subsection (5) above shall be given by the president and general secretary (or persons occupying positions equivalent to those of president and general secretary) of the union or association to which the instrument relates and, in the case of an instrument to which the list of securities is attached, shall appear both on the instrument and on the list.

(7) Nothing done for the purposes of or in pursuance of subsection (4) above shall be taken to affect any person with notice of any trust or to impose on any person a duty to inquire into any matter.

(8) In relation to a trade union or an employers' association whose principal office is situated in Scotland, references in this section to the appointment and to the discharge of a trustee shall be construed as including respectively references to the assumption and to the resignation of a trustee, and references to an instrument appointing, and to an instrument discharging, a trustee shall be construed accordingly. [**526**]

5. Rights of workers as to arbitrary or unreasonable exclusion or expulsion from trade union

(1) Subject to the provisions of this section, every worker shall have the right not to be—

(*a*) excluded from membership

(*b*) expelled from membership

of a trade union or a branch or section of a trade union by way of arbitrary or unreasonable discrimination.

(2) The exclusion or expulsion of a worker from membership of a union, branch or section shall not be deemed to be arbitrary or unreasonable if the worker is of a description different from that or those of the majority of the members of that union, branch or section (as the case may be) or does not possess the appropriate qualifications for such membership.

(3) A worker aggrieved by his exclusion or expulsion from any trade union, branch or section may apply to an industrial tribunal in accordance with industrial tribunal regulations for a declaration that he is entitled to be a member of that union, branch or section.

(4) Where any such declaration has been made and has not been implemented by the union, branch or section concerned within any period specified in the declaration or if no such period is specified within a reasonable period, the worker may apply to the High Court or, in Scotland, the Court of Session for an injunction, interdict or such other relief (including compensation) as the Court may think just and expedient in all the circumstances of the case.

(5) Nothing in this section or section 2 (5) above shall prejudice or in any way reduce the common law rights of a person who has applied to join, but not been given membership of, or who claims to be and to remain a member of, or who has been expelled from, a trade union. [527]

6. Provisions as to rules of trade unions and employers' associations

(1) The rules of every trade union and employers' association shall contain provisions in respect of the matters mentioned in the following subsections of this section.

(2) The rules must specify the name of the trade union or employers' association, the address of its principal office and the objects for which it was established.

(3) The rules must make provision as to the purposes for which, and the manner in which, any property or funds of the trade union or employers' association are authorised to be applied or invested.

(4) If any financial benefits are to be available for members of the trade union or employers' association out of its property or funds, the rules must make provision as to the amounts of those benefits and the circumstances in which they are to be available to members.

(5) The rules must specify the manner in which any rules of the trade union or employers' association can be made, altered or revoked.

(6) The rules must make provision for the election or appointment of officers and for the manner in which officers can be removed from office.

(7) The rules must make provision:—

(*a*) for the election of a governing body and for its re-election at reasonable intervals;

(*b*) for the manner in which members of the governing body can be removed from office.

(8) If the trade union or employers' association has officials (whether they are shop stewards, workplace representatives or other officials) who are not officers of the trade union or employers' association, the rules must make

provision for their election or appointment and for the manner in which they can be removed from office.

(9) The rules must make provision as to the manner in which, for any purposes of the trade union or employers' association, elections are to be held or ballots taken, including the following:—

(*a*) notification of vacancies and qualification of candidates;
(*b*) making of nominations;
(*c*) canvassing or content of election addresses, where these are permitted;
(*d*) eligibility for voting in any such election or ballot;
(*e*) procedure preparatory to any election or ballot;
(*f*) the procedure for counting and scrutiny of the votes and ballot papers; and
(*g*) the procedure for the declaration or notification of the result of any such election or ballot.

(10) The rules must specify the descriptions of persons who are eligible for membership of the trade union or employers' association or a branch or section of the trade union or employers' association and the procedure for dealing with applications for membership, including provision for appeals against decisions of the committee or other body responsible for determining such applications.

(11) The rules must specify:—

(*a*) the offences for which the trade union or employers' association is entitled under the rules to expel a member or take other disciplinary action, and the penalties applicable for each of those offences;
(*b*) the procedure for the hearing of cases in which offences against the rules are alleged; and
(*c*) the procedure with respect to appeals against any decision on any such hearing.

(12) The rules must prescribe a procedure for settling disputes between a member and the trade union or employers' association or an officer of the trade union or employers' association.

(13) In making provision for any hearing or a determination of any question, whether in relation to an alleged offence, an appeal or a dispute, the rules shall be so framed as not to depart from, or permit any departure from, the rules of natural justice. [**528**]

7. Right to terminate membership of trade union

Every member of a trade union, or branch or section thereof, shall have the right, on giving reasonable notice and complying with any reasonable conditions, to terminate his membership at any time of the trade union or branch or section thereof. [**529**]

8. Lists of trade unions and employers' associations

(1) The Registrar of Friendly Societies (in this Act referred to as the Registrar) shall maintain a list of trade unions and a list of employers' associations containing the names of those organisations which are entitled to have their names entered therein under the following provisions of this section.

(2) The Registrar shall enter in the list of trade unions or employers' associations, as the case may be, the name of every organisation of workers or of employers which—

(*a*) was on 30th September 1971 registered (whether by that or any other name) as a trade union under the Trade Union Acts 1871 to 1964; or

(*b*) has since that date been formed by the amalgamation of a number of such organisations each of which was so registered; or

(*c*) was immediately before the commencement of this section affiliated to the Trade Union Congress; or

(*d*) was immediately before that commencement registered as a trade union under section 68 (4) of the 1971 Act or as an employers' association under section 72 (4) of that Act;

except an organisation which appears to him not to be a trade union or, as the case may be, employers' association within the meaning of this Act.

(3) Any organisation of workers or of employers, whenever formed, whose name is not entered in the relevant list may apply to the Registrar to have its name so entered and, subject to subsection (5) below, the Registrar shall, if satisfied that the organisation is a trade union or employers' association and that subsection (4) below has been complied with, enter the name of that organisation in the relevant list.

(4) An application under subsection (3) above shall be made in such form and manner as the Registrar may require and be accompanied by a fee of £10 or such other fee as may be prescribed by regulations made by the Secretary of State and also by—

(*a*) a copy of the rules of the organisation;

(*b*) a list of its officers;

(*c*) the address of its head or main office; and

(*d*) the name under which it is or is to be known.

(5) The Registrar shall not under subsection (3) above enter the name of an organisation in the relevant list if that name is—

(*a*) the same as a name under which another organisation was registered as a trade union under the Trade Union Acts 1871 to 1964 on 30th September 1971 or was registered at any time as a trade union or employers' association under the 1971 Act or is for the time being entered in either list; or

(*b*) a name so nearly resembling any such name as to be likely to deceive the public.

(6) If it appears to the Registrar, whether on application made to him or otherwise, that an organisation whose name is entered in the relevant list is not a trade union or employers' association or that its rules do not comply with the provisions of this Act, he may remove its name from the relevant list, but shall not do so without giving the organisation notice of his intention to do so and without considering any representations made to him by the organisation during a period specified in the notice (being not less than twenty-eight days beginning with the date of the notice).

(7) Any organisation aggrieved by the refusal of the Registrar to enter its name in the relevant list or by a decision of his to remove its name from that list may appeal to the High Court, or in Scotland the Court of Session, within the time and in the manner directed by rules of court; and on any such appeal the

Court, if satisfied that that name should be or remain so entered, shall declare that fact and give directions to the Registrar accordingly.

(8) Rules of court may provide for excluding, in the case of appeals under subsection (7) above, so much of section 63 (1) of the Supreme Court of Judicature (Consolidation) Act 1925 as requires appeals to the High Court to be heard and determined by a divisional court; but no appeal to the Court of Appeal shall be brought against a decision of the High Court on an appeal under that subsection except with the leave of the High Court or the Court of Appeal.

(9) The Registrar shall at all reasonable hours keep available for public inspection (free of charge) copies of the lists of trade unions and employers' associations, as for the time being in force, and a copy of each list shall be included in the annual report made by the Chief Registrar of Friendly Societies under section 6 of the Friendly Societies Act 1896.

(10) On the application of any organisation whose name is included in the list of trade unions or employers' associations the Registrar shall issue it with a certificate that its name is included in the relevant list; and any document purporting to be such a certificate shall be evidence (and in Scotland sufficient evidence) that the name of the organisation is entered in the relevant list and that the organisation is a trade union or employers' association, as the case may be. [**530**]

9. Application of existing Acts referring to registered trade unions, employers' associations, etc.

(1) An enactment passed, or an instrument made under an enactment, before the commencement of this section which refers (or is to be construed as referring) to a trade union registered under the Trade Union Acts 1871 to 1964 or a trade union or employers' association registered under the 1971 Act, shall, on and after that commencement, have effect as if it referred to a trade union or employers' association within the meaning of this Act.

(2) Where an enactment passed, or an instrument made under an enactment, before the commencement of this section refers (or is to be construed as referring) to an organisation of workers or to an organisation of employers (within the meaning of the 1971 Act), it shall, on and after that commencement, have effect as if it referred to a trade union or an employers' association, as the case may be.

(3) Subsections (1) and (2) above shall not apply to any enactment contained in the Income and Corporation Taxes Act 1970 or any other enactment relating to income tax or corporation tax. [**531**]

10. Duty to keep accounting records

(1) This section applies to every trade union and every employers' association except one which consists wholly or mainly of representatives of constituent or affiliated organisations (of the description referred to in subsection (1) (*b*) (ii) or subsection (2) (*b*) (ii) of section 28 below).

(2) Every trade union and every employers' association to which this section applies shall—

(*a*) cause to be kept proper accounting records with respect to its transactions and its assets and liabilities; and

(*b*) establish and maintain a satisfactory system of control of its accounting records, its cash holdings and all its receipts and remittances.

(3) For the purposes of paragraph (*a*) above proper accounting records shall not be taken to be kept with respect to the matters mentioned in that paragraph if there are not kept such records as are necessary to give a true and fair view of the state of the affairs of the trade union or employers' association and to explain its transactions.

(4) Where a trade union or employers' association consists of or includes branches or sections, then—

(*a*) any duty falling upon the union or association in relation to a branch or section under this section shall be treated as having been discharged to the extent to which a branch or section discharges that duty instead of the union or association; and

(*b*) any duty falling upon a branch or section under this section by reason of its being a trade union or employers' association shall be treated as having been discharged to the extent to which the union or association of which it is a branch or section discharges that duty instead of the branch or section. [**532**]

11. Duties as to annual returns, auditors and members' superannuation

(1) This section applies to every trade union and every employers' association to which section 10 above applies except a union or association which has been in existence for less than 12 months.

(2) Every trade union and every employers' association to which this section applies shall send the Registrar as respects every calendar year a return relating to its affairs.

(3) Every trade union and every employers' association to which this section applies shall appoint an auditor or auditors to audit the accounts contained in its annual return.

(4) Every trade union and every employers' association to which this section applies shall at the request of any person, supply him with a copy of its rules and of its most recent annual return either free of charge or on payment of a reasonable charge.

(5) The Registrar shall at all reasonable hours keep available for public inspection either free of charge or on payment of a reasonable charge, copies of all annual returns sent to him under this section.

(6) The provisions of Part I of Schedule 2 to this Act shall have effect with respect to the annual return and to the qualifications, appointment, removal and functions of auditors of trade unions and employers' associations to which this section applies.

(7) The provisions of Part II of Schedule 2 to this Act shall have effect with respect to members' superannuation schemes maintained or to be maintained by trade unions or employers' associations to which this section applies.

(8) Where a trade union or employers' association consists of or includes branches or sections, then—

(*a*) any duty falling upon the union or association in relation to a branch or section under this section or Schedule 2 to this Act shall be treated as having been discharged to the extent to which a branch or section discharges that duty instead of the union or association; and

(*b*) any duty falling upon a branch or section under this section or Schedule 2 to this Act by reason of its being a trade union or employers' association shall be treated as having been discharged to the extent to which the union or association of which it is a branch or section discharges that duty instead of the branch or section. [**533**]

12. Offences

(1) If a trade union or an employers' association refuses or wilfully neglects to perform a duty imposed on it by or under any of the provisions of section 10 or 11 above or Schedule 2 to this Act the trade union or employers' association shall be guilty of an offence.

(2) Subject to subsection (3) below, any offence committed by a trade union or an employers' association under subsection (1) above shall be deemed to have been also committed by—

(*a*) every officer of that trade union or employers' association who is bound by the rules of the union or association to discharge on its behalf the duty breach of which constitutes that offence; or

(*b*) if there is no such officer, every member of the general committee of management of the union or association.

(3) In any proceedings brought against an officer or member by virtue of subsection (2) above in respect of any breach of duty, it shall be a defence for him to prove that he had reasonable cause to believe, and did believe, that some other person who was competent to discharge that duty was authorised to discharge it instead of him and had discharged it or would do so.

(4) A person who wilfully alters or causes to be altered a document which is required for the purposes of any of the provisions of section 10 or 11 above or Schedule 2 to this Act, with intent to falsify the document or to enable a trade union or employers' association to evade any of those provisions, shall be guilty of an offence.

(5) For every offence committed under this section the trade union, employers' association or other person guilty of the offence shall be liable on summary conviction—

(*a*) in the case of an offence under subsection (1) above, to a fine not exceeding £100;

(*b*) in the case of an offence under subsection (4) above, to a fine not exceeding £400. [**534**]

Restrictions on legal liability and legal proceedings

13. Acts in contemplation or furtherance of trade disputes

(1) An act done by a person in contemplation or furtherance of a trade dispute shall not be actionable in tort on the ground only—

(*a*) that it induces another person to break a contract of employment; or

(*b*) that it consists in his threatening that a contract of employment (whether one to which he is a party or not) will be broken or that he will induce another person to break a contract of employment to which that other person is a party.

(2) For the avoidance of doubt it is hereby declared that an act done by a person in contemplation or furtherance of a trade dispute is not actionable in tort on the ground only that it is an interference with the trade, business or employment of another person, or with the right of another person to dispose of his capital or his labour as he wills.

(3) For the avoidance of doubt it is hereby declared that—

(*a*) an act which by reason of subsection (1) or (2) above is itself not actionable;

(*b*) a breach of contract in contemplation or furtherance of a trade dispute;

shall not be regarded as the doing of an unlawful act or as the use of unlawful means for the purpose of establishing liability in tort.

(4) An agreement or combination by two or more persons to do or procure the doing of any act in contemplation or furtherance of a trade dispute shall not be actionable in tort if the act is one which, if done without any such agreement or combination, would not be actionable in tort. [**535**]

14. Immunity of trade unions and employers' associations to actions in tort

(1) Subject to subsection (2) below, no action in tort shall lie in respect of any act—

(*a*) alleged to have been done by or on behalf of a trade union which is not a special register body or by or on behalf of an unincorporated employers' association; or

(*b*) alleged to have been done, in connection with the regulation of relations between employers or employers' associations and workers or trade unions, by or on behalf of a trade union which is a special register body or by or on behalf of an employers' association which is a body corporate; or

(*c*) alleged to be threatened or to be intended to be done as mentioned in paragraph (*a*) or (*b*) above;

against the union or association in its own name, or against the trustees of the union or association, or against any members or officials of the union or association on behalf of themselves and all other members of the union or association.

(2) Subsection (1) above shall not affect the liability of a trade union or employers' association to be sued in respect of the following, if not arising from an act done in contemplation or furtherance of a trade dispute, that is to say—

(*a*) any negligence, nuisance or breach of duty (whether imposed on them by any rule or by or under any enactment) resulting in personal injury to any person; or

(*b*) without prejudice to paragraph (*a*) above, breach of any duty so imposed in connection with the ownership, occupation, possession, control or use of property (whether real or personal or, in Scotland, heritable or moveable).

(3) In this section "personal injury" includes any disease and any impairment of a person's physical or mental condition. [**536**]

15. Peaceful picketing

It shall be lawful for one or more persons in contemplation or furtherance of a trade dispute to attend at or near—

(*a*) a place whether another person works or carries on business; or

(*b*) any other place where another person happens to be, not being a place where he resides,

for the purpose only of peacefully obtaining or communicating information, or peacefully persuading any person to work or abstain from working. [**537**]

16. No compulsion to work

No court shall, whether by way of—

(*a*) an order for specific performance or specific implement of a contract of employment, or

(*b*) an injunction or interdict restraining a breach or threatened breach of such a contract,

compel an employee to do any work or attend at any place for the doing of any work. [**538**]

17. Restriction on grant of ex parte injunctions and interdicts

Where an application for an injunction or interdict is made to a court in the absence of the party against whom the injunction or interdict is sought or any representative of his and that party claims, or in the opinion of the court would be likely to claim, that he acted in contemplation or furtherance of a trade dispute, the court shall not grant the injunction or interdict unless satisfied that all steps which in the circumstances were reasonable have been taken with a view to securing that notice of the application and an opportunity of being heard with respect to the application have been given to that party. [**539**]

Collective Agreements

18. Enforceability of collective agreements

(1) Subject to subsection (3) below, any collective agreement made before 1st December 1971 or after the commencement of this section shall be conclusively presumed not to have been intended by the parties to be a legally enforceable contract unless the agreement—

(*a*) is in writing, and

(*b*) contains a provision which (however expressed) states that the parties intend that the agreement shall be a legally enforceable contract.

(2) Any such agreement which satisfies the conditions in subsection (1) (*a*) and (*b*) above shall be conclusively presumed to have been intended by the parties to be a legally enforceable contract.

(3) If any such agreement is in writing and contains a provision which (however expressed) states that the parties intend that one or more parts of the agreement specified in that provision, but not the whole of the agreement, shall be a legally enforceable contract, then—

(*a*) the specified part or parts shall be conclusively presumed to have been intended by the parties to be a legally enforceable contract; and

(*b*) the remainder of the agreement shall be conclusively presumed not to have been intended by the parties to be such a contract, but a part of an agreement which by virtue of this paragraph is not a legally enforceable contract may be referred to for the purpose of interpreting a part of that agreement which is such a contract.

(4) Notwithstanding anything in subsections (2) and (3) above, any terms of a collective agreement (whether made before or after the commencement of this section) which prohibit or restrict the right of workers to engage in a strike or other industrial action, or have the effect of prohibiting or restricting that

right, shall not form part of any contract between any worker and the person for whom he works unless the collective agreement—

(*a*) is in writing; and
(*b*) contains a provision expressly stating that those terms shall or may be incorporated in such a contract; and
(*c*) is reasonably accessible at his place of work to the worker to whom it applies and is available for him to consult during working hours; and
(*d*) is one where each trade union which is a party to the agreement is an independent trade union;

and unless the contract with the worker expressly or impliedly incorporates those terms in the contract.

(5) Subsection (4) above shall have effect notwithstanding any provision to the contrary in any agreement (including a collective agreement or a contract with any worker). [**540**]

Miscellaneous

19. Transitional provisions for trade unions and employers' associations ceasing to be incorporated

(1) The provisions of this section shall have effect in relation to a trade union or an employers' association to which they are applied by section 2 (4) or 3 (3) above; and in this section "the relevant date" means the day on which, under section 2 (4) or 3 (3) above, such a trade union or employers' association ceases to be a body corporate.

(2) On the relevant date—

(*a*) all property vested in the trade union or in the employers' association immediately before that date shall by virtue of this paragraph (and without the execution of any instrument) vest in the trustees who, in accordance with subsection (3) below, are the appropriate trustees;
(*b*) all liabilities, obligations and rights of the trade union or of the employer's association subsisting immediately before that date shall, in so far as they are liabilities, obligations or rights affecting any property so vested (instead of continuing to be liabilities, obligations or rights of the union or association), become liabilities, obligations and rights of the trustees who, in accordance with subsection (3) below, are the appropriate trustees.

(3) The appropriate trustees for the purposes of subsection (2) above are—

(*a*) the trustees appointed in writing for the purposes of this section by or on behalf of the members of the trade union or employers' association;
(*b*) in a case where no such trustees are appointed, the official trustees of the trade union or employers' association.

(4) A certificate given by the official trustees of a trade union or employers' association that the persons named in the certificate are the appropriate trustees of that union or association for the purposes of subsection (2) above shall be conclusive evidence that those persons are the appropriate trustees of that union or association for those purposes; and a document which purports to be such a certificate shall be taken to be such a certificate unless the contrary is proved.

(5) In this section "official trustees", in relation to a trade union or an employers' association, means the two officers of the union or association who, on the relevant date, are the president and the general secretary of the union or

association or occupy a position equivalent to that of president and general secretary respectively of a trade union or employers' association.

(6) Nothing in section 12 of the Finance Act 1895 (which requires certain Acts to be stamped as conveyances on sale) shall be taken as applying to this Act. [**541**]

20. Power to alter certain rules of trade unions restricting the application of funds

(1) Where during the period commencing with 1st December 1970 and ending with the passing of this Act a trade union has—

(*a*) made or amended any rule of the union so as to preclude any particular fund belonging to or held in trust for the union from being used for financing strikes or other industrial action; and

(*b*) has declared in its rules that the rule or the rule as so amended shall be incapable of revocation or alteration;

then, notwithstanding the declaration, the rule so made or amended may, subject to subsection (2) below, be revoked or amended.

(2) No rule of a trade union shall be revoked or amended by virtue of subsection (1) above after the expiration of the period of four years beginning with the date of the passing of this Act; and nothing in that subsection shall be taken to authorise the amendment or revocation of a rule of a trade union otherwise than in accordance with the procedural rules of that union. [**542**]

21. Effect of abolition of National Industrial Relations Court on pending proceedings and decisions given

(1) In this section and sections 22 and 23 below—

"the Court" means the National Industrial Relations Court;

"abate", in relation to any proceedings, means that the proceedings shall be treated as discontinued and, in relation to any decision, means that the decision, so far as not enforced, shall be unenforceable;

"decision" includes a judgment, order or award and any reference to the giving of a decision shall be construed accordingly;

"pending" means pending immediately before the passing of this Act;

and for the purposes of this section and those sections proceedings shall be treated as pending in the Court or an industrial tribunal until a final decision is given in those proceedings by the Court or the tribunal, as the case may be.

(2) On the passing of this Act, except in so far as provision is made by subsections (3) to (7) below for proceedings of the descriptions mentioned in those subsections—

(*a*) proceedings commenced in the Court before 30th April 1974 and pending in the Court shall be transferred by virtue of this paragraph to the High Court or the Court of Session;

(*b*) proceedings commenced in the Court on or after 30th April 1974 or any decision in those proceedings shall abate;

(*c*) any right of appeal against any such decision other than a right saved by section 23 (1) below shall be extinguished and any appeal from any such decision or any decision on any such appeal shall abate.

(3) Where a complaint has been presented to the Court under section 103 of the 1971 Act (complaints by Registrar against registered union or employers'

association), then, if the complaint was presented before 30th April 1974 and is pending in the Court, the complaint shall, on the passing of this Act, be transferred by virtue of this subsection to an industrial tribunal.

(4) Where an appeal arising out of any proceedings or decision of an industrial tribunal has been instituted in the Court, then—

(*a*) in the case of an appeal which is pending in the Court and arose out of proceedings or a decision under the Contracts of Employment Act 1972 or the Redundancy Payments Act 1965 or on a complaint under the 1971 Act by an employee that he has been unfairly dismissed by his employer, the appeal shall on the passing of this Act be transferred by virtue of this paragraph, to the High Court or the Court of Session;

(*b*) in the case of an appeal of any other description, the appeal shall, if the proceedings in the industrial tribunal were commenced before 30th April 1974 and the appeal is pending in the Court, be transferred by virtue of this paragraph on the passing of this Act to the High Court or the Court of Session;

(*c*) in the case of an appeal of a description referred to in paragraph (*b*) above, where the proceedings in the industrial tribunal were commenced on or after 30th April 1974, the appeal or any decision on the appeal shall on the passing of this Act abate.

(5) Where an appeal arising out of proceedings before the Chief Registrar of Trade Unions and Employers' Associations or any assistant registrar of his has been instituted and is pending in the Court, then—

(*a*) if the decision appealed from was made under any provisions of the Trade Union Act 1913 (funds for political purposes), the appeal shall on the passing of this Act be transferred by virtue of this paragraph to the High Court or the Court of Session;

(*b*) if the appeal is by way of case stated in proceedings on a complaint under section 4 of the Trade Union (Amalgamations, etc.) Act 1964 (complaints about resolutions to amalgamate), the appeal shall on the passing of this Act be so transferred by virtue of this paragraph;

(*c*) if the appeal arises out of any other proceedings, the appeal or any decision on the appeal shall on the passing of this Act abate.

(6) Where a complaint has been transferred by an industrial tribunal to the Court by virtue of section 111 of the 1971 Act and is pending in the Court, then—

(*a*) in the case of a complaint by an employee that he has been unfairly dismissed by his employer, the complaint shall on the passing of this Act be transferred by virtue of this paragraph back to the tribunal from which it was so transferred;

(*b*) in the case of a complaint of any other description presented before 30th April 1974, the complaint shall on the passing of this Act be transferred by virtue of this paragraph back to the tribunal from which it was so transferred;

(*c*) in the case of a complaint of a description referred to in paragraph (*b*) above presented on or after 30th April 1974, the complaint or any decision on the complaint shall on the passing of this Act abate.

(7) Where, under any provision of the 1971 Act, proceedings have been commenced in the Court at any time with a view to the making of a reference or request to the Commission on Industrial Relations, then—

(*a*) if the proceedings are pending in the Court and no reference or request has been made in the proceedings, those proceedings shall on the passing of this Act abate;

(*b*) if a reference or request so made in those proceedings is outstanding immediately before the passing of this Act, the reference or request shall be treated as withdrawn on the passing of this Act, and, subject to subsection (10) below, those proceedings shall then abate;

(*c*) any order of the Court made in proceedings resulting from a reference or request to that Commission shall cease to have effect on the passing of this Act.

(8) Where proceedings are transferred by virtue of subsection (2), (4) or (5) above, the proceedings shall be transferred in the case of proceedings in England and Wales, to the High Court and, in the case of proceedings in Scotland, to the Court of Session and may be continued there accordingly.

(9) Rules of court relating to proceedings so transferred may provide for excluding so much of section 63 (1) of the Supreme Court of Judicature (Consolidation) Act 1925 as requires appeals to the High Court to be heard and determined by a divisional court; but no appeal to the Court of Appeal shall be brought against a decision of the High Court on an appeal transferred by virtue of any provision of this section except with the leave of the High Court or the Court of Appeal.

(10) Where a reference or a request by the Court to the Commission on Industrial Relations is treated as withdrawn by virtue of subsection (7) (*b*) above, the Secretary of State may authorise the Commission to make a report of its findings and recommendations on that reference or request to those persons appearing to the Commission to be directly concerned, and to arrange for the report to be published in such manner as the Commission consider appropriate; and paragraph 43 (1) of Schedule 3 to the 1971 Act (disclosure of information) shall not apply to that report. [**543**]

22. Effect of repeals on pending proceedings and decisions given by industrial tribunals

Where a complaint, other than a complaint that an employee has been unfairly dismissed by his employer, has been presented to an industrial tribunal under any provision of the 1971 Act on or after 30th April 1974, then, when the repeal of that provision by this Act takes effect—

(*a*) the complaint or any decision on the complaint shall abate;

(*b*) any right of appeal against any such decision which is exercisable before that repeal takes effect shall be extinguished;

(*c*) any appeal from any such decision or any decision on any such appeal shall abate. [**544**]

23. Provisions supplementary to sections 21 and 22

(1) A decision given by the Court before the passing of this Act—

(*a*) in proceedings commenced in the Court before 30th April 1974;

(*b*) on an appeal instituted in the Court on or after 30th April 1974 in proceedings in which, if the appeal had been pending in the Court immediately before the passing of this Act, the appeal would have been transferred by virtue of any provision of section 21 above; or

(*c*) on a complaint which, if it had been pending in the Court immediately before the passing of this Act, would have been transferred back to an industrial tribunal by virtue of section 21 (6) above;

may, so far as not enforced, be enforced after the passing of this Act as if it were a judgement of the High Court or the Court of Session, and any right of appeal from such a decision to the Court of Appeal or the Court of Session exercisable under paragraph 29 of Schedule 3 to the 1971 Act (appeals) shall continue to be exercisable, and any appeal from such a decision (whether instituted before or after the passing of this Act) shall be heard and determined accordingly, after the repeal of that paragraph by this Act takes effect.

(2) Without prejudice to section 38 of the Interpretation Act 1889 (effect of repeals) any decision given by any court or tribunal—

(*a*) in any proceedings (including proceedings under the 1971 Act) before the repeal by this Act of sections 153 and 154 of the 1971 Act (enforcement) takes effect, or

(*b*) in any proceedings transferred to any court by virtue of any provision of section 21 above;

and falling to be enforced to any extent after that repeal takes effect shall not be enforceable against property of any description against which it would not have been enforceable before that repeal takes effect by virtue of any provision of the said section 153 or 154, as the case may be.

(3) Where any right, obligation or liability has accrued or been incurred under any provision of the 1971 Act (other than a provision re-enacted in Schedule 1 to this Act) before the repeal of that provision by this Act takes effect, but no proceedings have been commenced in any court or tribunal to enforce that right, obligation or liability, no proceedings to enforce it (directly or indirectly and by whatever means) shall be commenced in any court or tribunal after that repeal takes effect.

(4) If on an appeal from the Court after the passing of this Act the Court of Appeal would have exercised a power to order a new trial by the Court, the Court of Appeal shall order the re-hearing to be by the High Court. [**545**]

24. Power to compensate for loss of office

(1) If it appears to the Secretary of State that a person who ceases to be a member of the Commission on Industrial Relations by reason of its abolition by this Act should receive compensation for loss of office, he may pay him out of moneys provided by Parliament such sum as he may with the approval of the Minister for the Civil Service determine.

(2) If it appears to the Lord Chancellor that a person who ceases to be a member of the National Industrial Relations Court by reason of its abolition by this Act should receive compensation for loss of office, he may pay him out of moneys provided by Parliament such sum as he may with the approval of the Minister for the Civil Service determine. [**546**]

25. Miscellaneous amendments, and transitional provisions and repeals

(1) Schedule 3 to this Act shall have effect for undoing certain amendments and repeals made by the 1971 Act in certain enactments specified in that Schedule, for continuing the effect of other amendments so made and for making minor amendments and amendments consequential on other provisions of this Act in other enactments so specified.

(2) The transitional provisions in Schedule 4 shall have effect.

(3) The enactments specified in Schedule 5 are hereby repealed to the extent specified in the third column of that Schedule. [**547**]

Supplementary

26. Regulations and orders

(1) The Secretary of State may make regulations for any purpose for which regulations are authorised or required to be made under this Act.

(2) Any power to make regulations under this Act shall be exercisable by statutory instrument.

(3) A statutory instrument containing any such regulations, other than regulations required to be laid in draft before Parliament before being made, shall be subject to annulment in pursuance of a resolution of either House of Parliament.

(4) Any power to make an order under any provision of this Act shall include power to revoke or vary the order by a subsequent order under that provision. [**548**]

27. Expenses

There shall be defrayed out of moneys provided by Parliament—

(*a*) any administrative expenses incurred by the Secretary of State in consequence of the provisions of this Act; and

(*b*) any increase attributable to the provisions of this Act in the sums payable out of moneys so provided under any other enactment. [**549**]

28. Meaning of trade union and employers' association

(1) In this Act, except so far as the context otherwise requires, "trade union" means an organisation (whether permanent or temporary) which either—

(*a*) consists wholly or mainly of workers of one or more descriptions and is an organisation whose principal purposes include the regulation of relations between workers of that description or those descriptions and employers or employers' associations; or

(*b*) consists wholly or mainly of—

(i) constituent or affiliated organisations which fulfil the conditions specified in paragraph (*a*) above (or themselves consist wholly or mainly of constituent or affiliated organisations which fulfil those conditions), or

(ii) representatives of such constituent or affiliated organisations;

and in either case is an organisation whose principal purposes include the regulation of relations between workers and employers or between workers and employers' associations, or include the regulation of relations between its constituent or affiliated organisations.

(2) In this Act, except so far as the context otherwise requires, "employers' association" means an organisation (whether permanent or temporary) which either—

(*a*) consists wholly or mainly of employers or individual proprietors of one or more descriptions and is an organisation whose principal purposes include the regulation of relations between employers of that description or those descriptions and workers or trade unions; or

(*b*) consists wholly or mainly of—

(i) constituent or affiliated organisations which fulfill the conditions specified in paragraph (*a*) above (or themselves consist wholly or mainly of constituent or affiliated organisations which fulfil those conditions), or

(ii) representatives of such constituent or affiliated organisations;
and in either case is an organisation whose principal purposes include the regulation of relations between employers and workers or between employers and trade unions, or include the regulation of relations between its constituent or affiliated organisations. [550]

29. Meaning of trade dispute

(1) In this Act "trade dispute" means a dispute between employers and workers, or between workers and workers, which is connected with one or more of the following, that is to say—

(*a*) terms and conditions of employment, or the physical conditions in which any workers are required to work;
(*b*) engagement or non-engagement, or termination or suspension of employment or the duties of employment, of one or more workers;
(*c*) allocation of work or the duties of employment as between workers or groups of workers;
(*d*) matters of discipline;
(*e*) the membership or non-membership of a trade union on the part of a worker;
(*f*) facilities for officials of trade unions; and
(*g*) machinery for negotiation or consultation, and other procedures, relating to any of the foregoing matters, including the recognition by employers or employers' associations of the right of a trade union to represent workers in any such negotiation or consultation or in the carrying out of such procedures.

(2) A dispute between a Minister of the Crown and any workers shall, notwithstanding that he is not the employer of those workers, be treated for the purposes of this Act as a dispute between an employer and those workers if the dispute relates—

(*a*) to matters which have been referred for consideration by a joint body on which, by virtue of any provision made by or under any enactment, that Minister is represented; or
(*b*) to matters which cannot be settled without the Minister exercising a power conferred on him by or under an enactment.

(3) There is a trade dispute for the purposes of this Act even though it relates to matters occurring outside Great Britain, so long as the person or persons whose actions in Great Britain are said to be in contemplation or furtherance of a trade dispute relating to matters occurring outside Great Britain are likely to be affected in respect of one or more of the matters specified in subsection (1) of this section by the outcome of that dispute.

(4) A dispute to which a trade union or employers' association is a party shall be treated for the purposes of this Act as a dispute to which workers or, as the case may be, employers are parties.

(5) An act, threat or demand done or made by one person or organisation against another which, if resisted, would have led to a trade dispute with that other, shall, notwithstanding that because that other submits to the act or threat or accedes to the demand no dispute arises, be treated for the purposes of this Act as being done or made in contemplation of a trade dispute with that other.

(6) In this section—

"employment" includes any relationship whereby one person personally does work or performs services for another;

"worker", in relation to a dispute to which an employer is a party, includes any worker even if not employed by that employer.

(7) In the Conspiracy, and Protection of Property Act 1875, "trade dispute" has the same meaning as in this Act. [**551**]

30. General provisions as to interpretation

(1) In this Act, except so far as the context otherwise requires,—

"act" and "action" each includes omission and references to doing an act or taking action shall be construed accordingly;

"collective agreement" means any agreement or arrangement made by or on behalf of one or more trade unions and one or more employers or employers' associations and relating to one or more of the matters mentioned in section 29 (1) above;

"contract of employment" means a contract of service or of apprenticeship, whether it is express or implied and (if it is express) whether it is oral or in writing;

"dismissal procedures agreement" means an agreement in writing with respect to procedures relating to dismissal made by or on behalf of one or more independent trade unions and one or more employers or employers' associations;

"employee" means an individual who has entered into or works under (or, where the employment has ceased, worked under) a contract of employment, otherwise than in police service;

"employers' association" includes a combination of employers and employers' associations;

"independent trade union" means a trade union which—

(*a*) is not under the domination or control of an employer or a group of employers or of one or more employers' associations; and

(*b*) is not liable to interference by an employer or any such group or association (arising out of the provision of financial or material support or by any other means whatsoever) tending towards such control;

"individual proprietor" means an individual who is the owner of an undertaking;

"1971 Act" means the Industrial Relations Act 1971;

"official", in relation to a trade union, means any person who is an officer of the union or of a branch or section of the union or who (not being such an officer) is a person elected or appointed in accordance with the rules of the union to be a representative of its members or of some of them, including any person so elected or appointed who is an employee of the same employer as the members, or one or more of the members, whom he is to represent;

"police service" means service—

(*a*) in England and Wales as a member of a police force or as a special constable;

(*b*) as a constable within the meaning of the Police (Scotland) Act 1967;

(*c*) as a member of any constabulary maintained by virtue of any enactment; or
(*d*) in any other capacity by virtue of which a person has the powers or privileges of a constable;

"position", in relation to an employee, means the following matters taken as a whole, that is to say, his status as an employee, the nature of his work and his terms and conditions of employment;

"Registrar" has the meaning assigned to it by section 8 (1) above;

"special register body" means an organisation whose name was immediately before the commencement of sections 2 and 3 above entered in the special register maintained under section 84 of the 1971 Act and which for the time being is a company registered under the Companies Act 1948 or is incorporated by charter or letters patent;

"tort", as respects Scotland, means any wrongful or negligent act giving rise to liability in reparation, and cognate expressions shall be construed accordingly;

"union membership agreement" means an agreement or arrangement which—

(*a*) is made by or on behalf of, or otherwise exists between, one or more independent trade unions and one or more employers or employers' associations; and
(*b*) relates to employees of an identifiable class; and
(*c*) has the effect of requiring the terms and conditions of employment of every employee of that class to include a condition that he must be or become a member of the union or one of the unions which is or are parties to the agreement or arrangement or of another appropriate independent trade union;

"worker" (subject to the following provisions of this section) means an individual regarded in whichever (if any) of the following capacities is applicable to him, that is to say, as a person who works or normally works or seeks to work—

(*a*) under a contract of employment; or
(*b*) under any other contract (whether express or implied, and, if express, whether oral or in writing) whereby he undertakes to do or perform personally any work or services for another party to the contract who is not a professional client of his; or
(*c*) in employment under or for the purposes of a government department (otherwise than as a member of the naval, military or air forces of the Crown or of any women's service administered by the Defence Council) in so far as any such employment does not fall within paragraph (*a*) or (*b*) above,

otherwise than in police service.

(2) Without prejudice to the generality of the definitions in subsection (1) of this section, in this Act—

(*a*) "worker" includes an individual regarded in his capacity as one who works or normally works or seeks to work as a person providing general medical services, pharmaceutical services, general dental services or general ophthalmic services in accordance with arrangements made by an Area Health Authority or Family Practitioner Committee under section 33, section 38, section 40 or section 41 of the National Health Service Act 1946 or by a Health Board under section 34, section 39, section 40, or section 42 of the National Health Service (Scotland) Act 1947; and

(*b*) "employer" includes any Area Health Authority, Family Practitioner Committee or Health Board in accordance with whose arrangements a person provides or has provided or normally provides or seeks to provide any such service as aforesaid.

(3) Subject to subsection (4) below, in this Act "successor", in relation to the employer of an employee, means a person who, in consequence of a change occurring (whether by virtue of a sale or other disposition or by operation of law) in the ownership of the undertaking or of part of the undertaking for the purposes of which the employee was employed, has become the owner of that undertaking or of that part of it, as the case may be.

(4) Subsection (3) above shall have effect (subject to the necessary modifications) in relation to a case where—

(*a*) the person by whom an undertaking or part of an undertaking is owned immediately before a change is one of the persons by whom (whether as partners, trustees or otherwise) it is owned immediately after the change, or

(*b*) the persons by whom an undertaking or part of an undertaking is owned immediately before a change (whether as partners, trustees or otherwise) include the persons by whom, or include one or more of the persons by whom, it is owned immediately after the change,

as that subsection has effect where the previous owner and the new owner are wholly different persons; and any reference in this Act to a successor of an employer shall be construed accordingly.

(5) For the purposes of this Act any two employers are to be treated as associated if one is a company of which the other (directly or indirectly) has control, or if both are companies of which a third person (directly or indirectly) has control; and in this Act "associated employer" shall be construed accordingly.

(6) For the purposes of this Act it is immaterial whether the law which (apart from this Act) governs any persons' employment is the law of the United Kindom, or of a part of the United Kingdom, or not.

(7) Except so far as the context otherwise requires, any reference in this Act to any enactment shall be construed as a reference to that enactment as amended or extended by or under any other enactment, including this Act. **[552]**

31. Short title, commencement and extent

(1) This Act may be cited as the Trade Union and Labour Relations Act 1974.

(2) This Act, except as provided by section 1 (3) above and except sections 21 to 23 above, shall come into operation on such day as the Secretary of State may appoint by order made by statutory instrument, and different days may be so appointed for different purposes.

(3) Any reference in this Act to the commencement of any provision of this Act shall be construed as a reference to the day appointed under this section for the coming into operation of that provision.

(4) An order made under this section may make such transitional provision

or savings as appear to the Secretary of State to be necessary or expedient in connection with the provisions of this Act which are thereby brought (wholly or in part) into operation, including such adaptations of those provisions or of any provision of this Act then in force as appear to the Secretary of State to be necessary or expedient in consequence of the partial operation of this Act (whether before, on or after the day appointed by the order).

(5) The following provisions of this Act shall extend to Northern Ireland, that is to say, sections 4 and 19 and any provision of Schedule 3 or 5 to this Act which amends or repeals any provision of the House of Commons Disqualification Act 1957, the Trade Union (Amalgamations, etc.) Act (Northern Ireland) 1965, the Insurance Companies Act (Northern Ireland) 1968, the Merchant Shipping Act 1970 or the Insurance Companies Amendment Act 1973 or repeals any provision of the 1971 Act which extends to Northern Ireland, but except as aforesaid this Act shall not extend there. **[553]**

SCHEDULES

Section 1

SCHEDULE 1

Re-Enacted Provisions of Industrial Relations Act 1971

Note: The cross heading in square brackets at the beginning of each paragraph of this Schedule indicates the provision of the 1971 Act which is re-enacted, with or without amendments, in that paragraph.

Part I

Introductory

Code of Practice

[*Section* 2]

1.—(1) It shall be the duty of the Secretary of State to maintain a code of practice, containing such practical guidance as would be helpful for the purpose of promoting good industrial relations.

(2) The last code of practice brought into effect under Part I of the Industrial Relations Act 1971 shall remain in effect for the purpose of this Part of this Schedule unless and until revised as hereinafter provided.

(3) The Secretary of State may from time to time revise the whole or any part of a code of practice which has been brought into effect under this Part of this Schedule.

(4) In preparing any proposed revision of that code the Secretary of State shall have regard to—

(*a*) the need for those who manage undertakings to accept the primary responsibility for the promotion of good industrial relations, and

(*b*) the need for providing practical guidance with respect to disclosure of information by employers, and with respect to the establishment and maintenance of effective means of negotiation, consultation and communication at all levels between those who manage undertakings and the workers employed in them. **[554]**

Revisions of Code of Practice

[*Section* 3]

2. (1) Where the Secretary of State proposes to revise the whole or part of the code of practice (in the form in which, whether as originally approved or as pre-

viously revised, the code or that part of it has effect for the time being) he shall consult with the Trades Union Congress and the Confederation of British Industry and prepare a draft of the revised code, or of that part of it, as the case may be, and shall transmit a copy of the draft to each of them for their consideration and advice.

(2) The Secretary of State shall take account of any advice given to him by the Trades Union Congress or the Confederation of British Industry with respect to a draft prepared under sub-paragraph (1) above and shall arrange for any such advice to be published in such manner as he may consider appropriate; and, if the Secretary of State determines to proceed with the draft, he shall lay the draft, or a modified draft, before both Houses of Parliament.

(3) If the draft laid under sub-paragraph (2) above is approved by a resolution of each House of Parliament, the Secretary of State shall issue the revised code, or part of the code as revised, as the case may be, in the form of the draft.

(4) On issuing any document under this paragraph (whether it is the code of practice as originally approved or a revised code or part of a revised code) the Secretary of State shall make by statutory instrument an order specifying the date on which the document is to be brought into effect. [**555**]

Use of code in proceedings under this Act

[*Section* 4]

3. A failure on the part of any person to observe any provision of a code of practice which is for the time being in force under this Part of this Schedule shall not of itself render him liable to any proceedings; but in any proceedings before an industrial tribunal under this Act—

(*a*) any such code of practice shall be admissible in evidence, and
(*b*) any provision of such a code of practice which appears to the tribunal to be relevant to any question arising in the proceedings shall be taken into account by the tribunal in determining that question. [**556**]

Part II

Unfair Dismissal

Right of employee not to be unfairly dismissed

[*Section* 22]

4.—(1) In every employment to which this paragraph applies every employee shall have the right not to be unfairly dismissed by his employer, and the remedy of an employee so dismissed for breach of that right shall be by way of complaint to an industrial tribunal under Part III of this Schedule, and not otherwise.

(2) This paragraph applies to every employment except in so far as its application is excluded by or under any provision of this Schedule. [**557**]

Meaning of "dismissal"

[*Section* 23]

5.—(1) In this Schedule "dismissal" and "dismiss" shall be construed in accordance with the following provisions of this paragraph.

(2) Subject to sub-paragraph (3) below, an employee shall be treated for the purposes of this Act as dismissed by his employer, if, but only if,—

(*a*) the contract under which he is employed by the employer is terminated by the employer, whether it is so terminated by notice or without notice, or
(*b*) where under that contract he is employed for a fixed term, that term expires without being renewed under the same contract, or

(*c*) the employee terminates that contract, with or without notice, in circumstances such that he is entitled to terminate it without notice by reason of the employer's conduct.

(3) Where an employer gives notice to an employee to terminate his contract of employment and, at a time within the obligatory period of that notice, the employee gives notice in writing to the employer to terminate the contract of employment on a date earlier than the date on which the employer's notice is due to expire, the employee shall for the purposes of this Schedule be taken to be dismissed by his employer, and the reasons for the dismissal shall be taken to be the reasons for which the employer's notice is given.

(4) For the purposes of sub-paragraph (3) above—

(*a*) if the actual period of the employer's notice (that is to say, the period beginning at the time when the notice is given and ending with the time when it expires) is equal to the minimum period which (whether by virtue of any enactment or otherwise) is required to be given by the employer to terminate the contract of employment, "the obligatory period", in relation to that notice, means the actual period of the notice;

(*b*) in any other case, "the obligatory period", in relation to an employer's notice, means that period which, being equal to the minimum period referred to in sub-paragraph (*a*) above, expires at the time when the employer's notice expires.

(5) In this Schedule "the effective date of termination"—

(*a*) in relation to an employee whose contract of employment is terminated by notice, whether given by his employer or by the employee, means the date on which that notice expires;

(*b*) in relation to an employee whose contract of employment is terminated without notice, means the date on which the termination takes effect; and

(*c*) in relation to an employee who is employed under a contract for a fixed term, where that term expires without being renewed under the same contract, means the date on which that term expires. [**558**]

Fair and unfair dismissal

[*Section* 24]

6.—(1) In determining for the purposes of this Schedule whether the dismissal of an employee was fair or unfair, it shall be for the employer to show—

(*a*) what was the reason (or, if there was more than one, the principal reason) for the dismissal, and

(*b*) that it was a reason falling within sub-paragraph (2) below, or some other substantial reason of a kind such as to justify the dismissal of an employee holding the position which that employee held.

(2) In sub-paragraph (1) (*b*) above the reference to a reason falling within this sub-paragraph is a reference to a reason which—

(*a*) related to the capability or qualifications of the employee for performing work of the kind which he was employed by the employer to do, or

(*b*) related to the conduct of the employee, or

(*c*) was that the employee was redundant, or

(*d*) was that the employee could not continue to work in the position which he held without contravention (either on his part or on that of his employer) of a duty or restriction imposed by or under an enactment.

(3) Where the employer has fulfilled the requirements of sub-paragraph (1) above, then, subject to paragraphs 7 and 8 below, the question whether the dismissal was fair or unfair shall be determined in accordance with the following provisions of this paragraph.

(4) For the purposes of this Schedule the dismissal of an employee by an employer shall be regarded as having been unfair if the reason for it (or, if more than one, the principal reason) was that the employee—

(*a*) was, or proposed to become, a member of an independent trade union;
(*b*) had taken, or proposed to take, part at any appropriate time in the activities of an independent trade union; or
(*c*) had refused, or proposed to refuse, to become or remain a member of a trade union which was not an independent trade union.

(5) Dismissal of an employee by an employer shall be regarded as fair for the purposes of this Schedule if—

(*a*) it is the practice, in accordance with a union membership agreement, for all the employees of that employer or all employees of the same class as the dismissed employee to belong to a specified independent trade union, or to one of a number of specified independent trade unions; and
(*b*) the reason for the dismissal was that the employee was not a member of the specified union or one of the specified unions, or had refused or proposed to refuse to become or remain a member of that union or one of those unions;

unless the employee genuinely objects on grounds of religious belief to being a member of any trade union whatsoever or on any reasonable grounds to being a member of a particular trade union, in which case the dismissal shall be regarded as unfair.

(6) Any reason by virtue of which a dismissal is to be regarded as unfair in consequence of sub-paragraph (4) or (5) above is hereafter in this Schedule referred to as an inadmissible reason.

(7) Where the reason or principal reason for the dismissal of an employee was that he was redundant, but it is shown that the circumstances constituting the redundancy applied equally to one or more other employees in the same undertaking who held positions similar to that held by him and who have not been dismissed by the employer, and either—

(*a*) that the reason (or, if more than one, the principal reason) for which he was selected for dismissal was an inadmissible reason; or
(*b*) that he was selected for dismissal in contravention of a customary arrangement or agreed procedure relating to redundancy and there were no special reasons justifying a departure from that arrangement or procedure in his case,

then, for the purposes of this Schedule the dismissal shall be regarded as unfair.

(8) Subject to sub-paragraphs (4) to (7) above, the determination of the question whether the dismissal was fair or unfair, having regard to the reason shown by the employer, shall depend on whether the employer can satisfy the tribunal that in the circumstances (having regard to equity and the substantial merits of the case) he acted reasonably in treating it as a sufficient reason for dismissing the employee.

(9) In this paragraph, in relation to an employee—

(*a*) "capability" means capability assessed by reference to skill, aptitude, health or any other physical or mental quality;
(*b*) "qualifications" means any degree, diploma or other academic, technical or professional qualification relevant to the position which the employee held; and
(*c*) any reference to redundancy or to being redundant shall be construed as a reference to the existence of one or other of the facts specified in paragraphs (*a*) and (*b*) of section 1 (2) of the Redundancy Payments Act 1965. **[559]**

Dismissal in connection with a lock-out

[*Section* 25]

7.—(1) The dismissal of an employee by way of a lock-out (whether the lock-out extends to all the employees of the employer or only to some of them, and whether the dismissal occurs at the beginning of the lock-out or during the course of it) shall not be regarded as unfair if the employee is offered re-engagement as from the date of resumption of work.

(2) Where an employee who has been so dismissed, and has not been offered re-engagement as from the date of resumption of work, claims that he was unfairly dismissed by his employer, the provisions of paragraph 6 above shall apply as if in that paragraph, for any reference to the reason or principal reason for which the employee was dismissed by his employer, there were substituted a reference to the reason or principal reason for which he was not offered re-engagement as from that date.

(3) In this paragraph any reference to an offer of re-engagement, in relation to an employee, is a reference to an offer (made either by the original employer or by a successor of that employer or by an associated employer) to re-engage that employee, either in the position which he held immediately before the effective date of termination or in a different position which would be reasonably suitable to him.

(4) In this paragraph—

(*a*) "the date of resumption of work" means the date as from which, at or after the termination of the lock-out, the other comparable employees of the original employer, or a majority of those employees, were offered re-engagement, and

(*b*) "the original employer", in relation to an employee, means the employer who dismissed him;

and in this sub-paragraph "comparable employees", in relation to an employee, means such of the employees of the original employer to whom the lock-out extended as, immediately before the effective date of termination, held positions similar to that held by that employee. [**560**]

Dismissal in connection with a strike or other industrial action

[*Section* 26]

8.—(1) The provisions of this paragraph shall have effect in relation to an employee who claims that he has been unfairly dismissed by his employer, where on the date of dismissal he was taking part in a strike or other industrial action.

(2) If the reason or principal reason for the dismissal was that the employee took part in the strike or other industrial action, the dismissal shall not be regarded as unfair unless it is shown—

(*a*) that one or more employees of the same employer (in this paragraph referred to as "the original employer"), who also took part in that action, were not dismissed for taking part in it, or

(*b*) that one or more such employees, who were dismissed for taking part in it, were offered re-engagement on the termination of the industrial action and that the employee was not offered such re-engagement,

and that the reason (or, if more than one, the principal reason) for which the employee was selected for dismissal, or not offered re-engagement was an inadmissible reason.

(3) In this paragraph any reference to the date of dismissal—

(*a*) where the employee's contract of employment was terminated by notice, whether given by his employer or by him, is a reference to the date on which that notice was given, and

(*b*) in any other case, is a reference to the effective date of termination;

and any reference to an offer of re-engagement, in relation to an employee, is a reference to an offer (made either by the original employer or by a successor of that employer or by an associated employer) to re-engage that employee, either in the position which he held immediately before the date of dismissal or in a different position which would be reasonably suitable to him. [**561**]

Excluded classes of employment

[*Section* 27]

9.—(1) Paragraph 4 above does not apply to any of the following, that is to say,—

(*a*) any employment in an undertaking in which immediately before the effective date of termination there were in the aggregate (including the dismissed employee) less than four employees who had been continuously employed for a period of not less than thirteen weeks, whether they are, or had been, all employed at the same place or are, or had been, employed at different places;

(*b*) any employment where the employer is the husband or wife or a close relative of the employee;

(*c*) any employment as a registered dock worker, as defined by any scheme for the time being in force under the Dock Workers(Regulation of Employment) Act 1946, not being employment by virtue of which the employee is wholly or mainly engaged in work which is not dock work as defined by the scheme;

(*d*) any employment as master or as a member of the crew of a fishing vessel, where the employee is not remunerated otherwise than by a share in the profits or gross earnings of the vessel;

(*e*) any employment as a teacher to whom section 85 of the Education (Scotland) Act 1962 (dismissal of teachers) applies;

(*f*) any employment under a contract which normally involves employment for less than twenty-one hours weekly.

(2) Paragraph 4 above does not apply to any employment where under his contract of employment the employee ordinarily works outside Great Britain.

(3) For the purposes of sub-paragraph (2) above a person employed to work on board a ship registered in the United Kingdom (not being a ship registered at a port outside Great Britain) shall, unless—

(*a*) the employment is wholly outside Great Britain, or

(*b*) he is not ordinarily resident in Great Britain,

be regarded as a person who under his contract ordinarily works in Great Britain.

(4) In this paragraph "close relative", in relation to a person means that person's father, mother, grandfather, grandmother, stepfather, stepmother, son, daughter, grandson, granddaughter, stepson, stepdaughter, brother, sister, half-brother or half-sister.

(5) The foregoing provisions of this paragraph shall have effect subject to any order made under paragraph 11 below. [**562**]

Qualifying period and upper age limit

[*Section* 28]

10. Subject to paragraph 11 below, paragraph 4 above does not apply to the dismissal of an employee from any employment if the employee—

(*a*) was not continuously employed for a period of not less than 26 weeks ending with the effective date of termination, or

(*b*) on or before the effective date of termination attained the age which, in the undertaking in which he was employed, was the normal retiring age for an employee holding the position which he held, or, if a man, attained the age of sixty-five, or, if a woman, attained the age of sixty;

but this paragraph shall have effect in a case where the effective date of termination falls within the period of six months beginning with the commencement of this Schedule as if the reference in sub-paragraph (*a*) to 26 weeks were a reference to 52 weeks. [**563**]

Supplementary provisions relating to paragraphs 9 and 10

[*Section* 29]

11.—(1) Paragraphs 9 (1) (*a*) and 10 above shall not apply to the dismissal of an employee if it is shown that the reason (or, if more than one, the principal reason) for the dismissal was an inadmissible reason.

(2) The Secretary of State may by order made by statutory instrument add to or vary any of the provisions of paragraphs 9 and 10 above or exclude the operation of any of those provisions.

(3) No order shall be made under this paragraph unless a draft of the order has been laid before Parliament and approved by a resolution of each House of Parliament. [**564**]

Exclusion of certain contracts for a fixed term

[*Section* 30]

12. Paragraph 4 above does not apply—

(*a*) to dismissal from employment under a contract for a fixed term of two years or more, where the contract was made before 28th February 1972 and is not a contract of apprenticeship, and the dismissal consists only of the expiry of that term without its being renewed, or

(*b*) to dismissal from employment under a contract for a fixed term of two years or more, where the dismissal consists only of the expiry of that term without its being renewed, if before the term so expires the employee has agreed in writing to exclude any claim in respect of rights under that paragraph in relation to that contract. [**565**]

Exclusion in respect of dismissal procedures agreement

[*Section* 31]

13.—(1) An application may be made jointly to the Secretary of State by all the parties to a dismissal procedures agreement to make an order designating that agreement for the purposes of this paragraph.

(2) On any such application the Secretary of State may make such an order if he is satisfied—

(*a*) that every trade union which is a party to the dismissal procedures agreement is an independent trade union;

(*b*) that the agreement provides for procedures to be followed in cases where an employee claims that he has been, or is in the course of being, unfairly dismissed;

(*c*) that those procedures are available without discrimination to all employees falling within any description to which the agreement applies;

(*d*) that the remedies provided by the agreement in respect of unfair dismissal are on the whole as beneficial as (but not necessarily identical with) those provided in respect of unfair dismissal by this Schedule;

(*e*) that the procedures provided by the agreement include a right to arbitration or adjudication by an independent referee, or by a tribunal or other independent body, in cases where (by reason of an equality of votes or for any other reason) a decision cannot otherwise be reached; and (*f*) that the provisions of the agreement are such that it can be determined with reasonable certainty whether a particular employee is one to whom the agreement applies or not.

(3) Where a dismissal procedures agreement is designated by an order under this paragraph which is for the time being in force, the provisions of that agreement relating to dismissal shall have effect in substitution for any rights under paragraph 4 above; and accordingly that paragraph shall not apply to the dismissal of an employee from any employment if it is employment to which, and he is an employee to whom, those provisions of the agreement apply. [**566**]

Revocation of exclusion under paragraph 13

[*Section* 32]

14.—(1) At any time when an order under paragraph 13 above is in force, any of the parties to the dismissal procedures agreement to which the order relates may apply to the Secretary of State for the order to be revoked.

(2) If on any such application the Secretary of State is satisfied either—

(*a*) that it is the desire of all the parties to the dismissal procedures agreement that the order should be revoked, or

(*b*) that the agreement has ceased to fulfil all the conditions specified in paragraph 13 (2) above,

the Secretary of State shall revoke the order by a further order made under this paragraph.

(3) Any order made under this paragraph may contain such transitional provisions as appear to the Secretary of State to be appropriate in the circumstances, and, in particular, may direct—

(*a*) that, notwithstanding paragraph 13 (3) above, an employee shall not be excluded from his rights under paragraph 4 above where the effective date of termination falls within a transitional period which is specified in the order and is a period ending with the date on which the order under this paragraph takes effect and shall have an extended time for presenting a complaint under Part III of this Schedule in respect of a dismissal where the effective date of termination falls within that period, and

(*b*) that in determining any complaint of unfair dismissal presented by an employee to whom the dismissal procedures agreement applies, where the effective date of termination falls within that transitional period, an industrial tribunal shall have regard to such considerations (in addition to those specified in Part III of this Schedule) as may be specified in the order. [**567**]

Pressure on employer to dismiss unfairly

[*Section* 33]

15. In determining, for the purposes of this Part of this Schedule any question as to the reason, or principal reason, for which an employee was dismissed or any question whether the reason or principal reason for which an employee was dismissed was a reason fulfilling the requirements of paragraph 6 (1) (*b*) above or whether the employer acted reasonably in treating it as a sufficient reason for dismissing him,—

(*a*) no account shall be taken of any pressure which, by calling, organising, procuring or financing a strike or other industrial action, or threatening to do so, was exercised on the employer to dismiss the employee, and

(*b*) any such question shall be determined as if no such pressure had been exercised. [**568**]

Part III

Jurisdiction and Procedure of Industrial Tribunals

Extended scope of industrial tribunals

[*Section* 100]

16. Tribunals established under section 12 of the Industrial Training Act 1964 shall, by the name of industrial tribunals, continue to exercise the jurisdiction conferred on them by or under that Act, the Redundancy Payments Act 1965, the Docks and Harbours Act 1966, the Selective Employment Payments Act 1966, the Equal Pay Act 1970 and the Contracts of Employment Act 1972 and also the jurisdiction conferred on them by or under this Act. [**569**]

Complaint to industrial tribunal of unfair dismissal

[*Section* 106]

17.—(1) A complaint may be presented to an industrial tribunal against an employer by any person (in this Part and Part IV of this Schedule referred to as the complainant) that he was unfairly dismissed by the employer or by a person acting on the employer's behalf.

(2) Where on a complaint under this paragraph the industrial tribunal—

(*a*) finds that the grounds of the complaint are well-founded, and

(*b*) considers that it would be practicable and in accordance with equity, for the complainant to be reinstated or re-engaged by the employer or to be engaged by a successor of the employer or by an associated employer,

the tribunal shall make a recommendation to that effect, stating the terms on which it considers that it would be reasonable for the complainant to be so reinstated, re-engaged or engaged.

(3) Where on such a complaint the industrial tribunal finds that the grounds of the complaint are well-founded, but—

(*a*) the tribunal does not make such a recommendation as aforesaid, or

(*b*) the tribunal makes such a recommendation, and (for whatever reason) the recommendation is not complied with,

the tribunal shall make an award of compensation, to be paid by the employer to the complainant, in respect of the dismissal. [**570**]

National security

[*Section* 159]

18.—(1) If on a complaint under paragraph 17 above it is shown that the action to which the complaint relates was taken for the purpose of safeguarding national security, the industrial tribunal shall dismiss the complaint.

(2) A certificate purporting to be signed by or on behalf of a Minister of the Crown, and certifying—

(*a*) that action specified in the certificate was taken for the purpose of safeguarding national security, or

(*b*) that a particular request for information could not be complied with except by disclosing information the disclosure of which would have been against the interests of national security,

shall for the purposes of this Schedule be conclusive evidence of the fact so certified. [**571**]

General principles as to assessment of compensation

[*Section* 116]

19.—(1) Where in any proceedings on a complaint under paragraph 17 above an industrial tribunal makes an award of compensation to be paid by a party to the proceedings (in this paragraph referred to as the party in default) to another party (in this paragraph referred to as the aggrieved party), the amount of the compensation shall, subject to paragraph 20 below, be such amount as the tribunal considers just and equitable in all the circumstances, having regard to the loss sustained by the aggrieved party in consequence of the matters to which the complaint relates, in so far as that loss was attributable to action taken by or on behalf of the party in default.

(2) The said loss shall be taken to include—

(*a*) any expenses reasonably incurred by the aggrieved party in consequence of the matters to which the complaint relates, and

(*b*) loss of any benefit which he might reasonably be expected to have had but for those matters,

subject, however, to the application of the same rule concerning the duty of a person to mitigate his loss as applies in relation to damages recoverable under the common law of England and Wales or of Scotland, as the case may be.

(3) Where the industrial tribunal finds that the matters to which the complaint relates were to any extent caused or contributed to by any action of the aggrieved party in connection with those matters, the tribunal shall reduce its assessment of his loss to such extent as, having regard to that finding, the tribunal considers just and equitable.

(4) Where, on a complaint under paragraph 17 above, the industrial tribunal has made a recommendation in accordance with sub-paragraph (2) of that paragraph and that recommendation is not complied with, then—

(*a*) if the tribunal finds that the reason for which it was not complied with was that the aggrieved party refused an offer of re-instatement, re-engagement or engagement on the terms stated in the recommendation, and the tribunal considers that he acted unreasonably in doing so, the tribunal (without prejudice to the generality of the rule mentioned in sub-paragraph (2) above) shall reduce the assessment of his loss, or

(*b*) if the tribunal finds that the reason for which the recommendation was not complied with was that the employer in question refused or failed to make such an offer, and the tribunal considers that he acted unreasonably in doing so, the tribunal shall increase that assessment,

to such extent (in either case) as in the circumstances the tribunal considers just and equitable.

(5) In determining, on a complaint under paragraph 17 above, how far any loss sustained by the aggrieved party was attributable to action taken by or on behalf of the employer, no account shall be taken of any pressure which was exercised on the employer as mentioned in paragraph 15 (*a*) above, and the question shall be determined as if no such pressure had been exercised. **[572]**

Limit on compensation

[*Section* 118]

20.—(1) The amount of compensation which is awarded to a person under paragraph 17 above shall not exceed—

(*a*) the amount which, in his case, represents 104 weeks' pay, or

(*b*) £5,200 (that is to say, 104 × £50),

whichever is the less.

(2) The Secretary of State shall make provision by regulations for calculating the amount of a week's pay for the purposes of this paragraph.

(3) The Secretary of State may by order made by statutory instrument provide that, subject to such transitional provisions (if any) as may be contained in the order, sub-paragraph (1) above shall have effect as if, for the references to £5,200 and £50,

there were substituted references to such larger sums as may be specified in the order.

(4) No order shall be made under this paragraph unless a draft of the order has been laid before Parliament and approved by a resolution of each House of Parliament. **[573]**

Regulations as to tribunal procedure

[Schedule 6, paragraphs 1 to 5 and 11]

21.—(1) Regulations (in this Part of this Schedule referred to as "the regulations") may make such provision as appears to the Secretary of State to be necessary or expedient with respect to proceedings before industrial tribunals.

(2) The regulations may in particular include provision—

(*a*) for determining by which tribunal any appeal, question or complaint is to be determined;

(*b*) for treating the Secretary of State (either generally or in such circumstances as may be prescribed by the regulations) as a party to any proceedings before an industrial tribunal, where he would not otherwise be a party to them, and entitling him to appear and to be heard accordingly.

(*c*) for requiring persons to attend to give evidence and produce documents, and for authorising the administration of oaths to witnesses;

(*d*) for granting to any person such discovery or inspection of documents or right to further particulars as might be granted by a county court in England and Wales or, in Scotland, for granting to any such person such recovery or inspection of documents as might be granted by the sheriff;

(*e*) for prescribing the procedure to be followed on any appeal, reference or complaint or other proceedings before an industrial tribunal, including provisions as to the persons entitled to appear and to be heard on behalf of parties to such proceedings, and provisions for enabling an industrial tribunal to review its decisions, and revoke or vary its orders and awards in such circumstances as may be determined in accordance with the regulations;

(*f*) for the appointment of one or more assessors for the purposes of any proceedings before an industrial tribunal, where the proceedings are brought under an enactment which provides for one or more assessors to be appointed;

(*g*) for the award of costs or expenses, including any allowances payable under section 12 (3) of the Industrial Training Act 1964 other than allowances payable to members of industrial tribunals or assessors;

(*h*) for taxing or otherwise settling any such costs or expenses (and, in particular, in England and Wales, for enabling such costs to be taxed in the county court); and

(*i*) for the registration and proof of decisions, orders and awards of industrial tribunals.

(3) In relation to proceedings on complaints under paragraph 17 above the regulations shall include provision—

(*a*) for requiring a copy of any such complaint, and a copy of any notice relating to it which is lodged by or on behalf of the employer against whom the complaint is made, to be sent to a conciliation officer;

(*b*) for securing that the complainant and the employer against whom the complaint is made are notified that the services of a conciliation officer are available to them; and

(*c*) for postponing the hearing of any such complaint for such period as may be determined in accordance with the regulations for the purpose of giving an opportunity for the complaint to be settled by way of conciliation and withdrawn.

(4) An industrial tribunal shall not consider a complaint under paragraph 17

above unless it is presented to the tribunal before the end of the period of three months beginning with the effective date of termination or within such further period as the tribunal considers reasonable in a case where it is satisfied that it was not reasonably practicable for the complaint to be presented within the period of three months.

(5) The regulations may enable an industrial tribunal to sit in private for the purpose of hearing evidence which in the opinion of the tribunal relates to matters of such a nature that it would be against the interests of national security to allow the evidence to be given in public or hearing evidence from any person which in the opinion of the tribunal is likely to consist of—

(*a*) information which he could not disclose without contravening a prohibition imposed by or under any enactment; or

(*b*) any information which has been communicated to him in confidence, or which he has otherwise obtained in consequence of the confidence reposed in him by another person; or

(*c*) information the disclosure of which would, for reasons other than its effect on negotiations with respect to any of the matters mentioned in section 29 (1) above, be seriously prejudicial to the interests of any undertaking of his or any undertaking in which he works.

(6) Any person who without reasonable excuse fails to comply with any requirement imposed by the regulations by virtue of sub-paragraph (2) (*c*) above or any requirement with respect to the discovery, recovery or inspection of documents so imposed by virtue of sub-paragraph (2) (*d*) above shall be liable on summary conviction to a fine not exceeding £100. [**574**]

Exclusion of Arbitration Act 1950

[*Schedule* 6, *paragraph* 7]

22. The Arbitration Act 1950 shall not apply to any proceedings before an industrial tribunal. [**575**]

Presumption as to dismissal for redundancy

[*Schedule* 6, *paragraph* 8]

23. Where in accordance with the regulations an industrial tribunal determines in the same proceedings—

(*a*) a question referred to it under Part I of the Redundancy Payments Act 1965, and

(*b*) a complaint presented under paragraph 17 above,

section 9 (2) (*b*) of that Act (whereby a dismissal is to be presumed, unless the contrary is proved, to have been by reason of redundancy) shall not have effect for the purposes of the proceedings in so far as they relate to the complaint under paragraph 17 above. [**576**]

Right of appearance

[*Schedule* 6, *paragraph* 9]

24. Any person may appear before an industrial tribunal in person or be represented by counsel or by a solicitor or by a representative of a trade union or an employers' association or by any other person whom he desires to represent him. [**577**]

Recovery of sums awarded

[*Schedule* 6, *paragraph* 10]

25.—(1) Any sum payable in pursuance of a decision of an industrial tribunal in England and Wales which has been registered in accordance with the regulations shall, if a county court so orders, be recoverable by execution issued from the county court or otherwise as if it were payable under an order of that court.

(2) Any order for the payment of any sum made by an industrial tribunal in Scotland may be enforced in like manner as a recorded decree arbitral.

(3) In this paragraph any reference to a decision or order of an industrial tribunal—

(*a*) does not include a decision or order which, on being reviewed, has been revoked by the tribunal, and

(*b*) in relation to a decision or order which, on being reviewed, has been varied by the tribunal, shall be construed as a reference to the decision or order as so varied. **[578]**

PART IV

CONCILIATION OFFICERS, AND MISCELLANEOUS AND SUPPLEMENTARY PROVISIONS

Conciliation officers

[*Section* 146]

26.—(1) The Secretary of State shall appoint conciliation officers to perform the functions specified in the following provisions of this paragraph, subject to the approval of the Minister for the Civil Service as to their numbers and as to their terms and conditions of service.

(2) Where a complaint has been presented to an industrial tribunal by the complainant under paragraph 17 above, and a copy of it has been sent to a conciliation officer, it shall be the duty of the conciliation officer—

(*a*) if he is requested to do so by the complainant and by the employer against whom it was presented, or

(*b*) if, in the absence of any such request, the conciliation officer considers that he could act under this sub-paragraph with a reasonable prospect of success,

to endeavour to promote a settlement of the complaint without its being determined by an industrial tribunal.

(3) For the purpose of promoting such a settlement, in a case where the complainant has ceased to be employed by the employer against whom the complaint was made,—

(*a*) the conciliation officer shall in particular seek to promote the reinstatement or re-engagement of the complainant by the employer, or his engagement by a successor of the employer or by an associated employer, on terms appearing to the conciliation officer to be equitable; but

(*b*) where such reinstatement, re-engagement or engagement is not practicable or cannot be agreed between the parties to the complaint, and they desire the conciliation officer to act under this paragraph, he shall seek to promote agreement between them as to a sum by way of compensation to be paid by the employer to the complainant.

(4) Where at any time—

(*a*) after the complainant has ceased to be employed by an employer, in circumstances where the employee claims that he was unfairly dismissed, but

(*b*) before any complaint relating to that claim has been presented by the claimant under paragraph 17 above,

a request is made to a conciliation officer (whether by the employer or by the employee) to make his services available to them, the conciliation officer shall act in accordance with sub-paragraphs (2) and (3) above as if a complaint had been presented in pursuance of that claim.

(5) Anything communicated to a conciliation officer in connection with the performance of his functions under this paragraph shall not be admissible in evidence

in any proceedings before an industrial tribunal, except with the consent of the person who communicated it to that officer. [**579**]

Teacher in aided school dismissed on requirement of local education authority

[*Section* 148]

27.—(1) Where a teacher in an aided school is dismissed by the governors or managers of the school in pursuance of a requirement of the local education authority under paragraph (*a*) of the proviso to section 24 (2) of the Education Act 1944, Parts II and III of this Schedule shall have effect in relation to the dismissal as if—

(*a*) the local education authority had at all material times been the teacher's employer, and

(*b*) the local education authority had dismissed him, and the reason or principal reason for which they did so had been the reason or principal reason for which they required his dismissal.

(2) For the purposes of a complaint under paragraph 17 above as applied by this paragraph, paragraph 19 above shall have effect as if—

(*a*) in sub-paragraph (4) (*b*), for the words "the employer in question refused or failed to make such an offer, and the tribunal considers that he acted unreasonably in doing so" there were substituted the words "the local education authority refused or failed to permit the aggrieved party to be re-engaged, and the tribunal considers that they acted unreasonably in doing so", and

(*b*) in sub-paragraph (5), any reference to the employer were a reference to the local education authority. [**580**]

Race Relations Act 1968

[*Section* 149]

28.—(1) Where under the Race Relations Act 1968 a complaint is made to the Secretary of State or the Race Relations Board that an act has been done which is unlawful by virtue of section 3 (1) of that Act, or a matter falling to be investigated by that Board raises the question whether any such act has been done, then, if it appears to the Secretary of State or the Board—

(*a*) that that act is one in respect of which a complaint of unfair dismissal has been presented to an industrial tribunal under paragraph 17 above, or in respect of which a complaint could be so presented (or could have been so presented if the requirements of industrial tribunal regulations relating to it had been complied with), and

(*b*) that a complaint so presented to an industrial tribunal has not been dismissed by virtue of any provision contained in or made under paragraphs 9 to 13 above or (as the case may be) would not fall or have fallen to be so dismissed,

the Secretary of State or the Board shall not proceed any further under that Act in relation to that act, except to the extent provided by the following provisions of this paragraph.

(2) If, on determining a complaint of unfair dismissal presented under paragraph 17 above, an industrial tribunal has recorded a finding that the dismissal of the claimant was unfair and also that the reason or one of the reasons for the dismissal was the complainant's colour, race or ethnic or national origin, then, sub-paragraph (1) above shall not preclude the Secretary of State or the Race Relations Board—

(*a*) from proceeding under that Act for the purpose of securing a written assurance against a repetition of that action, in accordance with section 15 (3) (*b*) of that Act or in accordance with paragraph 3 of Schedule 2 or paragraph 2 or 8 of Schedule 3 to that Act, or (*b*) from proceeding under that Act (whether by way of bringing proceedings or otherwise) in consequence of forming an opinion or receiving a report that a written assurance so secured has been broken.

(3) The Secretary of State or the Race Relations Board may proceed in accordance with sub-paragraph (2) (*a*) or (*b*) above notwithstanding any limitation imposed by the Race Relations Act 1968 as to the time within which anything may be done under that Act.

(4) In this paragraph any reference to the Race Relations Board shall be construed as including references—

(*a*) to any conciliation committee constituted under the Race Relations Act 1968, and

(*b*) to any other body of persons to whom a matter could be referred for investigation under Schedule 2 or Schedule 3 to that Act. [**581**]

Redundancy payments

[*Section* 150]

29.—(1) Regulations may make provision with respect to cases where a complaint of unfair dismissal is presented to an industrial tribunal under paragraph 17 above, and a redundancy payment or an equivalent payment has been paid, or has been or is claimed, in respect of the same dismissal.

(2) Any such regulations may make such modifications of the provisions of Part III of this Schedule or of the Redundancy Payments Act 1965, as the Secretary of State may consider appropriate, including—

(*a*) provisions excluding the right to a redundancy payment or equivalent payment, or requiring any such payment to be repaid, or

(*b*) provisions requiring a rebate under section 30 of that Act or a sum payable under section 41 (2) of that Act to be withheld or reduced, or (where already paid) to be recoverable in whole or in part, and on being so recovered to be paid into the Redundancy Fund,

in such circumstances as may be prescribed by the regulations.

(3) In section 21 of the Redundancy Payments Act 1965 (claims for redundancy payments), at the end of paragraph (*c*) there shall be added the words "or

(*d*) a complaint relating to his dismissal has been presented by the employee under paragraph 17 of Schedule 1 to the Trade Union and Labour Relations Act 1974".

(4) In this paragraph "equivalent payment" means any payment which is either—

(*a*) a payment made or falling to be made as mentioned in paragraph (*b*) or paragraph (*c*) of section 30 (1) of the Redundancy Payments Act 1965, or

(*b*) a payment in respect of the termination of a person's employment, made in accordance with a scheme under section 1 of the Superannuation Act 1972 or in accordance with any such arrangements as are mentioned in section 41 (3) of the Redundancy Payments Act 1965.

(5) No regulations shall be made under this paragraph unless a draft of the regulations has been laid before Parliament and approved by resolution of each House of Parliament. [**582**]

Period of continuous employment

[*Section* 151]

30.—(1) The provisions of Schedule 1 to the Contracts of Employment Act 1972 (computation of period of employment), and the provisions of any order for the time being in force under section 10 of that Act in so far as it modifies that Schedule, shall have effect for the purposes of this Act in determining for what period an employee has been continuously employed.

(2) For the purposes of any proceedings under this Schedule a person's employment during any period shall, unless the contrary is shown, be presumed to have been continuous.

(3) Regulations made by the Secretary of State may make provision—

(*a*) for preserving the continuity of a person's period of employment for the purposes of Schedule 1 to the Contracts of Employment Act 1972, or for the purposes of that Schedule as applied by or under any other enactment specified in the regulations, or

(*b*) for modifying or excluding the operation of section 24 of the Redundancy Payments Act 1965 (which requires the continuity of the period of employment to be treated as broken for the purposes of that Act where a redundancy payment is paid to an employee and he is subsequently re-engaged), subject to the recovery of any sum which, in accordance with subsection (3) of that section, is treated as payment of a redundancy payment,

in cases where, in consequence of action to which sub-paragraph (4) below applies, a dismissed employee is re-engaged by his employer or is engaged by a successor of that employer or by an associated employer.

(4) This sub-paragraph applies to any action taken in relation to the dismissal of an employee which consists—

(*a*) of the presentation by him of a complaint under paragraph 17 above, or

(*b*) of his making a claim in accordance with a dismissal procedures agreement designated by an order under paragraph 13 above, or

(*c*) of any action taken by a conciliation officer under paragraph 26 (4) above. **[583]**

Nominations by members of trade unions

[*Section* 155]

31.—(1) Regulations may make provision—

(*a*) for enabling members of trade unions who are not under sixteen years of age to nominate a person or persons to become entitled, on the death of the person making the nomination, to the whole or part of any money payable on his death out of the funds of the trade union of which he is a member; and

(*b*) for enabling any money payable out of the funds of a trade union on the death of a member of the trade union, to an amount not exceeding £500, to be paid or distributed on his death (whether in accordance with such a nomination or otherwise) without letters of administration, probate of any will or confirmation.

(2) Any regulations made in accordance with sub-paragraph (1) (*a*) above—

(*a*) may include provision as to the manner in which nominations may be made and as to the manner in which nominations may be varied or revoked, and

(*b*) may provide that, subject to such exceptions as may be prescribed, no nomination made by a member of a trade union shall be valid if at the date of the nomination the person nominated is an officer or employee of the trade union or is otherwise connected with the trade union in such manner as may be prescribed by the regulations.

(3) Any regulations under this section may include such incidental, transitional or supplementary provisions as the Secretary of State may consider appropriate and, in particular, any such regulations made in accordance with sub-paragraph (1) (*a*) above may include provision for securing, to such extent and subject to such conditions as may be prescribed in the regulations, that nominations made under the Trade Union Act Amendment Act 1876 shall have effect as if they have been made under the regulations and may be varied or revoked accordingly.

(4) The Secretary of State may by order made by statutory instrument direct that, in relation to deaths occurring after the end of the period of one month beginning with the date on which the order comes into force, sub-paragraph (1) (*b*) above shall have effect as if, for the reference to £500, there were substituted a reference to such higher amount as may be specified in the order.

(5) No order shall be made under sub-paragraph (4) above unless a draft of the order has been laid before Parliament and approved by a resolution of each House of Parliament. [**584**]

Restrictions on contracting out

[*Section* 161]

32.—(1) Except as provided by sub-paragraph (2) below, any provision in an agreement (whether a contract of employment or not) shall be void in so far as it purports—

(*a*) to exclude or limit the operation of any provision of this Act; or

(*b*) to preclude any person from presenting a complaint to or bringing any proceedings before an industrial tribunal under this Act.

(2) Sub-paragraph (1) above shall not apply—

(*a*) to any union membership agreement;

(*b*) to any provision of an agreement relating to dismissal from employment such as is mentioned in paragraph 12 (*b*) above;

(*c*) to any provision in a dismissal procedures agreement excluding rights under paragraph 4 above if that provision is not to have effect unless an order under paragraph 13 above is for the time being in force in respect of it;

(*d*) to any agreement to refrain from presenting a complaint under paragraph 17 above, where in compliance with a request under paragraph 26 (4) above a conciliation officer has taken action in accordance with that sub-paragraph;

(*e*) to any agreement to refrain from proceeding with a complaint presented under paragraph 17 above where a conciliation officer has taken action in accordance with paragraph 26 (2) and (3) above. [**585**]

Employment under the Crown

[*Section* 162]

33.—(1) Subject to the following provisions of this paragraph, the provisions of this Act shall have effect in relation to Crown employment and to workers in Crown employment as they have effect in relation to other employment and to other workers.

(2) In this paragraph (subject to sub-paragraph (4) below) "Crown employment" means employment under or for the purposes of a government department, otherwise than as a member of the naval, military or air forces of the Crown or of any women's service administered by the Defence Council, and "Crown employee" means a person who is for the time being in Crown employment or (where it has ceased) was in Crown employment.

(3) For the purposes of the application of the provisions of this Act in relation to Crown employment in accordance with sub-paragraph (1) above—

(*a*) any reference to an employee shall be construed as a reference to a Crown employee;

(*b*) any reference to dismissal shall be construed as a reference to the termination of Crown employment;

(*c*) any reference to redundancy shall be construed as a reference to the existence of such circumstances as, in accordance with any arrangements for the time being in force as mentioned in section 41 (3) of the Redundancy Payments Act 1965, are treated as equivalent to redundancy in relation to Crown employment;

(*d*) the reference in paragraph 21 (5) (*c*) above to any person's undertaking or an undertaking in which he works shall be construed as a reference to the national interest; and

(*e*) any other reference to an undertaking shall be construed, in relation to a Minister of the Crown, as a reference to his functions or (as the context may require) to the department of which he is in charge, and, in relation to a government department, shall be construed as a reference to the functions of the department or (as the context may require) to the department.

(4) For the purposes of this Act—

(*a*) none of the bodies specified in Schedule 3 to the Redundancy Payments Act 1965 (national health service employers) shall be regarded as performing functions on behalf of the Crown, and their employees shall not be regarded as being employed under or for the purposes of a government department, and accordingly employment by any such body shall not be Crown employment within the meaning of this paragraph;

(*b*) associations established for the purposes of the Auxiliary Forces Act 1953 shall be treated as if they were government departments, and accordingly employment by any such association shall be Crown employment within the meaning of this paragraph;

and for the purposes of this paragraph Crown employment does not include any employment in respect of which a certificate to which sub-paragraph (5) below applies is for the time being in force.

(5) This sub-paragraph applies to any certificate issued by or on behalf of a Minister of the Crown and certifying that employment of a description specified in the certificate, or the employment of a particular person so specified, is (or at a time specified in the certificate was) required to be excepted from sub-paragraph (1) above for the purpose of safeguarding national security; and any document purporting to be a certificate so issued shall be received in evidence and shall, unless the contrary is proved, be deemed to be such a certificate. **[586]**

SCHEDULE 2

Section 11

ADMINISTRATIVE PROVISIONS RELATING TO TRADE UNIONS AND EMPLOYERS' ASSOCIATIONS

PART I

ANNUAL RETURNS, AND QUALIFICATIONS, APPOINTMENT AND REMOVAL, AND FUNCTIONS, OF AUDITORS

Annual returns

1.—(1) Subject to paragraph 5 below, the annual return of a trade union or an employers' association required by section 11 (1) above shall be sent to the Registrar before 1st June and shall relate to the last preceding calendar year.

(2) The annual return shall be in such form and be signed by such persons as the Registrar may require. **[587]**

2. Every annual return shall contain—

(*a*) revenue accounts indicating the income and expenditure of the trade union or employers' association for the period to which the return relates;

(*b*) a balance sheet as at the end of that period;

(*c*) such other accounts (if any) as the Registrar may require; and

(*d*) a copy of the rules of the trade union or employers' association as in force at the end of that period;

and shall have attached to it a note of all changes in the officers of the union or association and of any change in the address of the head or main office of the union or association during the period to which the return relates. [**588**]

3. Every revenue account, every balance sheet and every other account contained in a return in accordance with paragraph 2 above shall give a true and fair view of the matters to which it relates. [**589**]

4. Every return, in addition to containing the accounts mentioned in paragraph 2 above, shall contain a copy of the report made by the auditor or auditors of the trade union or employers' association on those accounts under paragraph 18 below and such other documents relating to those accounts and such further particulars as the Registrar may require, subject in the case of the accounts contained in the return to such modifications (if any) as may be necessary to secure compliance with paragraph 3 above. [**590**]

5. The Registrar, if in any particular case he considers it appropriate to do so—

(*a*) may direct that the period for which a return is to be sent to him under section 11 (2) above shall be a period other than the calendar year last preceding the date on which the return is sent;

(*b*) whether a direction under sub-paragraph (*a*) above is given or not, may direct that the date before which any such return is to be sent to him shall be such date (whether before or after 1st June) as may be specified in the direction. [**591**]

Qualifications of auditors

6. Subject to paragraphs 7 to 9 below, a person shall not be qualified to be the auditor or one of the auditors of a trade union or employers' association unless he is either a member of one or more of the following bodies—

(*a*) the Institute of Chartered Accountants in England and Wales;

(*b*) the Institute of Chartered Accountants of Scotland;

(*c*) the Association of Certified Accountants;

(*d*) the Institute of Chartered Accountants in Ireland;

(*e*) any other body of accountants established in the United Kingdom and for the time being recognised for the purposes of section 161 (1) (*a*) of the Companies Act 1948 by the Secretary of State,

or a person who is for the time being authorised by the Secretary of State under section 161 (1) (*b*) of that Act as being a person with similar qualifications obtained outside the United Kingdom. [**592**]

7. Notwithstanding anything in paragraph 6 above, a Scottish firm may act as auditor of a trade union or employers' association if, but only if, every partner of the firm is qualified so to act. [**593**]

8. A person who is not qualified under paragraph 6 above may act in respect of any accounting period as auditor of a trade union or employers' association if—

(*a*) it was registered under the Trade Union Acts 1871 to 1964 on 30th September 1971;

(*b*) he acted as its auditor in respect of the last period in relation to which it was required to make an annual return under section 16 of the Trade Union Act 1871;

(*c*) he has acted as its auditor in respect of every accounting period since that period; and

(*d*) he is for the time being authorised by the Secretary of State under section 161 (1) (*b*) of the Companies Act 1948 otherwise than as mentioned in paragraph 6 above. [**594**]

9.—(1) Two or more persons who are not qualified under paragraph 6 above may act as auditors of a trade union or employers' association in respect of any accounting period of that union or association if—

(*a*) its receipts and payments in respect of its last preceding accounting period did not in the aggregate exceed £5,000;

(*b*) the number of its members at the end of its last preceding accounting period did not exceed 500; and

(*c*) the value of its assets at the end of its last preceding accounting period did not in the aggregate exceed £5,000.

(2) Where by virtue of sub-paragraph (1) above persons who are not qualified under paragraph 6 above act as auditors in respect of any accounting period of a trade union or employers' association, the Registrar may at any time (whether during that period or after it comes to an end) direct the trade union or employers' association to appoint a person who is so qualified to audit its accounts for that period.

(3) Regulations may—

(*a*) substitute for any sum or number for the time being specified in sub-paragraph (1) above such sum or number as may be specified in the regulations; and

(*b*) prescribe what receipts and payments shall be taken into account for the purposes of that sub-paragraph. **[595]**

10.—(1) None of the following persons shall act as auditor of a trade union or employers' association, that is to say—

(*a*) an officer or employee of the trade union or employers' association or of any of its branches or sections;

(*b*) a person who is a partner of, or in the employment of, or who employs, such an officer or employee;

(*c*) a body corporate.

(2) References in this paragraph to an officer shall be construed as not including an auditor. **[596]**

Appointment and removal of auditors

11. The rules of every trade union and every employers' association shall contain provision for the appointment and removal of auditors. **[597]**

12. Notwithstanding anything in the rules of a trade union or employers' association, its auditor or auditors shall not be removed from office except by resolution passed at a general meeting of its members, or of delegates of its members. **[598]**

13.—(1) Notwithstanding anything in the rules of a trade union or employers' association, a qualified auditor appointed to audit its accounts for the preceding year of account shall (subject to sub-paragraph (2) of this paragraph) be re-appointed as auditor for the current year of account unless—

(*a*) a resolution has been passed at a general meeting of the trade union or employers' association appointing somebody instead of him or providing expressly that he shall not be re-appointed, or

(*b*) he has given to the trade union or employers' association notice in writing of his unwillingness to be re-appointed, or

(*c*) he is ineligible for appointment as its auditor or one of its auditors for the current year of account, or

(*d*) he has ceased to act as its auditor or one of its auditors by reason of incapacity.

(2) Where notice is given of an intended resolution to appoint some person or persons in place of a retiring auditor and the resolution cannot be proceeded with at the meeting because of the death or incapacity of that person or persons, or because he or they are ineligible for appointment as auditor or auditors for the current year of account, the retiring auditor shall not be automatically re-appointed by virtue of this paragraph.

(3) For the purposes of this paragraph a person is ineligible for appointment as auditor of a trade union or employers' association for the current year of account if, but only if,—

(*a*) he would be precluded by paragraph 10 above from acting as its auditor for that year, or (*b*) he is not a qualified auditor at the time when the question of his appointment falls to be considered.

(4) In this paragraph "qualified auditor", in relation to a trade union or employers' association, means a person qualified to be its auditor or one of its auditors in accordance with paragraphs 6 to 9 above, "the current year of account", in relation to the appointment of a person as auditor, means the year of account in which the question of that appointment arises, and "the preceding year of account" means the year of account immediately preceding the current year of account. [**599**]

14. Regulations may make provision as to the procedure to be followed when it is intended to move a resolution—

(*a*) appointing another auditor or other auditors in place of a retiring auditor or retiring auditors of a trade union or an employers' association, or

(*b*) providing expressly that a retiring auditor or auditors of a trade union or an employers' association shall not be re-appointed,

and as to the rights of auditors and members of a trade union or an employers' association in relation to such a motion. [**600**]

15.—(1) Where any regulations made under paragraph 14 above require copies of any representations made by a retiring auditor to be sent out, or require any such representations to be read out at a meeting, the High Court or the Court of Session, on the application of the trade union or employers' association or of any other person, may dispense with that requirement if satisfied that the rights conferred on the retiring auditor by the regulations are being abused to secure needless publicity for defamatory matter.

(2) On any such application the High Court or the Court of Session may order the costs or expenses of the trade union or employers' association to be paid, in whole or in part, by the retiring auditor, whether he is a party to the application or not. [**601**]

Auditor's right of access to books and information and right to be heard at meetings

16. Every auditor of a trade union or an employers' association—

(*a*) shall have a right of access at all times to its accounting records and to all other documents relating to its affairs, and

(*b*) shall be entitled to require from its officers, or the officers of any of its branches or sections, such information and explanations as he thinks necessary for the performance of his duties as auditor. [**602**]

17. Every auditor of a trade union or an employers' association shall be entitled—

(*a*) to attend any general meetings of its members, or of delegates of its members, and to receive all notices of and other communications relating to any general meeting which any such member or delegate is entitled to receive, and

(*b*) to be heard at any meeting which he attends on any part of the business of the meeting which concerns him as auditor. [**603**]

Auditors' reports

18. The auditor or auditors of a trade union or an employers' association shall make a report to it on the accounts of the trade union or employers' association audited by him or them and contained in its annual return. [**604**]

19. The report shall state whether, in the opinion of the auditor or auditors, those accounts give a true and fair view of the matters to which they relate. [**605**]

20. It shall be the duty of the auditor or auditors, in preparing a report under

paragraph 18 above, to carry out such investigations as will enable him or them to form an opinion as to the following matters, that is to say—

(*a*) whether the trade union or employers' association has kept proper accounting records in accordance with the requirements of section 10 above;

(*b*) whether it has maintained a satisfactory system of control over its transactions in accordance with the requirements of that section; and

(*c*) whether the accounts to which the report refers are in agreement with the accounting records;

and if in the opinion of the auditor or auditors the trade union or employers' association has failed to comply with section 10 (2) (*a*) or (*b*) above or if the accounts to which the report relates are not in agreement with the accounting records, the auditor or auditors shall state that fact in the report. **[606]**

21. If an auditor fails to obtain all the information and explanations which, to the best of his knowledge and belief, are necessary for the purposes of an audit, he shall state that fact in his report. **[607]**

22. In this Part of this Schedule, "accounting period", in relation to a trade union or an employers' association, means any period in relation to which it is required under section 11 (2) above to send a return to the Registrar. **[608]**

Part II

Members' Superannuation Schemes

Examination of superannuation schemes

23. Subject to paragraphs 29 to 31 below, every trade union and every employers' association which at the commencement of this Part of this Schedule is maintaining a members' superannuation scheme shall arrange for the scheme, as it has effect at a date not later than two years from the commencement of this Part of this Schedule, to be examined by an appropriately qualified actuary, and for the actuary to make a report to the trade union or employers' association on the results of his examination of the scheme. **[609]**

24. Where a members' superannuation scheme to which paragraph 23 above applies includes provision for the maintenance of a separate fund for the purpose of the scheme, the examination under that paragraph shall include a valuation (as at the date by reference to which the examination is carried out) of the assets comprised in that fund and of the liabilities falling to be discharged out of it. **[610]**

25. The report made by the actuary on the results of his examination of any such scheme—

(*a*) shall state whether in his opinion the premium or contribution rates are adequate and whether the accounting or funding arrangements are suitable, and

(*b*) if the scheme provides for the maintenance of a separate fund for the purposes of the scheme, shall state whether in his opinion the fund is adequate. **[611]**

26. A copy of any report made by an actuary under paragraph 23 above, signed by the actuary, shall be sent to the Registrar; and it shall be the duty of the trade union or employers' association to make such arrangements under that paragraph as will enable the report to be sent to the Registrar before the end of the period of one year from the date by reference to which the actuarial examination was carried out. **[612]**

27. Subject to paragraphs 30 and 31 below, no trade union or employers' association shall after the commencement of this Part of this Schedule begin to maintain a members' superannuation scheme unless, before the date on which the scheme begins to be maintained,—

(*a*) the proposals for the scheme have been examined by an appropriately qualified actuary; and (*b*) a copy of a report made to the trade union or employers' association by the actuary on the results of his examination of the proposals, signed by the actuary, has been sent to the Registrar;

and the provisions of paragraph 25 above shall have effect in relation to a report under this paragraph on the proposals for a scheme as they have effect in relation to a report on a scheme under paragraph 23 above. [**613**]

28. A copy of any report made to a trade union or employers' association under paragraph 23 or paragraph 27 above shall, on the application of any of its members, be supplied to him free of charge. [**614**]

29. Where on the application of the trade union or employers' association the Registrar is satisfied—

(*a*) that a members' superannuation scheme maintained by it, as it had effect at a date not more than two years before the commencement of this part of this Schedule, has been examined by an actuary;

(*b*) that the qualifications of the actuary were adequate for the purpose of carrying out the examination; and

(*c*) that the examination, and the report made by the actuary on its results, fulfil the requirements of paragraphs 24 and 25 above,

the Registrar may direct that paragraph 23 above shall have effect, in relation to that scheme, as if for the reference to two years from the commencement of this Part of this Schedule there were substituted a reference to five years from the date by reference to which that examination was carried out. [**615**]

30. The Registrar, on the application of a trade union or employers' association, may exempt any members' superannuation scheme which it maintains or proposes to maintain from the requirements of paragraph 23 or (as the case may be) paragraph 27 above, if he is satisfied that, by reason of the small number of members to which the scheme is or would be applicable or for any other special reasons, it is unnecessary for the scheme to be examined in accordance with those requirements. [**616**]

31. The Registrar may at any time revoke any exemption granted under paragraph 30 above if it appears to him that the circumstances by reason of which the exemption was granted have ceased to exist. [**617**]

Periodical re-examination of schemes

32.—(1) Where a trade union or employers' association for the time being maintains a members' superannuation scheme, and either—

(*a*) the scheme has been examined in pursuance of paragraph 23 above or in pursuance of this paragraph, or

(*b*) the scheme itself has not been so examined but the proposals for the scheme have been examined in pursuance of paragraph 27 above,

the trade union or employers' association in question shall arrange for that scheme, as it has effect at each successive relevant date, to be examined by an appropriately qualified actuary, and for a report to be made to it by the actuary on the result of his examination of the scheme.

(2) Subject to the next following sub-paragraph, in this paragraph "relevant date", in relation to a members' superannuation scheme, means such date as the trade union or employers' association in question may determine, not being later than five years after the date by reference to which the last examination of the scheme, or (as the case may be) the examination of the proposals for the scheme, was carried out in accordance with paragraph 23 or paragraph 27 above or in accordance with the preceding sub-paragraph.

(3) In the case of any trade union or employers' association the Registrar may direct that, in relation to any time after the making of the direction, sub-paragraph (2) of this paragraph shall have effect as if, for the reference to five years there was substituted a reference to such shorter period as may be specified in the direction.

[**618**]

33. The provisions of paragraphs 24 to 26 and paragraph 28 above shall have effect in relation to the examination of a scheme under paragraph 32 above as they have effect in relation to the examination of a scheme under paragraph 23 above. [**619**]

Separate fund for members' superannuation scheme

34. After the commencement of this Part of this Schedule no trade union or employers' association shall maintain a members' superannuation scheme which was not established before the commencement of this Part of this Schedule unless it maintains a separate fund for the payments of benefits in accordance with the scheme. [**620**]

35. After the end of the period of five years beginning with the date on which paragraph 34 above comes into operation no trade union or employers' association shall maintain a members' superannuation scheme (whenever established) unless it maintains a separate fund for the payment of benefits in accordance with the scheme. [**621**]

Interpretation of Part II

36. In this Part of this Schedule—

(*a*) "members' superannuation scheme" means any scheme or arrangement made by or on behalf of a trade union or employers' association (including any scheme or arrangement shown in the rules of a trade union or employers' association) in so far as it provides for benefits to be paid by way of pension (including any widows' or children's pensions or dependants' pensions) to or in respect of members or former members of the trade union or employers' association and to be so paid either out of the funds (whether the general funds or any other fund) of the trade union or employers' association or under any insurance scheme maintained out of those funds;

(*b*) "appropriately qualified actuary" in relation to a trade union or employers' association, means a person who is either a Fellow of the Institute of Actuaries or a Fellow of the Faculty of Actuaries or is approved by the Registrar on the application of the trade union or employers' association as a person having actuarial knowledge; and

(*c*) "separate fund" means a fund separate from the general funds of the trade unions or employers' association. [**622**]

SCHEDULE 3

Section 25

Miscellaneous Amendments

The Conspiracy, and Protection of Property Act 1875 (*c.* 86)

1. In section 3 of the Conspiracy, and Protection of Property Act 1875, for the words from "an industrial dispute" to "1971" substitute the words "a trade dispute". [**623**]

The Trade Union Act 1913 (2 & 3 Geo. 5 *c.* 30)

2.—(1) The Trade Union Act 1913 shall be amended in accordance with the following provisions of this paragraph.

(2) For section 2 (1), substitute as new subsections (1) and (1A) two subsections in the same terms as subsections (1) and (2) respectively of section 28 of this Act, but with the insertion in the definition of "employers' association" in subsection (2), after the words "temporary) which", of the words "is unincorporated and".

(3) In sections 3 to 6, for the words substituted by Schedule 8 to the 1971 Act substitute the words contained in those sections immediately before the substitutions

were effected by that Act except in the contexts specified in sub-paragraph (4) below.

(4) In sections 3 (1) and 4 (1) omit the words from "whether the" to "is registered or not" and in section 4 (2) the words "whether registered or not".

(5) After section 6, insert—

"6A. Application of sections 3 to 6 to employers' associations

Sections 3 to 6 of, and the Schedule to, this Act shall apply, with the necessary modifications, in relation to unincorporated employers' associations as they apply in relation to trade unions."

(6) For section 7 substitute—

"**7.** In any enactment relating to trade unions or employers' associations, unless the context otherwise requires, the expression 'the Registrar of Friendly Societies' means, in relation to a trade union or employers' association whose office or head or main office is situated in England or Wales, the Chief Registrar of Friendly Societies, and in relation to a trade union or employers' association whose office or head or main office is situated in Scotland, the assistant registrar for Scotland." [**624**]

The Industrial Courts Act 1919 (9 *&* 10 *Geo.* 5. *c.* 69)

3. In sections 1, 2, 3, 7 and 9, for the words "Industrial Court" and "the Court", wherever they occur (being words which appeared in those subsections before being amended by Schedule 8 to the 1971 Act) there shall continue to be substituted the words "Industrial Arbitration Board" and "the Board" respectively.

[**625**]

The Road Haulage Wages Act 1938 (*c.* 44)

4. In section 15 (1) of the Road Haulage Wages Act 1938, for the definition of "Trade Union" substitute the words " 'Trade Union' has the same meaning as in the Trade Union and Labour Relations Act 1974". [**626**]

The Industrial Assurance and Friendly Societies Act 1948 (*c.* 39)

5.—(1) The Industrial Assurance and Friendly Societies Act 1948 shall be amended in accordance with the following provisions of this paragraph.

(2) In section 6 (1), for the words from "an organisation of workers" to "that Act" substitute the words "a trade union or an employers' association".

(3) In section 16 (4), for the words substituted by the 1971 Act substitute the words "trade union or employers' association".

(4) In section 23 (1) insert the following—

"(*d*) the expressions 'trade union' and 'employers' association' have the same meanings respectively as they have in the Trade Union and Labour Relations Act 1974". [**627**]

The House of Commons Disqualification Act 1957 (*c.* 20)

6.—(1) In Part II of Schedule 1 to the House of Commons Disqualification Act 1957, both in its application to the House of Commons of the United Kingdom and in its application to the Northern Ireland Assembly,—

(*a*) there shall (at the appropriate place in alphabetical order) be re-inserted the following entry—

"The Industrial Arbitration Board"; and

(*b*) the entries relating to the Commission on Industrial Relations and the National Industrial Relations Court shall be omitted.

(2) In Part III of that Schedule, in its application to the House of Commons of the United Kingdom, the entry relating to the Chief Registrar or Assistant Registrar of Trade Unions and Employers' Associations shall be omitted and, in its application both to the House of Commons of the United Kingdom and to the Northern Ireland Assembly, at the end of the entry relating to members of wages councils and other persons appointed under the Wages Councils Act 1959 insert the words "or Member of a Commission of Inquiry appointed under paragraph 1 (a) of Schedule 4 to that Act". **[628]**

The Insurance Companies Act 1958 (*c.* 72)

7. In section 1 of the Insurance Companies Act 1958, after subsection (5) insert as a new subsection (5A) in place of that inserted by Schedule 8 to the 1971 Act the following—

"(5A) Where a trade union or an employers' association carries on insurance business, this Act does not apply to it as an insurance company if the insurance business is limited to the provision for its members of provident benefits or strike benefits.

In this subsection 'trade union' and 'employers' association' have the same meanings respectively as they have in the Trade Union and Labour Relations Act 1974." **[629]**

The Terms and Conditions of Employment Act 1959 (*c.* 26)

8. In section 8 (2) of the Terms and Conditions of Employment Act 1959, for the words from "which is registered" to "1971, and is, or is" inserted by paragraph 2 of Schedule 7 to the 1971 Act substitute the words "being or". **[630]**

The Wages Councils Act 1959 (*c.* 69)

9.—(1) The Wages Councils Act 1959 shall be amended in accordance with the following provisions of this paragraph.

(2) The functions of commissions of inquiry under the Wages Councils Act 1959 transferred to the Commission on Industrial Relations by paragraph 40 of Schedule 3 to the 1971 Act shall become again functions of commissions of inquiry under the 1959 Act and accordingly any reference in sections 1, 2, 3, 6, 7 and 9 of, and Schedule 1 to, that Act which, by virtue of the 1971 Act, became a reference to the Commission shall become again a reference to a commission of inquiry under the said Act of 1959.

(3) In section 5, at the end of subsection (1) there shall be re-inserted the words—

"or

(*c*) by any organisation of workers which represents a substantial proportion of the workers with respect to whom that wages council operates";

and in subsection (2) for the words from "the council" to the end of the subsection there shall continue to be substituted the words "the existence of a wages council is no longer necessary for the purpose of maintaining a reasonable standard of remuneration for the workers with respect to whom that wages council operates".

(4) Section 9 (1) and Schedule 4 (which were repealed by the 1971 Act) are hereby revived.

(5) In section 22 (3), for the words "any report" substituted by Schedule 8 to the 1971 Act there shall continue to be substituted the words "the report".

(6) In section 23 the words "a commission of inquiry" repealed by the 1971 Act are hereby revived.

(7) In section 24, there are hereby revived the definitions of "wages council" and "commission of inquiry" for which a definition of "wages council" was substituted by Schedule 8 to the 1971 Act.

(8) In Schedule 1, after paragraph 2 there shall be reinserted the following paragraph:—

"2A. In relation to the making of an order under section 4 of this Act in pursuance of an application made in accordance with section 5 (1) (*c*) of this Act, paragraph 2 of this Schedule shall have effect as if, before the words 'shall publish', there were inserted the words 'after consultation with the wages council concerned and with all such organisations of employers as in his opinion represent a substantial proportion of employers with respect to whom the wages council operates'." [**631**]

The Trade Union (Amalgamations, etc.) Act 1964 (*c.* 24)

10.—(1) The Trade Union (Amalgamations, etc.) Act 1964 shall be amended in accordance with the following provisions of this paragraph.

(2) In sections 1 to 11 (and the Schedules), for the expressions "organisation to which this Act Applies" or "organisation" substituted by Schedule 8 to the 1971 Act, wherever they occur, substitute the words contained in those sections (and Schedules) immediately before the substitutions were effected by that Act.

(3) In section 1, for the subsection (1A) inserted by Schedule 8 to the 1971 Act substitute—

"(1A) Subject to any express provision of this Act with respect to employers' associations, this Act shall apply, with the necessary modifications, in relation to unincorporated employers' associations as it applies in relation to trade unions."

(4) In section 4, for subsection (8) substitute—

"(8) In the course of proceedings on a complaint under this section the Registrar may, if he thinks fit, at the request of the complainant or of the trade union, state a case for the opinion of the High Court, or in relation to proceedings in Scotland the Court of Session, on any question of law arising in the proceedings.

The decision of the High Court or the Court of Session, as the case may be, on a case stated under this subsection shall be final."

(5) For section 6 (2) substitute—

"(2) If the name of a trade union or employers' association is for the time being entered in the list of trade unions or employers' associations under section 8 of the Trade Union and Labour Relations Act 1974, a change of its name shall not take effect until approved by the Registrar under this Act; and the Registrar shall not approve a change of name if it appears to him that the proposed new name is the same as one entered in either list as the name of another trade union or employers' association or is a name so nearly resembling such a name as to be likely to deceive the public."

(6) In section 7 (1) (*c*) the words "or by any assistant registrar" repealed by the 1971 Act are hereby revived.

(7) Section 8 (which was repealed by the 1971 Act) is hereby revived.

(8) In section 9, for subsection (1) substitute—

"(1) In this Act, unless the context otherwise requires—

'amalgamating unions' and 'amalgamated union', in relation to a proposed amalgamation, mean respectively the trade unions proposing to amalgamate and the trade union which is to result from the proposed amalgamation;

'assistant registrar' means any assistant registrar of friendly societies appointed under section 1 of the Friendly Societies Act 1896;

'employers' association' has the same meaning as in the Trade Union and Labour Relations Act 1974;

'Northern Ireland union' has the meaning assigned to it by section 10 of this Act;

'the Registrar' means the Chief Registrar of Friendly Societies;

'trade union' has the same meaning as in the Trade Union and Labour Relations Act 1974;

'transferor trade union' and 'transferee trade union', in relation to a proposed transfer of engagements, mean respectively the trade union proposing to transfer its engagements and the trade union proposing to accept them." [**632**]

The Trade Union (*Amalgamations etc.*) *Act* (*Northern Ireland*) 1965 (*c.* 2) (*N.I.*)

11. For section 9 (2) of the Trade Union (Amalgamations etc.) Act (Northern Ireland 1965 substitute—

"(2) In this Act 'Great Britain union' means a trade union or employers' association within the meaning of the Trade Union and Labour Relations Act 1974, being either—

(*a*) a union whose name is for the time being entered in the list of trade unions or of employers' associations under section 8 of that Act; or

(*b*) a union or association whose name is not so entered, but whose principal office is situated in England, Wales or Scotland." [**633**]

The Companies Act 1967 (*c.*81)

12. In section 60 (1) of the Companies Act 1967 for the paragraph (*e*) inserted by Schedule 8 to the 1971 Act substitute the following—

"(*e*) a trade union or employers' association (within the meaning of the Trade Union and Labour Relations Act 1974) where the insurance business carried on by the union or association is limited to the provision for its members of provident benefits or strike benefits". [**634**]

The Insurance Companies Act (*Northern Ireland*) 1968 (*c.* 6) (*N.I.*)

13.—(1) The Insurance Companies Act (Northern Ireland) 1968 shall be amended in accordance with the following provisions of this paragraph.

(2) In section 1 (2) (*a*) omit the words "or trade unions".

(3) In section 1 (2) after paragraph (*c*) insert— "or

(*d*) any insurance company which is, or is deemed to be, registered under the Acts relating to trade unions or to any insurance company which is a Great Britain union if in either case the insurance business is limited to the provision for its members of provident benefits or strike benefits.".

(4) In section 3 (1) (*c*) omit the words "or trade unions".

(5) In section 3 (1) after paragraph (*d*) insert:—

"(*e*) a body which is, or is deemed to be, registered under the Acts relating to trade unions, or is a Great Britain union and in either case limits its insurance business to the provision for its members of provident benefits or strike benefits.".

(6) In section 72 (1) at the appropriate place in alphabetical order insert:—
" 'Great Britain union' means a trade union or employers' association within

the meaning of the Trade Union and Labour Relations Act 1974, being either—

(*a*) a union whose name is for the time being entered in the list of trade unions or of employers' associations under section 8 of that Act; or

(*b*) a union or association whose name is not so entered, but whose principal office is situated in England, Wales or Scotland." [**635**]

The Merchant Shipping Act 1970 (*c.* 36)

14. In section 42 of the Merchant Shipping Act 1970, in subsection (2), for the words "industrial dispute" substitute the words "trade dispute (within the meaning of the Trade Union and Labour Relations Act 1974)" and omit subsection (3). [**636**]

The Tribunals and Inquiries Act 1971 (*c.* 62)

15. Section 13 of the Tribunals and Inquiries Act 1971 (which, among other things, makes provision for appeals from and the statement of cases by industrial tribunals to the High Court or Court of Session) shall, in its application to industrial tribunals, be taken as referring to those tribunals when exercising any jurisdiction whatsoever, notwithstanding the effect of any order which was made under section 114 of the 1971 Act (appeals from industrial tribunals to the National Industrial Relations Court). [**637**]

The Contracts of Employment Act 1972 (*c.* 53)

16. In section 4 (2) of the Contracts of Employment Act 1972, omit paragraph (*a*) and in section 11 (1) omit the definitions of "agency shop agreement" and "approved closed shop agreement". [**638**]

The Administration of Justice (Scotland) Act 1972 (*c.* 59)

17. In section 3 (3) of the Administration of Justice (Scotland) Act 1972, for the words "an industrial dispute within the meaning of the Industrial Relations Act 1971" substitute the words "a trade dispute within the meaning of the Trade Union and Labour Relations Act 1974", for the words "Act of 1971" substitute the words "Act of 1974" and omit the words "described in section 124 of that Act". [**639**]

SCHEDULE 4

Section 25

TRANSITIONAL PROVISIONS

1. Schedule 1 to this Act shall apply to dismissals where the effective date of termination (within the meaning of that Schedule) falls on or after the commencement of that Schedule. [**640**]

2. Subject to any provision to the contrary contained in section 21 or 23 above, sections 22 to 33 of the 1971 Act (unfair dismissals) and the other provisions of that Act relating to proceedings for unfair dismissal shall, notwithstanding the repeal of that Act by this Act, continue to apply to dismissals where the effective date of termination falls before the commencement of Schedule 1 to this Act. [**641**]

3. Parts III and IV of Schedule 1 to this Act shall apply to any act (other than a dismissal) done before the commencement of that Schedule in respect of which an industrial tribunal continues to have jurisdiction as if they had been in force when the act was done. [**642**]

4. As respects proceedings pending in the National Industrial Relations Court immediately before the passing of this Act and transferred by section 21 above to the High Court or Court of Session, rules made by virtue of paragraph 24 of Schedule 3 to the 1971 Act (costs and expenses of parties) shall, notwithstanding the repeal of

that Schedule by this Act, continue to have effect and shall with any necessary modifications, apply to the High Court and Court of Session as they applied before the passing of this Act to the National Industrial Relations Court. [**643**]

5. Schedule 2 to this Act shall apply to a trade union's or employers' association's return and accounts for 1974 or the period substituted therefor by a direction under paragraph 5 of that Schedule, notwithstanding that that Schedule was not in force for the whole of that year or period. [**644**]

6.—(1) In so far as anything done or treated as done under any enactment contained in the 1971 Act, which is re-enacted, with or without amendment, in a corresponding provision of Schedule 1 or Schedule 2 to this Act, could have been done under that provision, then, subject to sub-paragraph (3) below, it shall on the commencement of that Schedule have effect as if done under that provision.

(2) In particular, sub-paragraph (1) above applies to the following things done under any such enactment, that is to say—

any complaint presented;

any application, determination, recommendation, award, order, regulations, appointment, request or report made;

any certificate, exemption or notice given.

(3) Sub-paragraph (1) above shall not apply to anything done under those provisions of the 1971 Act which continue to apply to dismissals by virtue only of paragraph 2 above.

(4) Without prejudice to sub-paragraph (1) above, any regulations made wholly or partly under Section 46 of the Redundancy Payments Act 1965 and in force immediately before the passing of this Act shall so far as so made continue in force and have effect as if made under paragraph 21 of Schedule 1 to this Act. [**645**]

7. Any enactment or document which refers, whether specifically or by means of a general description, to an enactment contained in the 1971 Act which is re-enacted, with or without amendment, in a corresponding provision of Schedule 1 or Schedule 2 to this Act shall, except so far as the context otherwise requires, be construed as referring, or as including a reference, to that corresponding provision. [**646**]

8. Nothing in this Schedule shall be construed as prejudicing section 38 of the Interpretation Act 1889 (effect of repeals). [**647**]

Section 25

SCHEDULE 5

ENACTMENTS REPEALED

Chapter	Short Title	Extent of Repeal
2 & 3 Geo. 5 c. 30	The Trade Union Act 1913	In sections 3 (1) and 4 (1), the words from "whether the" to "is registered or not". In section 4 (2), the words "whether registered or not".
1957 c. 20	The House of Commons Disqualification Act 1957	In Part II of Schedule 1, both in its application to the House of Commons of the United Kingdom and in its application to the Northern Ireland Assembly, the entries relating to the Commission on Industrial Relations and the National Industrial Relations Court. In Part III of Schedule 1, in its application to the House of Commons of the United Kingdom, the entry relating to the Chief Registrar or Assistant Registrar of Trade Unions and Employers' Associations.
1968 c. 6 (N.I.)	The Insurance Companies Act (Northern Ireland) 1968	In section 1 (2) (*a*), the words "or trade unions". In section 3 (1) (*c*), the words "or trade unions".
1970 c. 36	The Merchant Shipping Act 1970	Section 42 (3).
1971 c. 72	The Industrial Relations Act 1971	The whole Act.
1972 c. 53	The Contracts of Employment Act 1972	In section 4 (2), paragraph (*a*). In section 11 (1), the definitions of "agency shop agreement" and "approved closed shop agreement".
1972 c. 59	The Administration of Justice (Scotland) Act 1972	In section 3 (3), the words "described in section 124 of that Act".
1973 c. 58	The Insurance Companies Amendment Act 1973	Section 40. In Schedule 3, paragraph 31.

[**648**]

INDEX

All references are to paragraph numbers

All references are to paragraph numbers

All references are to paragraph numbers

All references are to paragraph numbers

All references are to paragraph numbers